Guerrilla Capacity Planning

Neil J. Gunther

Guerrilla Capacity Planning

A Tactical Approach to Planning
for Highly Scalable Applications and Services

With 108 Figures and 37 Tables

 Springer

Neil J. Gunther
Performance Dynamics Company
4061 East Castro Valley Blvd.
Suite 110, Castro Valley
California 94552
USA
http://www.perfdynamics.com/

Library of Congress Control Number: 2006935329

ACM Computing Classification (1998): C.4, K.6.2, D.2.8

ISBN-10 3-540-26138-9 Springer Berlin Heidelberg New York
ISBN-13 978-3-540-26138-4 Springer Berlin Heidelberg New York

Springer is a part of Springer Science+Business Media

springer.com

© Springer-Verlag Berlin Heidelberg 2007

Typesetting: by the Author
Production: LE-TEX Jelonek, Schmidt & Vöckler GbR, Leipzig
Cover: KünkelLopka, Heidelberg

Printed on acid-free paper   45/3100YL - 5 4 3 2 1 0

Go forth and Kong-ka!

Preface

This book is based largely on the material used in the professional training course of the same name. Currently, the *Guerrilla Capacity Planning* (GCaP) classes are usually conducted every calendar quarter by Performance Dynamics Educational Services (`www.perfdynamics.com`) in Pleasanton, California. The same course has also been taught privately at such international organizations as: Amdahl Corporation, AT&T Wireless, Boeing Companies, Federal Express, Peter Harding and Associates (Australia), Sun Microsystems (USA and France), System Administrators Guild of Australia, and Thales Naval (Holland).

Some of the material originates from 1997, when I began teaching a similar class under the title *Practical Performance Methods*, at the Stanford University *Western Institute for Computer Science* summer extension program. My class replaced a similar one that had been taught jointly for many years by Ed Lazowska, Ken Sevcik, and John Zahorjan. Their course and the accompanying book (Lazowska et al. 1984) (now out of print) has provided much inspiration for all my books. Sadly, while writing this book, I learned that Ken Sevcik had passed away.

A major motivation for writing this book was to provide GCaP graduates with a more detailed version of the lecture notes for their later review and reference. Another motivation is to make the same material available to a wider audience who, although they may not be able to attend the GCaP classes, could nonetheless benefit from applying GCaP methods. In these days of ever-shortening planning horizons and contracting times to market, traditional approaches to capacity planning are often seen as inflationary for production schedules. Rather than giving up in the face of this kind of relentless economic pressure to get things done more quickly, GCaP tries to facilitate it through opportunistic and rapid forecasting of capacity requirements. A more detailed list of the advantages of GCaP and guidelines for applying it can be found in the *Guerrilla Manual* located in Appendix F.

Book Structure

This book is not broken into conventional sections, rather there are several themes running concurrently throughout all the chapters. These themes can be grouped as follows:

Guerrilla Tactics

This is the dominant theme that provides the rationale for the title of the book. Put bluntly, the planning horizon has now been reduced to about three months (i.e., a fiscal quarter), thanks to the influence of Wall Street on project cycle times, and only GCaP-style *tactical planning* is crazy enough to be compatible with that kind of insanity.

The Guerrilla theme explains and motivates the GCaP approach to capacity management by identifying opportunistic circumstances in team meetings where capacity planning issues can be brought up, whether they were part of the meeting agenda or not; key concepts, such as the performance homunculus and the universal law of computational scalability; and the use of lightweight tools, such as spreadsheets and operational formulae. The core of this theme is introduced in Chap. 1.

Chapter 2 continues the introduction to the GCaP theme by demonstrating how it is also a natural fit with other standardized IT management frameworks such as ITIL (Information Technology Infrastructure Library). Chapter 11 presents an entirely independent report written by contributing author James Yaple, who took the GCaP theme and tailored it to meet the immediate capacity management needs of his data center.

Guerrilla Scalability

Another major theme is the concept of *scalability* assessment in the context of capacity management, and in particular, the scalability of *application software*. Many people use the word "scalability" without defining it clearly. Most people cannot define it *quantitatively*, and if you cannot quantify it, you cannot guarantee it!

Chapters 4, 5, and 6 address that need by presenting *the universal law of computational scaling*. The notion of ideal parallelism, as it relates to hardware scalability, is used as a springboard to go beyond such well-known models as Amdahl's law and multiuser concurrency, to arrive at the universal law of scalability for hardware. A queue-theoretic argument, based on Theorem 6.2 in Chap. 6, which states:

> *Amdahl's law for parallel speedup is equivalent to the synchronous throughput bound of the repairman queueing model of a multiprocessor*

is invoked to extend the universal law to the prediction of application software scalability. Many examples, based on difficult to obtain hardware and software scalability measurements, are discussed in these three core chapters. The universal scaling law is also applied, in GCaP style, to the analysis of capacity planning data in later chapters. Although many of these ideas have been developed and applied by the author since about 1991, this book represents the first time they have been brought together and demonstrated in one place.

An important advantage of this universal scaling law is that it provides the underpinnings for a *virtual load testing* environment. It allows the reader to take a sparse set of load measurements (e.g., 4–6 data points) and determine how an application will scale under larger user loads than can be generated in the physical test lab. Moreover, and in keeping with the GCaP theme, much of this scalability analysis can be done in a spreadsheet like Excel.

Guerrilla Victories

The remaining chapters comprise detailed examples of successful applications of the other two themes. Chapter 8 presents the author's success in applying GCaP to a large-scale Web site capacity planning in the Silicon Valley. In particular, it demonstrates how some more traditional capacity planning techniques that originated on mainframe computer systems can be adapted to modern servers. Chapter 9 presents GCaP techniques for planning the capacity of gargantuan computing environments such as peer-to-peer systems.

Chapter 10 provides an overview of the peculiar impact of certain Internet packet behavior on buffer sizing for routers and servers. The reason this is potentially very important for capacity planning is due the veritable "paper mill" of academic papers written on so-called *self-similar* Internet traffic. This self-similarity refers to long-term clustering of Internet packets first observed in the famous Bellcore measurements circa 1990. Many of these papers, however, are mathematically very sophisticated and impenetrable to the typical network capacity planner. This chapter attempts to provide a simpler mathematical treatment than is generally available, but without any loss in accuracy. The chapter concludes with some recent measurements and analysis done in the U.K. that indicates the severity of these self-similar packet-clustering effects may have been overplayed.

Intended Audience

Each of the three themes just described can be used to advantage by a broad diversity of IT professionals. At the executive level there are chief information officers (CIOs), chief technology officers (CTOs), and vice presidents (VPs). Mid-level management that could benefit from understanding and championing GCaP concepts include directors, senior management, and project managers. GCaP methodologies are useful for mainframe capacity planners in the process of broadening their skills, performance engineers, and software engineers, system architects, software developers, system analysts and system administrators.

One suggested grouping of themes with professional expertise is shown in the following table.

Theme	Audience	Chapters
Guerrilla tactics	CIOs, CTOs, directors, VPs, senior managers, project managers	Chaps. 1–2
Guerrilla scalability	Mainframe capacity planners, performance and software engineers, QA and test engineers, system architects, software developers, system administrators and analysts	Chaps. 4–6
Guerrilla victories	CTOs, project managers, mainframe capacity planners, performance and Software engineers, software developers, software and performance engineers, system administrators and analysts	Chaps. 1–11, Chaps. 4–10

Acknowledgments

This book has benefited from the insight and assistence of several people, and they deserve my explicit thanks for their contributions.

Steve Jenkin inspired me to put together *The Guerrilla Manual* in Appendix F by pointing out that employees in the trenches often find themselves in the position where being able to point to an authoritative list of methods and aphorisms can make the difference between getting their point across or not. He also suggested the organization of workload types in Table 6.9 based on the range of values for the contention (σ) and coherency (κ) parameters of the universal scalability law for software in Chap. 6.

Ken Christensen performed the event-based simulations that provided empirical support for Theorem 6.2. He also corroborated the findings of Field et al. (2004) regarding self-similar packetization using his own IEEE-validated Ethernet simulation model.

Greg Dawe, Jamie Rybicki, and Andrew Sliwkowski at RSA Security performed the painstaking application measurements which enabled me to develop the PDQ performance models used in Chap. 7. In typical eclectic fashion, Andrew Sliwkowski also drew my attention to the software variant of Amdahl's law, which provided the bridge to open Chap. 6.

Finally, it is my pleasure to thank Giordano Beretta, Ken Christensen, Mark Friedman, Kathy Hagedon, Jim Holtman, J. Scott Johnson, Scott John-

son, Robert Lane, Pedro Vazquez and Lloyd Williams for providing feedback
on early drafts of various chapters, and otherwise improving the overall content of this book. Any remaining shortcomings are mine alone.

Warranty Disclaimer

No warranties are made, express or implied, that the information in this book
and the associated computer programs are error free, or are consistent with
any particular standard of merchantability, or that they will meet your requirements for any particular application. They should not be relied upon for
solving a problem the incorrect solution of which could result in injury to
a person or loss of property. The author disclaims all liability for direct or
consequential damages resulting from the use of this book.

In Sect. 5.6.2 some precision problems with the values computed by Excel
are noted. A more careful analysis is provided in Appendix B. Because of its
potential precision limitations, as noted by Microsoft (support.microsoft.
com/kb/78113/), you are advised to validate any numerical predictions made
by Excel against those calculated by other high-precision tools, such as *Mathematica*, R, S-PLUS or Minitab.

Palomares Hills, California   N.J.G.
October 12, 2006

Contents

Preface VII

1 **What Is Guerrilla Capacity Planning?** 1
   1.1 Introduction 1
   1.2 Why Management Resists Capacity Planning 1
        1.2.1 Risk Management vs. Risk Perception 2
        1.2.2 Instrumentation Just Causes Bugs 3
        1.2.3 As Long as It Fails on Time 4
        1.2.4 Capacity Management as a Homunculus 5
   1.3 Guerrilla vs. Gorilla 6
        1.3.1 No Compass Required 7
        1.3.2 Modeling Is Not Like a Model Railway 8
        1.3.3 More Like a Map Than the Metro 8
   1.4 Tactical Planning as a Weapon 9
        1.4.1 Scalability by Spreadsheet 10
        1.4.2 A Lot From Little 11
        1.4.3 Forecasting on the Fly 13
        1.4.4 Guerrilla Guidelines 14
   1.5 Summary 16

2 **ITIL for Guerrillas** 17
   2.1 Introduction 17
   2.2 ITIL Background 17
        2.2.1 Business Perspective 19
        2.2.2 Capacity Management 21
   2.3 The Wheel of Capacity Management 21
        2.3.1 Traditional Capacity Planning 21
        2.3.2 Running on the Rim 23
        2.3.3 Guerrilla Racing Wheel 24
   2.4 Summary 25

3 Damaging Digits in Capacity Calculations 27
  3.1 Introduction 27
  3.2 Significant Digits 28
     3.2.1 Accuracy 28
     3.2.2 Precision 29
  3.3 Sifting for SigDigs 30
     3.3.1 Count by Zeros 30
     3.3.2 Significance and Scale 32
  3.4 Rounding Rules 32
     3.4.1 Golden Rule 34
     3.4.2 Sum Rule 34
     3.4.3 Product Rule 34
  3.5 Planning With Dollars and Sense 35
     3.5.1 Cost Metric 35
     3.5.2 Significant Digits 36
  3.6 Expressing Errors 37
     3.6.1 Absolute Error 37
     3.6.2 Relative Error 37
     3.6.3 Standard Deviation 37
     3.6.4 Standard Error 38
     3.6.5 Error Bars 38
     3.6.6 Instrumentation Error 39
  3.7 Interval Arithmetic 39
  3.8 Summary 40

4 Scalability—A Quantitative Approach 41
  4.1 Introduction 41
  4.2 Fundamental Concepts of Scaling 41
     4.2.1 Geometric Scaling 42
     4.2.2 Allometric Scaling 43
     4.2.3 Critical Size 44
     4.2.4 Sizing Examples 45
  4.3 Hardware Scalability 47
     4.3.1 Ideal Parallelism 48
     4.3.2 Amdahl's Law 49
     4.3.3 Multiuser Scaleup 52
     4.3.4 Serial-Parallel Duality 55
     4.3.5 Scaled Speedup 56
  4.4 Universal Scalability Model 56
     4.4.1 The Role of Coherency 58
  4.5 Other Scalability Models 63
     4.5.1 Geometric Model 63
     4.5.2 Quadratic Model 63
     4.5.3 Exponential Model 64
  4.6 Multicores and Clusters 66

4.7   Summary... 68

5   **Evaluating Scalability Parameters** 71
    5.1   Introduction 71
    5.2   Benchmark Measurements 72
        5.2.1   The Workload 72
        5.2.2   The Platform 74
        5.2.3   The Procedure 75
    5.3   Minimal Dataset 75
        5.3.1   Interpolating Polynomial 76
        5.3.2   Regression Polynomial 76
    5.4   Capacity Ratios 77
    5.5   Transforming the Scalability Equation 77
        5.5.1   Efficiency 78
        5.5.2   Deviation From Linearity.......................... 78
        5.5.3   Transformation of Variables 79
        5.5.4   Properties of the Regression Curve 80
    5.6   Regression Analysis..................................... 82
        5.6.1   Quadratic Polynomial............................ 82
        5.6.2   Parameter Mapping 83
        5.6.3   Interpreting the Scalability Parameters.............. 85
        5.6.4   Error Reporting................................. 86
    5.7   Less Than a Full Deck 87
        5.7.1   Sparse Even Data 88
        5.7.2   Sparse Uneven Data 90
        5.7.3   Missing $X(1)$ Datum 91
    5.8   Summary... 94

6   **Software Scalability** 97
    6.1   Introduction 97
    6.2   Amdahl's Law for Software 98
    6.3   Universal Software Scalability 100
    6.4   Concurrent Programming and Coherency 102
    6.5   UNIX Multitasking Application 103
        6.5.1   The Workload 103
        6.5.2   The Platform 104
        6.5.3   Regression Analysis..............................104
    6.6   Windows-Based Applications 107
        6.6.1   The Workload 107
        6.6.2   The Platform 108
        6.6.3   Regression Analysis..............................109
    6.7   Multitier Architectures.................................110
        6.7.1   The Workload 111
        6.7.2   The Platform 111
        6.7.3   Regression Analysis..............................112

6.7.4   Why It Works 114
6.8   Classification by Workload 115
6.9   Summary 116

7   **Fundamentals of Virtualization** 117
7.1   Introduction 117
7.2   The Spectrum of Virtual Machines 118
7.2.1   VM Spectroscopy 118
7.2.2   Polling Rates and Frequency Scales 119
7.3   Microlevel Virtual Machines: Hyperthreading 119
7.3.1   Micro-VM Polling 122
7.3.2   Thread Execution Analysis 123
7.3.3   Missing MIPS Explained 124
7.3.4   Windows 2000 Production Server 126
7.3.5   Guerrilla Capacity Planning 127
7.4   Mesolevel Virtual Machines: Hypervisors 127
7.4.1   Fair-Share Scheduling 129
7.4.2   Meso-VM Polling 132
7.4.3   VMWare Share Allocation Analysis 134
7.4.4   J2EE WebLogic Production Application 135
7.4.5   VMWare Scalability Analysis 137
7.4.6   Guerrilla Capacity Planning 138
7.5   Macrolevel Virtual Machines: Hypernets 138
7.5.1   Macro-VM Polling 139
7.5.2   Bandwidth Scalability Analysis 140
7.5.3   Remote Polling Rates 141
7.5.4   Guerrilla Capacity Planning 142
7.6   Summary 142

8   **Web Site Planning** 143
8.1   Introduction 143
8.2   Analysis of Daily Traffic 144
8.2.1   The Camel and the Dromedary 144
8.2.2   Unimodal but Bicoastal 146
8.3   Effective Demand 148
8.3.1   Modeling Assumptions 149
8.3.2   Statistical Approach 149
8.4   Selecting Statistical Tools 150
8.4.1   Spreadsheet Programming 150
8.4.2   Online Support 150
8.5   Planning for Data Collection 151
8.5.1   Commercial Collectors: Use It or Lose It 151
8.5.2   Brewing in the Background 151
8.6   Short-Term Capacity Planning 152
8.6.1   Multivariate Regression of Daily Data 152

8.6.2   Automation Using Spreadsheet Macros 153
8.7   Long-Term Capacity Planning 155
8.7.1   Nonlinear Regression of Weekly Data 155
8.7.2   Procurement Curves 156
8.7.3   Estimating Server Scalability 157
8.7.4   Calculating Capacity Gains 158
8.7.5   Estimating the Doubling Period 161
8.8   Summary 162

9   Gargantuan Computing—GRIDs and P2P 165
9.1   Introduction 165
9.2   GRIDs vs. P2P 166
9.3   Analysis of Gnutella 167
9.4   Tree Topologies 168
9.4.1   Binary Tree 169
9.4.2   Rooted Tree 169
9.4.3   Cayley Tree 169
9.5   Hypernet Topologies 169
9.5.1   Hypercube 170
9.5.2   Hypertorus 170
9.6   Capacity Metrics 170
9.6.1   Network Diameter 170
9.6.2   Total Nodes 171
9.6.3   Path Length 171
9.6.4   Internal Path Length 171
9.6.5   Average Hop Distance 171
9.6.6   Network Links 172
9.6.7   Network Demand 172
9.6.8   Peer Demand 172
9.6.9   Bandwidth 173
9.7   Relative Bandwidth 173
9.7.1   Cayley Trees 173
9.7.2   Trees and Cubes 174
9.7.3   Cubes and Tori 175
9.7.4   Ranked Performance 176
9.8   Summary 176

10   Internet Planning 179
10.1   Introduction 179
10.2   Bellcore Traces 180
10.3   Fractals and Self-Similarity 182
10.4   Fractals in Time 186
10.4.1   Short-Range Dependence 186
10.4.2   Long-Range Dependence 188
10.5   Impact on Buffer Sizing 190

        10.5.1 Conventional Buffer Sizing..........................190
        10.5.2 LRD Buffer Sizing................................192
    10.6 New Developments 193
        10.6.1 Ethernet Packetization............................194
        10.6.2 LRD and Flicker Noise............................196
    10.7 Summary...197

11 **Going Guerrilla—A Case Study** 199
    11.1 Introduction 199
    11.2 Guerrilla Monitoring Phase 199
    11.3 The Basic Solution 201
        11.3.1 Implementation Details 202
        11.3.2 Orca Output Examples 203
        11.3.3 Round-Robin Database 203
    11.4 Extending the Basic Solution 206
        11.4.1 Mainframe Data Processing........................206
        11.4.2 Guerrilla Planning Phase..........................207
        11.4.3 Monitoring With ORCAlerts........................208
    11.5 Future Developments 209
    11.6 Summary...210

Appendix

A **Amdahl and the Repairman** 213
    A.1 Repairman Queueing Model 213
    A.2 Amdahl's Law for Parallel Subtasks......................214
        A.2.1 Single Task 215
        A.2.2 Two Subtasks....................................215
        A.2.3 Multiple Subtasks 215
    A.3 Amdahl's Law for Concurrent Multitasks 217
    A.4 Note On Nelson's Approach..............................217

B **Mathematica Evaluation of NUMA Parameters** 219
    B.1 Mathematica Packages 219
    B.2 Import the Data 219
    B.3 Tabulate the Data 220
    B.4 Plot Normalized Data....................................220
    B.5 Nonlinear Regression....................................221
    B.6 ANOVA Report 221
    B.7 Maximal CPU Configuration.............................222
    B.8 Plot of Regression Model 222

C   Abbreviations and Units 223
    C.1 SI Prefixes 223
    C.2 Time Suffixes 223
    C.3 Capacity Suffixes 224

D   Programs for Chapter 3 225
    D.1 Determine SigDigs in VBA 225
    D.2 Determine SigDigs in Mathematica 226
    D.3 Determine SigDigs in Perl 227

E   Programs for Chapter 8 229
    E.1 Example Data Extractor in Perl 229
    E.2 VBA Macro for Calculating U_{eff} 231

F   The Guerrilla Manual 235
    F.1 Weapons of Mass Instruction 235
    F.2 Capacity Modeling Rules of Thumb 238
    F.3 Scalability on a Stick 240
        F.3.1 Universal Law of Computational Scaling 240
        F.3.2 Areas of Applicability 241
        F.3.3 How to Use It 241

Bibliography 243

Index 249

1

What Is Guerrilla Capacity Planning?

The enemy advances, we retreat; the enemy camps, we harass; the enemy tires, we attack; the enemy retreats, we pursue.

—Mao Tse-tung

1.1 Introduction

Performance experts, like any other group, have a tendency to regurgitate certain performance clichés to each other, and to anyone else who will listen. Here are two such clichés:

1. Acme Corporation just lost a $40 million sale because their new application cannot meet service level targets under heavy load. How much money do they need to lose before they do capacity planning?
2. Company XYZ spent a million dollars buying performance management tools but they won't spend $10,000 on training to learn the capacity planning functionality. They just produce endless strip-chart plots without regard for what that data might imply about their future.

Several years ago I stopped mindlessly reiterating statements like these and took a hard look at what was happening around me. It was then that I realized not only were people not gravitating toward capacity planning, they actually seemed to be avoiding it at any cost! From this standpoint, we performance experts appeared more like clergy preaching from the pulpit after the congregation had well and truly vacated the church.

In trying to come to grips with this new awareness, I discovered some unusual reasons why capacity planning was being avoided. Later, I began to ponder what might be done about it (Gunther 1997). My thinking has evolved over the years (Gunther 2002b), and my current position is presented in this chapter. Since I see performance management differently from most, you may find my conclusions rather surprising and, it is hoped, inspiring.

1.2 Why Management Resists Capacity Planning

Capacity planning has long been accepted as a necessary evil in the context of mainframe upgrades and network device procurement. The motivation is simple: The hardware components are expensive and budgets are always limited. Why then has capacity planning become less accepted today? Once again the reason is simple: Hardware is far less expensive than it used to be (even for mainframes!). So there is no need to plan, because you can just throw more hardware at any bottlenecks when they arise or, better yet, simply over engineer the system in the first place. If you are trying to do capacity planning in the trenches, I am sure this kind of management resistance is very familiar to you.

Underlying this general resistance from management is a set of unspoken assumptions, which, if you fail to recognize them, will pretty much doom you to periodic bouts of despair. Some of the assumptions are:

1. The new performance limits are in software, not hardware.
2. There is a big difference between perceiving risk and managing it.
3. Product production is more important than product performance.
4. Schedules are the only measure of success.
5. There are plenty of commercial tools that can do capacity planning.
6. Most software is plug-and-play, so it does not need to be measured.
7. We do not need instrumentation in our software. It just causes bugs!

Well, you know how it goes. On the other hand, when you do recognize these assumptions and consider them more carefully, you will quickly realize that management is not simply behaving like a brain-dead curmudgeon, although it often appears that way. Some of these assumption present very real constraints, and they are not likely to change. You can go on trying to fight them and lose, or you can factor them into your capacity planning and succeed in spite of them. This book is about the latter approach, and it forms the basis of the Guerrilla capacity planning methodology. Let us look at some of these assumptions in more detail.

1.2.1 Risk Management vs. Risk Perception

Consider an executive manager who has to fly to another city for an important executive meeting. While he is getting ready to go to the airport, he hears a news report about a plane crash where many people were killed. Now, he starts to feel nervous because he is about to board an aircraft and he cannot help thinking that he might suffer the same fate. Moreover, his knuckles start to turn white as he continues to turn over the aircraft disaster while he is driving on the freeway to the airport. What's wrong with this picture?

You probably already know that common statistics indicates that there is a greater risk of being killed on the freeway than on any airline (by a factor of more than 30 times, it turns out). Our intrepid traveler has also heard these same statistics. He is not dumb, he is an executive, after all. So, why does he not simply remind himself that the statistics are in his favor on the aircraft and look forward to his flight? Try it yourself. It does not work. We all get a little apprehensive when a plane crashes, particularly if we are about to get on one. This is not an issue of rational thought, it is a psychological issue.

On the freeway, our intrepid driver feels like he is in control because he has *his* hands firmly on the steering wheel. But on the aircraft, he is just another fearful passenger strapped into his seat. This fear is registered at a deep personal level of (false) insecurity. He remains oblivious to the possibility that he could have been completely obliterated by another careless driver on the freeway.

This is the essential difference between risk perception and risk management. Managers are paid to be in control. Therefore, the perception is that bad things will not happen to their project because that would be tantamount to admitting that they were not really in control. Incidentally, our traveler's best strategy is actually to *fly* to the airport!

Nowadays, however, hardware has become relatively cheap—even mainframe hardware. The urge to launch an application with over engineered hardware has to be tempered with the less obvious caution that bottlenecks are more likely to arise in the application design than in the hardware. Throwing more hardware at it will not necessarily improve performance. In this sense, capacity planning has not gone away. Time is money, even if you have all the hardware in the world. The new emphasis is on software scalability, and that impacts the way capacity planning needs to be done. The traditional approach to capacity planning on a monolithic mainframe can no longer be supported. In the brave new world of distributed computing we have many software pieces in many hardware places.

1.2.2 Instrumentation Just Causes Bugs

To make a difficult environment even more confusing, we have the following limitations to contend with:

- Little or no instrumentation in third-party applications.
- No such thing as UNIX. Rather, we have: AIX, HPUX, Solaris, BSDI, FreeBSD, MacOS X, RedHat Linux, Debian Linux, ... pick one.
- No such thing as Windows. Rather, we have: 2000, XP, and Vista.
- Scripts built on one platform are almost guaranteed not to work on another.
- Multiple commercial off-the-shelf (COTS) software running on multiple platform types.
- No universal performance database such as that available on mainframes.
- Most commercial performance management software has mainframe roots and thus is server-centric in its data collection capabilities. Additional tools are needed to incorporate network and application data.
- Comprehending resource consumption across hundreds of platforms and tiers is still problematic.

The Universal Measurement Architecture (UMA) standard from The Open-Group (1997) might have helped to surmount some of these difficulties by normalizing both performance data and the functionality of performance management tools (Gunther 1995; Gunther and Traister 1995), but vendors saw no significant financial returns for investing in the UMA standard. Even worse, they foresaw the possibility of their own proprietary performance tools losing ground in the marketplace to UMA-based tools. But the real the coup de grâce probably came from the fact that UMA was designed by committee and therefore, almost by definition, was *dead on arrival*. Similarly, the Application Resource Measurement (ARM) standard, also from The OpenGroup (2002), has had better but still limited success.

The wholesale adoption of performance measurement standards like ARM and UMA has been thwarted to a large degree by the necessity of compiling their instrumentation code into each application. Most software developers have a real problem with this approach. One objection is that the instrumentation code simply opens up the opportunity to introduce more bugs into the application, thus inflating the release schedule. This argument is not without merit. Since ARM and UMA were designed, less intrusive technniques have been developed, e.g., instrumenting Java bytecodes (See Gunther 2005a, Appendix D), and this newer approach may help to disseminate the notion that performance instrumentation is a necessary evil.

So today, we build more complex architectures with less instrumentation available to manage them. I do not know about you, but I am glad Boeing does not build aircraft this way.

1.2.3 As Long as It Fails on Time

Some managers believe they do not need to do anything about capacity planning, but this is a misperception about risk. Risk management is often subverted by a false perception of risk. It will always be someone else that loses $40 million because of poor performance.

Management is generally employed to oversee schedules. To emphasize this fact to my students, I tell them that managers will even let a project fail—as long as it fails on time! Many of my students are managers and none of them has disagreed with me yet. In other words, managers are often suspicious that capacity planning will interfere with project planning. Under such scheduling pressures, the focus is on functionality first. Unfortunately, new functionality is often overprescribed because it is seen as a competitive differentiator. All the development time therefore tends to be absorbed by implementing and debugging the new functionality. In this climate, applications often fail to meet performance expectations as a result of management pressure to get the new functionality to market as fast as possible.

Let us face it, Wall Street rules our culture. Time-to-market dictates the schedules that managers must follow. This is a fact of life in the new millennium, and a performance analyst or capacity planner who ignores that fact puts his or her career in peril. It is therefore imperative that any capacity planning methodology not inflate project schedules.

Remark 1.1. When Einstein was asked by the press what he considered to be the greatest force in the universe, he quipped "Compound interest!" Today, he might well have said "Wall Street!"

1.2.4 Capacity Management as a Homunculus

Capacity management can be thought of as a subset of general systems management activities. Systems management typically includes areas like:

- backup/recovery
- chargeback management
- security management
- distribution of software
- capacity management

Looked at in this way, capacity management is simply another bullet item on the list. But this is another of those risk misperceptions. In terms of complexity, it is arguably the most significant item. It is more like the difference between the human body and the medical homunculus in Fig. 1.1.

Fig. 1.1. The homunculus shows the human body in sensory proportion rather than the usual geometric proportion

Indicating the location of an ailment to your doctor has meaning because references are made to your body in geometric proportion. The homunculus, on the other hand, represents the sensate proportion of our bodies. Reflecting this sensory weight, the hands and the mouth become huge, whereas the thorax and head appear relatively small (Fig. 1.1). This is because we receive vastly more sensory information through our fingers and tongue than we do via the skin on our chest, for example.

The same proportionality argument can be applied to capacity management. Capacity management is to systems management as the homunculus is to the human corpus. Almost every other item on the above list can be accommodated by purchasing the appropriate COTS package and installing it. Not so for capacity management.

In terms of coverage, capacity management can be broken into three major subareas:

1. performance monitoring
2. performance analysis
3. performance planning

Most attention is usually paid to level 1, performance monitoring, because it is generally easiest to address. If you want to manage performance and capacity, you have to measure it. Naturally, this is the activity that the majority of commercial tool vendors target. As a manager, if you spend $250,000 on tools, you feel like you must have accomplished something. Alternatively, UNIX and Microsoft Windows system administrators are very good at writing scripts to collect all sorts of data as part of their system administration duties. Since almost nobody sports the rank of *Performance Analyst* or *Capacity Planner* on their business card these days, that job often falls to the system administrator as part of the systems management role. But data collection just generates data. The next level is performance analysis. The usual motivation for doing any analysis these days is to *fire-fight* an unforeseen performance problem that is impacting a release schedule or deployed functionality. With a little more investment in planning (level 3), those unforeseen "fires" can minimized. But, level 3 is usually skipped for fear of inflating project schedules. How can this Gordian knot be cut?

1.3 Guerrilla vs. Gorilla

In my view, a more opportunistic approach to capacity planning is needed. Enter *Guerrilla Capacity Planning!* The notion of planning tactically may seem contradictory. At the risk of mixing metaphors, we can think of traditional capacity planning as being the 800-pound gorilla! That *gorilla* needs to go on a diet to produce a leaner approach to capacity planning in the modern business environment (Table 1.1). By *lean*, I do not mean *skinny*. Skinny means remaining stuck at level 1, where there is a tendency to simply monitor everything that moves in the false hope that capacity issues will never arise and thus, planning can be avoided altogether. Monitoring requires that someone watch the "meter needles" wiggle. Inherent in this approach is the notion that no action need be taken unless the meter redlines. But performance "meters" can only convey the current state of the system. Such a purely reactive approach does not provide any means for forecasting what lies ahead. You cannot forecast the weather by listening to leaves rustle.

Table 1.1. Comparison of traditional (800-lb. gorilla) and Guerrilla methods

Attribute	Gorilla	Guerrilla
Planning Horizon	Strategic	Tactical
Horizon	12 to 24 months	3 mins to 3 months
Focus	Hardware performance	Application performance
Budget	Not an issue	None that you know of (see Chap. 11)
Title	On your office door	Not even on your business card
Style	Opulent and ponderous	Lean and mean
Tools	Expensive commercial	Mix of commercial and open-source (see Table 1.3)
Reporting	Routine, written, formal	Opportunistic, verbal, informal
Skills	Specialized, more quantitative	Eclectic, more qualitative (Sect. 1.3.1)

The irony is that a lot of predictive information is likely contained in the collected monitoring data. But, like panning for gold, some additional processing must be done to reveal the hidden gems about the future. Keeping in mind the economic circumstances outlined earlier, moving to levels 2 and 3 must not act as an inflationary pressure on the manager's schedules. Failure to comprehend this point fully is, in my opinion, one of the major reasons that traditional capacity planning methods have been avoided.

1.3.1 No Compass Required

Traditional capacity planning has required relatively high precision because hardware was expensive and many thousands of dollars were attached to each significant digit of the calculation (see Chap. 3). Today, however, the price of hardware has declined dramatically, even for traditional mainframe planning. Predicting capacity with high precision is much less of a requirement than it used to be historically. Managers are generally looking for a sense of direction rather than the actual compass bearing. In other words, should we go this way or that way? In this sense, the precision of capacity predictions has become less important than its accuracy. There is little virtue in spending several months debugging and validating a complex simulation model if the accuracy of a simple spreadsheet model will suffice.

Let us not overlook the fact that any performance model is only as accurate as the data used to parameterize it. Performance data provided by kernel instrumentation in operating systems such as Windows, UNIX (Vahalia 1996), or Linux, can only be assumed to be accurate to within a margin of about

±5%. Such operating system instrumentation was originally implemented for the benefit of operating system developers (Gunther 2005a), not for the grand purpose of capacity planning. Nonetheless, every capacity planning tool in existence today primarily relies on those same operating system counters with little modification.

1.3.2 Modeling Is Not Like a Model Railway

Sometimes the compass bearing is required, if not by management, by you. It may be desirable for you to check your results with higher accuracy than you are going to present them. The goal of capacity planning is to be predict ahead of time that which cannot be known or measured now. Prediction requires a consistent framework in which to couch the assumptions. That framework is called a model. The word model, however, is one of the most overloaded terms in the English language. It can mean everything from a model railway to a fashion mannequin. Consider the model railway. The goal there is to cram in as much detail as the scale will allow. The best model train set is usually judged as the one that includes not just a scale model of the locomotive, and not just a model of an engineer driving the scaled locomotive, but the one that includes the pupil painted on the eyeball of the engineer driving the scaled locomotive!

This is precisely what a capacity planning model is not. For capacity planning, the goal is to discard as much detail as possible while still retaining the essence of the system's performance characteristics. This tends to argue against the construction and use of detailed simulation models, in favor of the use of spreadsheets or even automated forecasting. The skill lies in finding the correct balance. Linear trending models may be too simple in many cases, while event-based simulation models may be overkill. To paraphrase Einstein: *Keep the model as simple as possible, but no simpler.*

1.3.3 More Like a Map Than the Metro

Sometimes we need a compass and a map. To take the model railway analogy a step further, a capacity plan and the capacity models which support it are more like a map of the metro railway than the metro railway itself. A map of the San Francisco Bay Area Rapid Transit (BART) rail system offers an excellent example of this difference. The map in Fig. 1.2 is an abstraction containing just enough detail for a commuter to visually decipher the correct route between their departure and destination. It easy to tell if you need to change trains, and how far you can go by train versus other modes of public transportation. There is just enough encoded information and this achieved by suppressing all realistic details. In fact, the map is not even close to the *real* railway system. A more realistic representation would require a satellite image, e.g., `maps.google.com/maps?ll=37.579413,-122.343750&spn=.755799,.960205&t=h&hl=en`, but this kind of additional information does

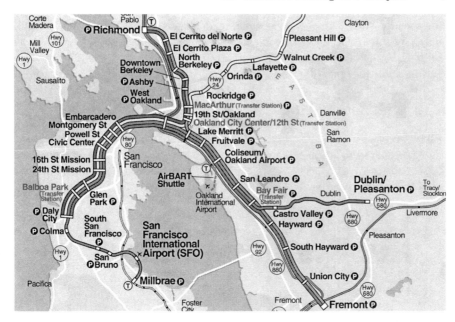

Fig. 1.2. A metro railway map that encodes the rail lines and the respective stations with just enough information to allow a commuter to visually decipher the correct route between their departure and destination. All other realistic details are suppressed (© 2005 Bay Area Rapid Transit System. Used with permission)

not help in finding your way around on BART. In fact, it is too much information and is more likely to confusing than helpful. Guerrilla capacity planning models have the same requirement: abstract simplicity.

To summarize, so far, Guerrilla Capacity Planning (GCaP) tries to facilitate rapid forecasting of capacity requirements based on available performance data in such a way that management schedules are not inflated. Let us look at a brief description of guerrilla capacity planning in action.

1.4 Tactical Planning as a Weapon

As I have already indicated, tools alone are not the answer. In fact, the tools can be quite cheap. Furthermore, the tools needed are likely to be less sophisticated the better trained are the people who use them. If the people doing the performance analysis and capacity planning have the appropriate training in capacity planning methods, they are more likely to be able to improvize with tools like Excel. Consistent investment in a human capacity planning infrastructure is one of the more cost-effective things a company can do.

An important reason for doing any capacity planning is the need to stay ahead in the procurement cycle. If capacity demand is not forecast sufficiently far ahead the additional servers, when they are finally procured and installed, may have their capacity consumed instantly by latent user-demand that has built up in the meantime. The next three examples show how that problem can be avoided, Guerrilla style.

1.4.1 Scalability by Spreadsheet

First, we briefly outline a relatively simple and fast method for quantitatively determining application scalability. Application scalability is a perennial hot topic that involves concepts of performance and planning, yet few people are able to quantify the term.

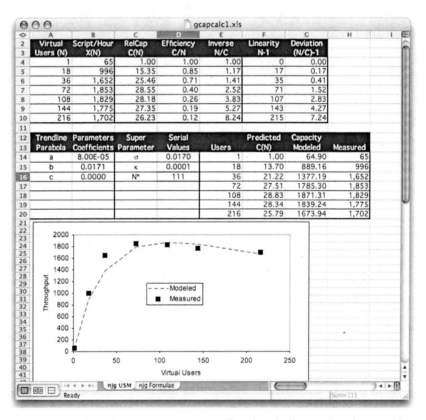

Fig. 1.3. Virtual load-test environment in Excel including a plot showing the results of performing regression analysis (*dashed curve*) on measured throughput data (*squares*)

Scalability has to do with laws of diminishing returns and therefore can be expressed as a mathematical function (Chaps. 4–6). Figure 1.3 shows an example of actual load test measurements of application throughput plotted against the number of users or load generators on the x-axis.

gcapcalc1.xls

	D	E	F	G
12	Serial		Predicted	Capacity
13	Values	Users	C(N)	X(N)
14	=B15-B14	=A4	=E14/(1+$D$14*(E14-1)+$D$15*E14*(E14-1))	=F14*$B$4
15	=B14	=A5	=E15/(1+$D$14*(E15-1)+$D$15*E15*(E15-1))	=F15*$B$4
16	=FLOOR(SQRT((1-D15)/D15), 1)	=A6	=E16/(1+$D$14*(E16-1)+$D$15*E16*(E16-1))	=F16*$B$4
17		=A7	=E17/(1+$D$14*(E17-1)+$D$15*E17*(E17-1))	=F17*$B$4
18		=A8	=E18/(1+$D$14*(E18-1)+$D$15*E18*(E18-1))	=F18*$B$4
19		=A9	=E19/(1+$D$14*(E19-1)+$D$15*E19*(E19-1))	=F19*$B$4
20		=A10	=E20/(1+$D$14*(E20-1)+$D$15*E20*(E20-1))	=F20*$B$4
21				

Fig. 1.4. Quantitative scalability model equations set up in Excel. The theoretical foundations of this model are presented in Chap. 4

Superimposed on these data (*squares*) is the corresponding scalability function (*dashed curve*) defined in Chap. 4. Since it takes the form of a simple equation, it does not require any queueing theory or event-based simulations. Therefore, sizing server capacity for applications can be accomplished relatively quickly by entering the scalability equation into a spreadsheet (Fig. 1.4).

This scalability equation involves just two parameters the values of which can be determined using the regression tools built into Excel (See, e.g., Levine et al. 1999). An example of the entire setup is shown in Fig. 1.3. The two model parameters have clear physical interpretations. One is identified with contention delays, e.g., time spent waiting on a database lock, while the other is identified with coherency delays, e.g., time to fetch a cache-miss. The actual cause of these delays can reside in hardware, software, or a combination of both. The details of this technique are presented in Chap. 5.

Another way to look at this approach is that it represents a *virtual load test* environment (Fig. 1.3). The required input data for Excelregression analysis can come from a test platform comprising a relatively small processor and user configuration. For example, Fig. 1.3 shows only a few hundred users executing on a 16-way multiprocessor. Since it is neither a production platform (a "real simulation") nor an event-based simulation, it is a virtual test platform.

An essential feature of this capacity model is that it can predict retrograde throughputs like those shown in Fig. 1.3. Retrograde throughput means that the throughput decreases as the load on the system increases. This effect cannot be modeled easily using conventional queueing solvers or simulators without a lot of additional work. As noted in Sect. 1.3, this amount of effort tends to be more gorilla than Guerrilla.

1.4.2 A Lot From Little

Einstein is purported to have said about physical models that if the data does not fit the model, change the data. What he meant was that there are certain fundamental laws that cannot be violated and if some measurements disagree with those laws, the measured data must be wrong. Let us look at an example of how that can happen in the context of capacity planning.

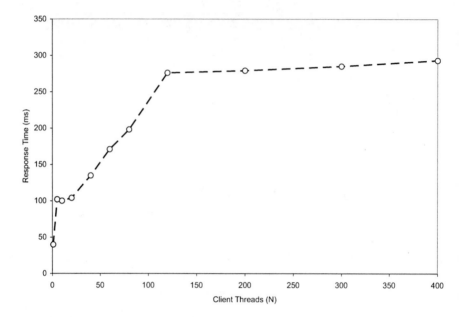

Fig. 1.5. Measured times R that client requests spend in the test system as a function of increasing load N

A fundamental law in computer performance analysis is Little's law:

$$N = XR \,, \tag{1.1}$$

which states that the number of active requests N in the system is given by the product of the throughput X and the time spent in the system R (Gunther 2005a). Consider the load-test data plotted in Fig. 1.5. These data show that above about $N = 120$ clients driving the test system, the response time data R becomes constant.

That the response time can remain essentially constant under higher and higher loads defies all the laws of queueing theory, and Little's law in particular. Put simply, these data are wrong! The measurements need to be repeated, but as Guerrilla capacity planners we would like to make the case for doing that. We can employ Little's law to that end.

In Table 1.2 N_{init} is the number of client threads that are assumed to be running. The number of active threads should also be equal to the product of the measured X and R data according to Little's law (1.1). We see immediately in the fourth column of Table 1.2 that no more than 120 threads (in boldface)

Table 1.2. Distinguishing intitiated from running client threads. The last three entries in column four show that only about 120 threads are actually running even though up to 400 threads have been initiated

Client threads N_{init}	System throughput X_{init}	Response time R_{init}	Running threads N_{active}	Idle threads N_{idle}
1	24	40	0.96	0.04
5	48	102	4.90	0.10
10	99	100	9.90	0.10
20	189	104	19.66	0.34
40	292	135	39.42	0.58
60	344	171	58.82	1.18
80	398	198	78.80	1.20
120	423	276	116.75	3.25
200	428	279	**119.41**	80.59
300	420	285	**119.70**	180.30
400	423	293	**123.94**	276.06

are actually active on the client side, even though up to 400 client processes were initiated. In fact, there are $N_{\text{idle}} = N_{\text{init}} - N_{\text{active}}$ threads that remain idle in the pool. This throttling by the client thread pool shows up in the response data of Fig. 1.5. By the way, if your company does produce a product with a response time like that in Fig. 1.5, ship it!

A common fallacy is to treat data as divine. The significant cost and effort required to set up a load-test system can lead to a false sense of security that the more complex it is, the more sacrosanct are the data it produces. As we shall see in Chap. 3, nothing could be further from the truth. As the example above demonstrates, such reverence is not only misplaced, if the data are not changed it almost certainly guarantees a sure ticket to production hell when the application finally goes live.

1.4.3 Forecasting on the Fly

The spreadsheet equations in Fig. 1.4 can also be applied to Web site traffic analysis where the rapid increase in traffic growth demands a more tactical approach to capacity planning. Although the number of high-growth Web sites has diminished since the "dot.bomb" period of several years ago, server capacity still needs to keep pace with demand. As already noted, Web site architects know they need capacity, but the concept of *planning* is not typically part of that culture.

A useful metric that I have devised for this high growth Web sites is the capacity doubling period (Gunther 2001). This is simply the time until the amount of processing capacity consumed becomes twice that which is being consumed currently. In some cases this can be as short as six months. That is about ten times faster than typical data processing centers and four times faster than Moore's Law. Such exponential demand for server capacity can lead to a new definition of bankruptcy—if you have to purchase a lot of cheap servers, pretty soon, you are talking real money! This forces the need to plan capacity well in advance of the procurement cycle.

Once again, the capacity doubling period can be determined with the use of elementary tools like spreadsheets. For example, if the processor utilization ρ is measured at regularly scheduled intervals, the long term in consumption can be estimated by assuming an exponential trend:

$$\rho_W = \rho_0 \, e^{\Lambda W} \, , \tag{1.2}$$

where Λ is the growth rate determined by using the *Add Trendline* facility in Excel, and W is the number of weeks over which the data are being fitted. The doubling time τ_2 is then given by

$$\tau_2 = \frac{\ln(2)}{\Lambda} \, . \tag{1.3}$$

An exponential growth model was chosen because it is the simplest function that captures the notion of *compounded* growth. It is also reflective of supra-linear *revenue* growth models. The details of this technique are presented in Chap. 8. If you decide to get more involved in statistical models, you might want to consider using more robust tools like *Minitab* or *R*, which are listed in Table 1.3.

The next task is to translate these trends into procurement requirements. Since the trend lines only pertain to the measurements on the current system configuration, we need a way to extrapolate to other possible system configurations. For that purpose, I used the scalability functions in Fig. 1.4. The details of how this is done can be found in Chap. 8.

1.4.4 Guerrilla Guidelines

What are the benefits of this guerrilla sizing methodology? Apart from avoiding queueing theory or simulation models, perhaps the most significant benefit is not the technical merits of the model but the fact that a framework is created against which the consistency of the load measurements can be checked. If the data do not fit your capacity planning model, there is very likely a problem with the measurement process that may be worth a more detailed investigation. For example, each of the parameters in the scalability model (Fig. 1.4) has a well-defined physical interpretation (the details are presented in Chap. 4). It has been my experience that engineers, when presented with performance information based on those parameters, quickly identify the specific parts of the application or platform that need to be tuned to improve scalability. In this way, scalability can be forecast without inflating the release schedule.

Table 1.3. Some weapons of choice used by Guerrilla planners

Weapon	Remarks
Excel	Well-known commercial spreadsheet application.
	You probably have it already as part of Microsoft Office.
	office.microsoft.com (See, e.g., Levine et al. 1999)
Mathematica	Commercial symbolic and numerical computation application.
	Uses its own C-like functional programming language.
	Gold standard with a golden price tag around $2000.
	www.wolfram.com/products/mathematica/index.html
Minitab	Commercial statistical package.
	A step beyond Excel priced around $1200
	www.minitab.com
Net-SNMP	Open source data acquisition using SNMP MIBs.
	net-snmp.sourceforge.net
PDQ	*Pretty Damn Quick.* Open-source queueing modeler.
	Supporting textbook with examples (Gunther 2005a)
	www.perfdynamics.com/Tools/PDQ.html
R	Open source statistical analysis package.
	Uses the *S* command-processing language.
	Capabilities far exceed Excel (Holtman 2004).
	www.r-project.org
SimPy	Open-source discrete-event simulator
	Uses Python as the simulation programming language.
	simpy.sourceforge.net

As I hope the examples in this section have demonstrated, GCaP does provide an approach to assessing application scalability that matches management's requirement to keep a tight rein on project schedules. In many situations where there is a tendency to avoid traditional capacity planning, the Guerrilla approach can provide management with a simple framework whereby disparate groups can be brought together and unforeseen performance issues revealed. Once revealed, they can then be addressed within the context of existing schedules. In this way, GCaP can help to keep projects on schedule and minimize revisions. Think of it as a way of managing hidden time-sinks. It is also a way of replacing risk perceptions with risk management. Sometimes, the biggest hurdle preventing the introduction of GCaP is simply getting started.

Aspects of capacity planning that have not been discussed here include: floor-space, power, cooling, disk storage, tape storage, etc. Many of these issues can be addressed with spreadsheet models similar to those presented in this chapter.

1.5 Summary

So, what is GCaP? Here are the primary attributes that distinguish the Guerrilla approach from traditional capacity planning:

Tactical Planning: Prima facie, this looks like an oxymoron because planning, by definition, is strategic. But strategic planning essentially has no role in today's business environment. It is 2006, not 1966. Most planning horizons rarely extend beyond the next financial quarter, if that. Rather than trying to fight these economic constraints, GCaP tries to embrace them.

Opportunistic Intervention: Given the need for tactical planning, and generally little support for any kind of capacity planning in many work environments, a more opportunistic approach is required. Rather then proselytizing the virtues of what could be achieved with capacity planning, just look for opportunities to demonstrate it on the spot. One simple way to start this process is to ask the right kind of performance questions in your next "Tiger Team" meeting. If there is resistance to your intervention, retreat and try another day.

Rapid Analysis: Opportunistic intervention means you need to be fast on your feet, and that is where light weight tools can help. Any capacity planning models should not be too complex: They should be more like a map than a metro (Sect. 1.3.3). I have given some examples based on Excel in Sect. 1.4. You may have your own preferred tools (Table 1.3).

Methods vs. Madness: All capacity planning, and GCaP in particular, is about methodologies rather than recipes. Methods are generalizable to many different circumstance. Recipes tend to be case-specific. Methods applied consistently can help to reduce the madness of short planning horizons. In this chapter, and throughout the rest of this book, I present general methods that I hope can be easily translated to meet your particular capacity planning requirements.

A much more extensive list of GCaP attributes and guidelines can be found in Appendix F, the Guerrilla Manual. You may also come up with some of your own attributes based on aspects of Table 1.1 and the case study presented in Chap. 11.

To paraphrase the words of a more notorious guerrilla planner: [1]

Management resists, the guerrilla planner retreats.
Management dithers, the guerrilla planner proposes.
Management relents, the guerrilla planner promotes.
Management retreats, the guerrilla planner pursues.

Finally, after reading the remaining chapters with this book's epigraph in mind, I hope that you too will become another Guerrilla capacity planner able to go forth and "Kong-ka!"

---

[1] See the rubric for this chapter (Taber 1969, p. 27).

2

ITIL for Guerrillas

2.1 Introduction

This chapter is the only place in the book where I emphasize the *process* of capacity planning and how it relates to the business side of the operation, rather than the tools and techniques that support the discipline of capacity planning. An internationally recognized framework that emphasizes business processes for IT is called *ITIL*. The acronym ITIL stands for *Information Technology Infrastructure Library*; ITIL is quite literally a collection of related manuals and copyrighted books. The objective of this chapter is to outline the ITIL framework and provide some ideas for how Guerrilla capacity planning (GCaP) can be included within the ITIL framework.

One of the more significant benefits that derive from understanding the ITIL framework is that it forces you think about the business impact of capacity planning rather than remaining narrowly focused on the tools and technologies used to achieve capacity planning. One example is to avoid using overly technical capacity planning terminology when presenting the conclusions of your analysis to your ITIL customers. Use their business terminology and units rather than performance metrics like throughput and utilization.

2.2 ITIL Background

Historically, ITIL was initiated in the 1980's by British *Office of Government Commerce* (OGC) as a set of best practices for IT Service Management (ITSM), and they own the copyright. The original outcome has now come to be known as ITIL version one. Since then it has been updated and published as version two. Although it has been used widely in the UK, allied British Commonwealth countries, and some European countries, it has found much slower adoption in the USA. To further ITIL promotion, a number of user groups have been established. The IT Service Management Forum (itSMF) is an international user group with a Web site at www.itsmf.com, whereas www.itsmfusa.org is the corresponding USA Web site. ITIL is intended to integrate with other standards such as:

ISO: (International Organization for Standardization, www.iso.org) Perhaps best known for the ISO 9000 standard, which has become an international reference for quality requirements in business-to-business dealings; ISO 14000 looks set to achieve at least as much, if not more, in helping organizations to meet their environmental challenges.

COBIT: (Control Objectives for Information and Related Technology) www.isaca.org COBIT is an IT governance framework and supporting toolset that allows managers to bridge the gap between control requirements, technical issues and business risks.

CMM: (Capability Maturity Model) CMM for Software, Carnegie Mellon Software Engineering Institute (SEI), has been a model used by many organizations to identify best practices useful in helping them increase the maturity of their processes.

MOF: (Microsoft Operations Framework) A set of Microsoft publications containing their guidelines for IT service management. Although MOF is not the same as ITIL, the framework is built on best practices from ITIL, but directed at the Windows Server platform.

The ITIL framework (Fig. 2.1) addresses seven management areas:

1. service support
2. service delivery
3. planning to implement service management
4. information communication technology infrastructure management
5. applications management
6. the business perspective
7. security management

In this chapter, we focus on ITIL management area 2 (service delivery), because that is where the capacity management processes are defined.

Recall from Sect. 1.2.4 that the performance and capacity planning components do not have equal weighting in terms of significance or resources with these other areas of systems management. Capacity management can rightly be regarded as just a subset of systems management, but the infrastructure requirements for successful capacity planning (both the tools and knowledgeable humans to use them) are necessarily out of proportion with the requirements for simpler systems management tasks like software distribution, security, backup, etc. It is self-defeating to try doing capacity planning on the cheap.

Remark 2.1. The adoption rate for ITIL in the USA runs the gamut from those companies adopting it wholesale, to others seeing it as just another fad. As a GCaP planner, it should be pretty obvious which environment you are in. Nonetheless, it may be prudent for you to become conversant with

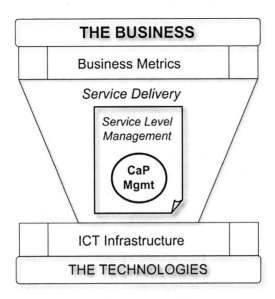

Fig. 2.1. The ITIL framework showing the relative location of the service level management process and the capacity management process

some of the ITIL framework. There are barriers to entry, unfortunately. One of the greatest that I ran into was trying to obtain introductory literature on ITIL, just to see whether I needed to investigate it more thoroughly or not. The published manuals and books comprising the ITIL library are not written at an introductory level and are also prohibitively expensive for an individual to purchase. The closest I came to an "ITIL for Dummies" type of exposition was a complimentary booklet (Rudd 2004) published by *it*SMF. Try requesting it via email: publications@itsmf.com. The ITIL Toolkit (www.itil-toolkit.com) is another resource designed to guide the novice through the ITIL diagram and acronym jungle. It contains a whole series of resources to help simplify, explain, and manage the process.

2.2.1 Business Perspective

ITIL views IT as a business, so it emphasizes process rather than tools, in order to provides an appropriate interface between business processes and technology. Internal IT shops that were accustomed to having a captive audience or customer base, now find this is no longer true because of the advent of such things as outsourcing. To encompass the broader scope imposed by these recent developments, requires a broader framework. Part of the ITIL framework is to recognize that IT products, such as application hosting, are actually comprised of services that utilize devices, such as servers, storage, and networks.

Within the context of ITIL management area 2 (service delivery), service level management (SLM) provides the interface to the business (Fig. 2.2). The SLM process negotiates, agrees to, and reviews service requirements for the business side such as SLAs (service level agreements). SLM further specifies service targets that are contained in a set OLAs (Operational Level Agreements).

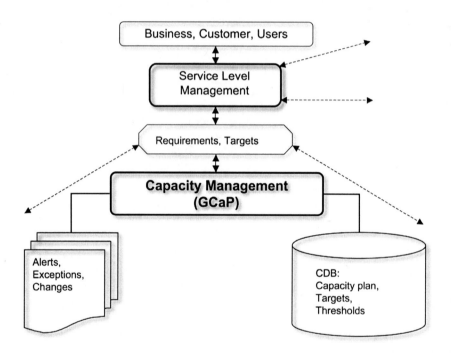

Fig. 2.2. The relationship of the capacity management process (and its possible GCaP implementation) to other immediate ITIL processes and the capacity management database (CDB)

Although ITIL is quite literally a collection of related manuals and copyrighted books that document best practices for ITSM, these materials should not be regarded as providing stepwise procedure manuals. ITIL is more about *what* needs to be done to provide and efficient coupling between IT and business rather than *how* that coupling is to be achieved. The actual implementation details are left open. Therefore, a lot is left to individual interpretation. In many respects, best practices are really an admission of failure. Copying someone else's apparent success is like cheating on a test. You may make the grade, but how far is the bluff going to take you? Very quickly you reach the point where the implementation details are needed, and in the area of ITIL capacity management, that is where GCaP comes in.

2.2.2 Capacity Management

The capacity manager is an ITIL process owner responsible for such things as supply and demand, cost-benefit analysis, capability, and requirements. To satisify these responsibilities under ITIL requires structure, discipline, and organization. Compare this with the *capacity homunclulus* discussed in Chap. 1. To implement the ITIL capacity management process requires skills, technology, and enterprise wide support. The idea is that the ITIL processes should surmount typical organizational boundaries.

One of the most important components with the ITIL specification for capacity management is the Capacity Management Database (CDB) shown in Fig. 2.2. This repository is intended to be far more encompassing than the typical database of operating system performance metrics supplied with commercial performance management products. It can and should include previous capacity reports, various statistical analsyes, and capacity planning models.

2.3 The Wheel of Capacity Management

Modern business practice demands rapid product development to meet narrow market windows. Time to market is everything, so management is constantly forced to seek ways of shrinking product development schedules. Traditional engineering practices, such as design reviews, prototyping, and performance analysis, have become common casualties of such schedule squeezing. This creates a dilemma for the performance analyst. The product is expected to perform, but performance analysis tends to get squeezed out of product design. In this climate, performance analysis is reduced to mere post mortem evaluation long after the crucial design decisions have been made, or even long after the product has actually been released. Here I am using the terms business, market, customer, and product in their most generic sense. A product may be a full-blown commercial offering or an artifact for internal consumption only. The product may be a piece of computer hardware, a software application, or an integrated computer system.

2.3.1 Traditional Capacity Planning

The frustration of today's capacity planner stems from trying to combat these business pressures. The purist's position, that capacity management is the "right thing to do" because it helps to ensure a more cost-effective product, tends to fall on deaf ears. On the other hand, it is relatively easy to cite an ongoing litany of multimillion-dollar computer projects that have failed as a consequence of a more short-sighted approach to system design. To help clarify the nature of this paradox, we introduce a visual aid: the *wheel of capacity management* in Fig. 2.3.

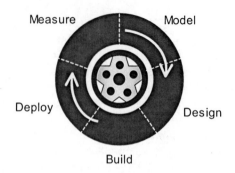

Fig. 2.3. The *gorilla* wheel of capacity management

The wheel is read clockwise starting at any position and consists of five segments corresponding to nominal phases in the development cycle any product:

Measure: Measurements are made on the current product, if it exists, or when a completely new product line is being developed. Back-of-the-envelope estimates (with appropriate fudge factors) can be based on the previous generation of product. These measurements might be made as part of quality assurance, for example, and these data are are fed into the modeling phase.

Model: Since capacity planning involves predictions (by definition), performance models are a natural part of any capacity plan. Relevant parameters are extracted from performance data collected in the measurement phase and are used to define the inputs of the performance model, e.g., the spreadsheet scalability models discussed in Chaps. 1 and 5.

Design: Architectural design decisions should be inclusive of capacity and performance projections from the modeling phase. Elsewhere (Gunther 2000) I have called this approach *performance-by-design* because it is a cost-effective way to build performance into the product, which, in turn, increases the chances that it will meet performance expectations. That keeps costs down and customers happy.

Build: In general, the capacity planner will be less involved during this engineering phase, but it is still worthwhile to participate in the relevant engineering meetings, where useful information may be acquired for use in modeling phases of the future, e.g., unit test or functional test data.

Deploy: The day of reckoning. The greater the investment in the modeling and design phases, the more likely the product will meet performance expectations and remain on track for the capacity plan. Like the build phase, measurements should be made where possible, and that is more easily facilitated if some degree of instrumentation (data collection points) is built into the product as part of the design phase.

The phases apply to either hardware or software artifacts, no matter whether those artifacts are built for internal use or as part of a commercial product. Figure 2.3 is meant to convery the more traditional approach as practiced in the heyday of centralized mainframe computing—what I referred to as gorilla capacity planning in Chap. 1. The appropriate visual, therefore, would seem to be a big, fat, tractor tire capable of doing a lot of heavy lifting.

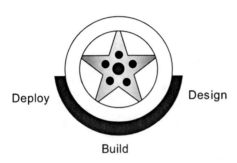

Deploy   Design

Build

Fig. 2.4. Running the wheel of capacity management (Fig. 2.3) on the rim because the important capacity planning phases have been dismissed as inflationary for the product schedule (Sect. 1.2.3)

2.3.2 Running on the Rim

To much of modern management, capacity planning conjures up this image of tractor tire, viz., a cumbersome expander of time that tends to inflate precious product development schedules. Under prevailing business pressures, managers tend to react to this "tractor tire" image by rushing to the other extreme, whereby the measurement and modeling phases are dropped altogether (or are never included in the first place), and decision making is largely reduced to guesswork. As Fig. 2.4 shows, it certainly shortens the skeletonized development cycle of guess, build, and guess again, but it also makes for a rather bumpy and uncertain ride because the development cycle is running partly on the rim.

Remark 2.2. As if this were not bad enough, there are other compelling incentives for pursuing this approach. The strategy in Fig. 2.4 is aimed exclusively at releasing a product within a narrow market window. Once the product becomes available and adopted, so-called performance enhancements merely provide additional revenue as part of the customer service contract. Therefore, management can hardly be faulted for concluding that, if customers are willing to pay more for the next "performance version," why design it in? In short, performance analysis gets dropped on the proverbial floor, products are released with inferior performance, and the customer ends up financing the enhancements. Against this kind of economic incentive, the purist does not stand a chance.

Things look bleak for the modern capacity planner. Is there any hope? As the old adage goes, *if you can't beat 'em, join 'em!* In Chap. 1 we pointed out that your management might be more receptive to your input if you can offer them capacity management that is streamlined to meet their own high-pressure constraints.

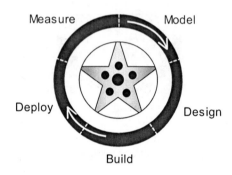

Fig. 2.5. The leaner and meaner GCaP wheel of performance. It has exactly the same periodic phases, in exactly the same order (cf. Fig. 2.3), but with an emphasis on higher planning efficiency (see Table 1.1)

2.3.3 Guerrilla Racing Wheel

Enter the *racing wheel* of GCaP (Fig. 2.5). It repairs the broken wheel of performance (Fig. 2.4) by reinstating the modern capacity planner as an active player in today's fast-paced development process. Notice also that Figs. 2.3 and 2.5 look similar. That is because the basic methodologies are very similar. In fact, in Chap. 8 I discuss a GCaP approach to Web site capacity planning that derives from a mainframe technique called *latent demand*. Mainframe methods are mature, and many of them (e.g., queueing models) can be adapted to the analysis of modern computing environments (Gunther 2005a). The important difference between Figs. 2.3 and 2.5 is that no matter which capacity planning techniques you choose, they must be a good match for the high-pressure demands of shortened development cycles. Since management is unlikely to change its ways, you have to change yours.

Assuming that the GCaP approach to capacity planning depicted in Fig. 2.4 is actually implemented, one has to remain vigilant against unbridled enthusiasm in the measure and model phases, otherwise the GCaP wheel

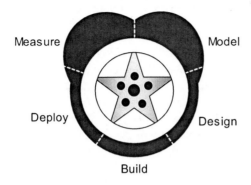

Fig. 2.6. The GCaP wheel becoming overweight because of unbridled enthusiasm in the capacity planning phases

can end up looking more like Fig. 2.6. In other words, those phases can become overinflated. It is important to keep in mind that management today is very sensitive to such inflationary expansion of their schedules (Sect. 1.2.3). Management no longer focuses on the speed of the product as much as the speed of producing the product. Nowadays, production performance matters more than product performance. GCaP requires that you remain cognizant of this management constraint and, accordingly, keep your capacity planning style lean and mean.

Clearly, I have somewhat oversimplified things to make a point. The real world is usually more confused than I have described it here. These days, when it comes to the trade-off between the speed with which a decision can be made and its accuracy, speed wins. Purists find this point difficult to accept. Most design decisions, however, do not require fine detail, and the decision makers are usually just looking for a sense of direction rather than a precise compass bearing. If they do no want precision, why waste time providing it? Moreover, design decisions are often revised many times throughout the product development cycle, so precision gets lost in the flux.

2.4 Summary

This chapter has provided a brief overview of the ITIL framework and its history. How widely it is adopted, and for how long, remains to be seen. The formal copyright structure, expense, and lack of early regional advocate groups have slowed the adoption of ITIL in the USA. This has started to change over the last few years.

Our focus in this chapter was on the position of capacity management within the ITIL framework. We saw (Fig. 2.1) that it resides within the service level management process, which, in turn, resides within the service delivery area, one of the seven top-level components of the ITIL framework. Although the ITIL framework emphasizes process over procedure, and the actual implementation details are left open to interpretation, we suggested in Sect. 2.3 that GCaP was intrinsically compatible with ITIL processes and best practices.

Perhaps one of the most significant benefits to come out of understanding the ITIL framework is that it forces you think about the business impact of capacity planning rather than remaining narrowly focused on the tools and technologies of capacity planning. Having acknowledged that point in this chapter, we now go on to examine in detail the tools and methodologies that can be applied to Guerrilla capacity planning.

3

Damaging Digits in Capacity Calculations

> *O, pardon! Since a crooked figure may*
> *Attest in little place a million;*
> *And let us, ciphers to this great accompt,*
> *On your imaginary forces work.*
>
> —William Shakespeare, *Henry V*

3.1 Introduction

In this chapter, we are going to discuss something that all engineers do: measure, measure, measure, end up with a set of different numbers, and finally use them to calculate something. For the Guerrilla planner the measurements might comprise certain performance metrics. Inevitably, the measurements are used to calculate a final result. This presents a subtle and often overlooked problem. For example, suppose you have the following three measurements: 2.95, 32.7, 1.414 (the units are not important here), and you want to add them together. How many digits should appear after the decimal point in the final result? The answer to that question (see Example 3.6) depends on something called *significant digits* or "sigdigs," and that is what we shall discuss in this chapter.

Note that in this chapter we shall be discussing the manipulation of digits within numbers, not the representation of those numbers in a finite amount of computer memory, e.g., whether to use fixed-point or floating-point representations. However, when it comes to questions of precision and accuracy there is some overlap between these topics, so we visit that briefly in Sect. 3.7.

Possibly, you have heard of the *sin of omission*, where you omit some details because you were not explicitly asked about them, but you also know that declaring them would alter the outcome. The problem of significant digits is more akin to a *sin of precision*, where more detail gets included in the outcome than is justified by the preciseness of the initial information.

Sins of precision can occur in a variety of ways, but each of them arises out of a failure to recognize two possible classes of numbers:

1. Exact numbers. These are numbers identified with the positive *integers*, e.g., 42, 137, also known as cardinal or *counting* numbers in mathematics.
2. Measured numbers. These numbers, e.g., 12.345, 3.14, are identified with the *real* numbers in mathematics.

Exact numbers are numbers that are exact by definition, e.g., there are 3600 seconds in one hour (Table C.2 in Appendix C). There can be no question about it because it is true by definition. Mathematically, exact numbers are associated with the integers. When you ask for seating at a restaurant, the number of people you give the maître d' is an integer—an exact number— because people only come in integral multiples, not fractions.

Measured numbers, on the other hand, are *estimates* that do not have the benefit of any integer multiplier. Mathematically, measured values are associated with the real numbers. The real number π refers to the measurement of a circle's circumference using the diameter as the yard stick. As the Greeks discovered to their dismay, the circumference is not an exact multiple of the diameter. It cannot be expressed as an integer, and therefore it is given the Greek meta name, π, instead.

Averaging is another process closely associated with measurements and estimates. For example, even though people occur naturally in integral multiples, the *average* family size in the USA during the 2000 census (`factfinder. census.gov`) was found to be 3.14 members. This is an estimate, not an exact number, and is expressed here to 3 significant digits, or 3 sigdigs.

Remark 3.1. The process of averaging causes information to be lost. In fact, the simpler process of adding numbers together loses information. If you are presented with the addends 3 and 4, you know unequivocally that the sum is $3 + 4 = 7$. However, if the situation is reversed and you are presented with the number 7, you no longer know with certitude which one of the 15 possible combinations of addends, e.g., $3 + 4$, $6 + 1$, $5 + 2$, was used. That information has been lost.

Performance monitoring tools of the type discussed in Chaps. 1, 8, and 11 collect data and report them as time-based averages over some specified sampling interval. Once again, these number are not and cannot be exact numbers. To make these distinctions clearer, we now define some terms more precisely.

3.2 Significant Digits

A significant digit is one that is actually measured. The number of significant digits in a measurement depends on the type of measuring device. No matter what the measuring device, there will always be some uncertainty in the measurement. Both the device and the observer add their own uncertainty to the measurement. This point reached world wide *significance* during the confusion surrounding the Florida vote count in the 2000 US presidential elections (see Example 3.2).

3.2.1 Accuracy

In everyday parlance, we tend to use the words *accuracy* and *precision* synonymously, but in science and engineering they are clearly distinguished. Accuracy

Fig. 3.1. Archery target analog of accuracy. Holes are grouped together around the bull's eye

refers to how close a measurement is to the expected value. Using an archery analogy (Fig. 3.1), where an arrow hole represents a measurement and the bull's eye represents the expected (or accepted) value, *accuracy* corresponds to the distance between the arrows and the bull's eye. Mathematically speaking, it is the maximum error we introduce because we truncate the digits. By convention, this is taken to be one half of the value of the least significant digit.

3.2.2 Precision

Again, using the archery target analogy, **precision** is *the distance between each hole,* irrespective of where they lie on the target with respect to the bull's eye. The grouping of arrow holes could be tightly clustered but a long way from the bull's eye. Mathematically, it is the number of digits available to

Fig. 3.2. Archery target analog of precision. Holes are grouped together but well away from the bull's eye

represent the mantissa. [1] Exact numbers (or integers) have infinite precision. But beware! As Fig. 3.2 shows, it is possible to have high precision with poor accuracy.

Example 3.1 (Calculating π).
In 1853 William Shanks published a calculation of π to 607 decimal places.

---

[1] The part of the number after the decimal point.

Twenty years later he published a result that extended this precision to 707 decimal places. It was the most precise numerical definition of π for its time and adorned many classroom walls.

In 1949 a computer was used to calculate π, and it was discovered that William Shanks's result was in error, starting at a point near the 500th decimal place all the way to the 707th decimal place. Nowadays, with the benefit of a value for π correct to 100,000 decimal places, we can say that William Shanks's techniques generated a *precise* value, but not an *accurate* value.   □

Example 3.2 (Voting and Precision).
Prior to the year 2000 presidential election in the USA, voting was assumed to have infinite precision, i.e., it was a straightforward counting problem. As noted in Sect. 3.1, counting is exact but measurement is not. The gross count in Florida had roughly the same number of votes in favor of each presidential candidate, and this led to the problem of determining the very small difference between two very large numbers. The precision required was on the order of 1 part in 6 million, or 0.0000166667%. The measurement process, including ballot machines and human inspectors, was not capable of producing this kind of precision, and gave rise to the infamous "hanging chad" and "pregnant dimple" ballot classifications. The Florida component of the presidential election degenerated into a philosophical question of, What is a vote? rather than addressing the narrow margin of measurement error by using the scientific process of repeated measurement.   □

3.3 Sifting for SigDigs

We now write down the steps for manually assigning significance to a digit. The first thing to remember is that all nonzero digits are counted as significant. We also need to consider if the number is exact (integer) or a decimal fraction (real).

3.3.1 Count by Zeros

The steps required to correctly determine the number of significant digits can be expressed by the following algorithm.

Algorithm 3.1 (Significance).
Scan the number left → right.
Is there an explicit decimal point?

Yes: Scan and locate the first nonzero digit.
    Count it and all digits to its right. (including zeros)
No: Append a decimal point.
    Scan and locate the last nonzero digit prior to the decimal point.
    All zeros trailing that digit should be ignored.

We consider some examples that demonstrate how to apply Algorithm 3.1.

Example 3.3. Let 200300 be the number. There are two nonzero digits: 2 and 3, shown in bold:

$$2\ 0\ 0\ \mathbf{3}\ 0\ 0$$

So, we have at least 2 sigdigs, so far. Is there a decimal point? No. So, we append it to produce:

$$2\ 0\ 0\ \mathbf{3}\ 0\ 0\ .$$

Now we scan from left to right and locate the *last* nonzero digit prior to the decimal point. That is the digit 3.

$$2\ 0\ 0\ \overset{\smile}{3}\ 0\ 0\ .$$

Every digit to the right of the 3 is now ignored and what remains is

$$2\ 0\ 0\ 3$$

which has 4 significant digits.   □

Consider another example, using a real number this time.

Example 3.4. Suppose 0.000050 is the number. There is one nonzero digit: the 5 shown in bold.

$$0\ .\ 0\ 0\ 0\ 0\ \mathbf{5}\ 0$$

Is there a decimal point? Yes. Hence, we scan from left to right and locate the *first* nonzero digit. Once again, that is the 5. We start counting from there and include any zeros. Therefore, there are two significant digits.   □

Finally, here is a table of examples for you to practice with at any time.

Example 3.5. Cover up everything in the following table of numbers except the first column, and using the above procedure, determine the number of sigdigs.

Number	SigDigs	Remark
50	1	See Sect. 3.5 for an application
0.00341	3	
1.0040	5	
50.0005	6	
6.751	4	
0.157	3	
28.0	3	
40300	3	Implicit decimal point
0.070	2	
30.07	4	
65000	2	Implicit decimal point
0.0067	2	
6.02×10^{23}	3	Explicit decimal point in scientific notation

This skill of determining the number of significant digits can be honed with a little consistent practice.   □

That is it in a nutshell! As you might expect, this manual process gets rather tedious, and if you do not use it frequently you might forget the algorithm altogether. Surprisingly, the above algorithm is not readily available in tools like calculators, spreadsheets, or mathematical codes. To help help rectify this situation Appendix D contains the sigdigs algorithm in several languages. It should be clear from those examples how to translate sigdigs into your favorite programming dialect, e.g., SAS, APL, etc.

3.3.2 Significance and Scale

According to Algorithm 3.1, each of the numbers 1100, 11 and 0.011 have the *same* number of significant digits. But, how can that be? Surely more effort was put into *measuring* the second and third decimal places of the third number.

To understand why this is an illusion, imagine you are getting a doctor's prescription filled at a pharmacy. The pharmacist may be required to measure out 11 milliliters of a liquid to make up your prescription. A *milliliter* means one one-thousandth of a liter, so 0.011 liter is the same as 11 milliliters (often abbreviated to ml). The pharmacist would use a graduated cylinder that has milliliter (ml) intervals marked on it. If the size of the cylinder held a total of 100 ml of liquid, there would be 100 major intervals marked on the side. With this device, it is very easy to sight and read off 11 ml (and even fractions of a milliliter, using the minor intervals).

Similarly, 1100 ml is the same as one and one-tenth of a liter. In that case, the pharmacist might use a liter-size graduated cylinder to measure 1100 ml in two steps. First, a full liter (1000 ml) is measured out. Then, the same graduated cylinder is used to measure out one tenth of a liter (a deciliter), and the two volumes are added together to produce 1100 ml. There are two things to notice about these measurements:

- The amount of reading effort is about the same in each case.
- The real difference is the size of the measuring device used.

In other words, the quantities 1100, 11, and 0.011 only distinguish scale, not precision. The precision is the same in each case (2 sigdigs), but the scale or measurement unit to which they refer is different. Hence, it makes no difference to the precision whether I write 0.011 liters or 11 milliliters.

3.4 Rounding Rules

Consider the number 7.246, which has 4 sigdigs. We would like to express it correctly with only 3 sigdigs. We need to eliminate the "6". We round up the "4" because the "6" is greater than 5, and the result is 7.25, correct to 3 sigdigs. But what if the number was 7.245? I was also taught to round up the "4" when the next digit is "5" or greater. It turns out that this rule has been modified recently because the old rule was introducing a *bias* into the results.

Definition 3.1 (Parity). *The parity of an exact number N (integer) is even if Nmod 2 ≡ 0; otherwise N is odd.*

Remark 3.2. Definition 3.1 should not be confused with bit wise parity. If a binary string of digits contains an even number of 1's (bitwise XOR or mod-2 addition), it is said to have even parity. Otherwise, it has odd parity.

The new rounding rule requires that we look at digits beyond the "5" (if any exist) as well as determine if the digit preceding the "5" is odd or even. In this case, there are no digits beyond the "5" and the digit preceding it is *even*. The new rule says to drop the '5' and leave the "4" alone, producing 7.24 correct to 3 sigdigs; not 7.25 as you might have anticipated using the old rule. If the number had been 7.235, the digit preceding the "5" is *odd*, so the new rule requires that the "3" be incremented to a "4". Same result, different reason. Checking the parity compensates for the old rounding bias. In general, for a terminating string of digits:

$$\dots X\,Y\,Z$$

we can express the new rounding rules in the following Algorithm.

Algorithm 3.2 (Rounding).

a. Examine Y
b.   If $Y < 5$ then goto (i)
c.   If $Y > 5$ then set $X = X + 1$ and goto (i)
d.   If $Y \equiv 5$ then examine Z
e.   If $Z \geq 1$ then set $Y = Y + 1$ and goto (a)
f.   If Z is blank or a string of zeros then
g.   Examine the parity of X
h.   If X is odd then set $X = X + 1$
i. Drop Y and all trailing digits

The old rule corresponds to steps (a–c) and (i), whereas the new procedure introduces the parity checking steps (d–h).

Using the old rule, you would round *down* if the next digit was any of (1, 2, 3, or 4), but you would round *up* if the next digit was any of (5, 6, 7, 8, or 9). In other words, looked at over a large number of rounding samples, you would tend to round down four out of nine times but round up five out of nine times. This is where the bias comes from. By selecting out the "5" as a special case, we are left with rounding up if the next digit is one of (6, 7, 8, or 9), i.e., 4/9-ths of the time. In the case of "5" exactly, we only round up only half time based on whether or not the preceding digit is odd. The overall effect is to make the rounding process balanced.

Many tools, e.g., Excel use the old rule. You can check this by setting the Cell Format to General. Then:

$$\boxed{=\text{ROUND}(7.245, 2)} \rightarrow \boxed{7.25}$$

Be aware that the second parameter in the ROUND function indicates the number of places after the decimal point, and not the number of sigdigs.

3.4.1 Golden Rule

When a calculation involves measurements with different numbers of significant digits, the result should have the same number of significant digits as the least of those among the measurements.

3.4.2 Sum Rule

A sum or difference can never be more precise than the least precise number in the calculation. So, before adding or subtracting measured quantities, round them to the same degree of precision as the least precise number in the group to be summed.

Example 3.6 (Addition).
Sum the quantities $2.95, 32.7$, and 1.414 correct to three significant digits. The least precise values have 3 sigdigs. Setting the sigdigs under their respective columns, and using a *diamond* to indicate the absence of a digit in that column, we have:

$$
\begin{array}{r}
2.95\,\Diamond \\
32.7\,\Diamond\,\Diamond \\
+\quad 1.414 \\
\end{array}
$$

After rounding using Algorithm 3.2, the summands become:

$$
\begin{array}{r}
3.0\,\Diamond\,\Diamond \\
32.7\,\Diamond\,\Diamond \\
+\quad 1.4\,\Diamond\,\Diamond \\
\hline
37.1 \\
\end{array}
$$

and the result 37.1 is correct to 3 sigdigs. (cf. Algorithm 3.1)   □

3.4.3 Product Rule

When two numbers are multiplied, the result often has several more digits than either of the original factors. Division also frequently produces more digits in the quotient than the original data possessed, if the division is continued to several decimal places. Results such as these appear to have more significant digits than the original measurements from which they came, giving the false impression of greater accuracy than is justified. To correct this situation, the following rules are used:

1. **Equal Sigdigs.** In order to multiply or divide two measured quantities having an equal number of significant digits, round the answer to the same number of significant digits as are shown in one of the original numbers.
2. **Unequal Sigdigs.** If one of the original factors has more significant digits than the other, round the more accurate number to one more significant digit than appears in the less accurate number. The extra digit protects the answer from the effects of multiple rounding.
3. **Final Rounding.** After performing the multiplication or division, round the result to the same number of sigdigs as appear in the less accurate of the original factors.

Example 3.7 (Multiplication).
Suppose measured throughput is $X = 2.95$ transactions per second, and the measured service demand is $D = 904.62$ ms. We wish to calculate the server utilization using Little's law $U = X \times D$ (see, e.g., Gunther 2005a).

Converting the timebase to seconds, the product becomes 2.95×0.90462. Note there are 3 sigdigs in the first factor (the least precise number). However, applying product rule 2 we retain 4 sigdigs in the second factor, i.e., 0.9046. Hence, we find:

$$
\begin{aligned}
X \times D &= 2.95 \times 0.90462, \\
&\Rightarrow 2.95 \times 0.9046, \\
&= 2.66857, \\
U &\Rightarrow 2.67 (\text{rounded up}),
\end{aligned}
$$

or 267% busy, which also matches the least number of significant digits. The $\Rightarrow$ symbol should be read as "becomes" to distinguish it from the "=" sign since that step involves a nonmathematical transformation with regard to precision.   □

3.5 Planning With Dollars and Sense

In an interesting paper entitled "How to Communicate and Define the Value of Performance in Dollars and Cents," Acree et al. (2001) employ a quantity D_{100} to represent the number of dollars per 100th of a second [2] of response time amortized over a 218-day work-year.

3.5.1 Cost Metric

The formula for D_{100} is given by:

$$
D_{100} = \frac{\$50 \text{ per hour}}{3600x100} \times \frac{5,500,000 \text{ trans. per day}}{1 \text{ work day}} \times \frac{218 \text{ work days}}{\text{year}} \tag{3.1}
$$

---

[2] $/ms$ would be more consistent with SI units (Appendix C).

Based on this formula the authors claim that the cost of 100th of a second is $D_{100} = \$166,528$. Let us examine this claim more closely.

The number with the least significant digits is the first factor, viz., \$50. From Example 3.5, we know that 50 has only 1 sigdig. This number is not exact since it is not a defintion. It is actually a guess as to what a department might charge on an hourly basis for its services. Asking different people in different departments would produce different estimates for the hourly charge. In this sense, it is equivalent to a measurement that should be written as $50 \pm \epsilon$. However, no indication of the measurement error ϵ is provided by Acree et al. (2001).

Remark 3.3. It is noteworthy that financial people never include explicit error ranges in their calculations, even though a lot of the input data comes either from measurements or guesswork ("guesstimates"). For example, try asking your accountant for an estimate of the error on your income tax returns.

The number of transactions per day is also expected to have some errors associated with it. The value will differ statistically each day. But because it is a quantity that is measured directly by the computer system, the number of sigdigs is likely to be higher than the hourly charge estimate. However, no error margin was provided for that quantity either.

3.5.2 Significant Digits

Dropping the units in (3.1) for simplicity, leads to the following calculation where we take significant digits into account:

$$D_{100} = \frac{50}{360,000} \times 5,500,000 \times 218 \,, \tag{3.2a}$$

$$= 0.000138888 \times 5,500,000 \times 218 \,, \tag{3.2b}$$

$$\Rightarrow 0.0001389 \times 5,500,000 \times 218 \,, \tag{3.2c}$$

$$= 166,541.1 \,, \tag{3.2d}$$

$$\Rightarrow 200,000.0 \text{ (rounding up)} \,. \tag{3.2e}$$

In other words, the cost factor $D_{100} = \$200,000.00$, correct to one significant digit, thereby matching the least accurate of the measured or estimated quantities used in the calculation.

You may be thinking we could have reached this conclusion immediately by simply rounding up the published result for D_{100}. The above detailed calculation is needed, however, to confirm that we need to round up and not down. If the value in (3.2d) had turned out to be 136,541.1 instead of 166,541.1, we would have been justified in rounding down to $D_{100} = \$100,000.00$ as the final result.

Moreover, in (3.2c) we kept 4 sigdigs in the first factor (one more than the value with the most sigdigs, i.e., 218, which has three sigdigs). This shows the variant of product rule 2 in action. It is applied by convention to retain as much information as possible until the final rounding.

3.6 Expressing Errors

There are several acceptable ways to express the magnitude of errors. In general, we have some measured quantity Y and some discrepancy ΔY such that the reported should be expressed as:

$$Y \pm \Delta Y .\tag{3.3}$$

The most appropriate form of ΔY depends on the context.

3.6.1 Absolute Error

Denoting the actual or expected value by y and the measurement or estimated value by $\hat{y}$, the error is the difference:

$$\Delta y = \hat{y} - y .\tag{3.4}$$

The absolute error is $|\Delta y|$. Equation (3.4) is similar to the definition of the residual:

$$r_i = y_i - \hat{y}_i ,\tag{3.5}$$

which is used in statistical regression and analysis of variance. It provides a measure of the vertical displacement between a given data point y_i and the regression line.

3.6.2 Relative Error

$$\delta y \equiv \frac{\Delta y}{y} = \frac{\hat{y} - y}{y} .\tag{3.6}$$

The percentage error is 100 times the relative error.

3.6.3 Standard Deviation

The standard deviation σ is the square root of the variance:

$$\sigma^2 = \sum_i^N \frac{\Delta y_i}{N - 1} .\tag{3.7}$$

Choosing $\Delta Y \equiv \sigma$ in (3.3) gives the measure of the *precision* of the measurement. Often, the value of the standard deviation is used to serve as the error bars for the data (Sect. 3.6.5). Notice that the standard deviation is positive and has the same units as the estimated quantity itself.

It can be shown that there is a 68% probability that an individual measurement will fall within one standard deviation ($\pm 1\sigma$) of the true value. Furthermore, there is a 95% chance that an individual measurement will fall within two standard deviations ($\pm 2\sigma$) of the true value, and a 99.7% chance that it will fall within $\pm 3\sigma$ of the true value.

3.6.4 Standard Error

The standard error (SE) is the square root of the sample variance s divided by the number of samples (N):

$$SE = \sqrt{\frac{s}{N}}. \qquad (3.8)$$

3.6.5 Error Bars

Error bars are used in plots like Fig. 3.3.

Example 3.8. In the response time calculation of Sect. 3.5, the least precise input value of $50 has only 1 sigdig. That sigdig resides in the 10's column. An appropriate way to express the error is half that sigdig viz., $10/2 = 5$, using (3.9). The hourly rate then would be expressed as $50±$5, which corresponds to ±5/50 or ±10%, and gives the following range:

$$\$180,000 < D_{100} < \$220,000$$

for the cost per 100th of a second. Notice that the published value of D_{100} (Acree et al. 2001) lies *below* this range and is therefore an *underestimate* of the proposed metric, even though it has the appearance of being a more precise value. □

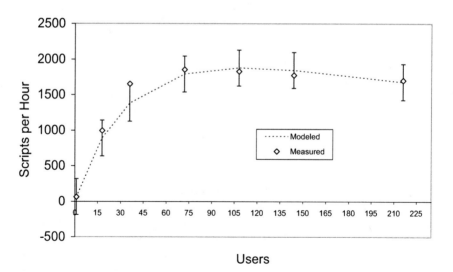

Fig. 3.3. Error bars associated with throughput measurements

Error bars can and should be included on all data plots. In reality, because the degree of error can differ for each data point, (vertical) error bars should have different heights to reflect that fact. The error bars in Fig. 3.3 simply used the *Y Error Bars* tab in Excel, which automatically computes the standard error. Although not entirely realistic, it is better than having no visual cue for error margins.

3.6.6 Instrumentation Error

Each instrument has an inherent amount of uncertainty in its measurement. Even the most precise measuring device cannot give the actual value because to do so would require an infinitely precise instrument. A measure of the precision of an instrument is given by its uncertainty. A good rule of thumb for determining instrument error (IE) is:

$$\text{IE} = \frac{1}{2} \text{ smallest sigdig} , \qquad (3.9)$$

Equation (3.9) states that the uncertainty of a measuring device is 50% of the smallest *subdivision* on the scale of the measuring device. The accuracy of an experimental value is expressed using its percent error (Sect. 3.6.2).

3.7 Interval Arithmetic

Some performance metrics, such as the *load average*, use fixed-point arithmetic (see e.g., Gunther 2005a, Chap. 4), while others use floating-point (see e.g., Hennessy and Patterson 1996, Appendix A). Each of these methods can run into precision problems.

One way around this problem is to use *interval arithmetic*. The idea behind interval arithmetic is to represent a real number by two numbers, a lower and an upper bound. This helps to avoid classical rounding errors of the type discussed in Sect. 3.4.

Remark 3.4. The rules for calculating with intervals look like this:

1. $[a, b] + [c, d] = [a + c, b + d]$.
2. $[a, b] \times [c, d] = [\, min(a {\times} c,\ a {\times} d,\ b {\times} c,\ b {\times} d),\ max(a {\times} c,\ a {\times} d,\ b {\times} c, `b {\times} d)\,]$.

Symbolic computation systems, such as *Mathematica* mentioned in Chap. 1, already have interval arithmetic capabilities built in. □

A large body of literature has emerged on numerical computing with real intervals. See e.g., `www.cs.utep.edu/interval-comp/books.html`.

3.8 Summary

All performance measurements contains errors that need to be tracked to avoid wrong conclusions and misleading results. The Golden Rule in Sect. 3.4.1 states that the result of a calculation should not have more significant digits than the least precise number used. If you have absorbed the points of this chapter, you now know there are 3 sigdigs in the number 50.0 but only 1 sigdig in the number 50. You can verify that by manually applying Algorithm 3.1 or using the programs in Appendix D. The rules for rounding numbers to the appropriate sigdigs have been modified in recent times and the latest conventions are incorporated in Algorithm 3.2. The NIST guidelines at physics.nist.gov/cuu/Uncertainty/index.html present even more complex expressions of uncertainty in measurement.

Now, you also appreciate why CPU utilization data is never displayed with more than 2 sigdigs. If you see a CPU busy reading of CPU% = 20 output by your favorite performance monitoring tools, you now know that it really should be reported with an error margin along the lines of CPU% = 20 ± 5. Ignoring error margins leads to the sin of precision, or possibly worse!

4

Scalability—A Quantitative Approach

> *You can drop a mouse down a mine shaft and on arriving at the bottom it gets a slight shock and walks away. A rat is killed, a man is broken, but a horse splashes.*
>
> —J. B. S. Haldane

4.1 Introduction

As the biologist J. B. S. Haldane pointed out in his famous essay entitled "On Being the Right Size," size does matter for biological systems (Haldane 1928). Haldane's essay (available online at `www.physlink.com/Education/essay_haldane.cfm`) is an elaboration on Galileo's observation, almost three hundred years earlier, that size also matters for mechanical structures like buildings and bridges. What Haldane could not have foreseen is that size also matters for computer systems.

In this chapter we explore the fundamental concept of *scaling* with a view to quantifying it for the purposes of doing Guerrilla-style capacity planning. In Chap. 6 we extend the same ideas to *software* scalability, and in Chap. 10 we shall see how recursive scaling in certain types of Internet traffic impacts the size of buffers.

4.2 Fundamental Concepts of Scaling

No doubt, you are familiar with the fairy tale of *Jack and the Beanstalk* from childhood. Did you ever wonder how big the giant was? It seems not to be mentioned in the original versions of the story. For that matter, did you ever wonder how big a beanstalk can be? It not only has to support Jack and the giant on the way down, it also has to support its own weight. Compared with the largest trees known, e.g., the giant redwoods in California, a beanstalk that reaches above the clouds is no mean feat. (See Examples 4.1 and 4.2 for a more quantitative discussion).

The first of the *Two New Sciences* discussed by Galileo Galilei (1638) is the science of materials and their strength. He recognized, over 350 years ago, that there was a natural limit to the size of physical structures; the inherent strength of materials does not permit arbitrary dimensions for real objects. Neither giant beanstalks nor a gorilla with the physical dimensions of King Kong is possible.

The simplest notion of scaling is to take every dimension, e.g., length, width, and height, and multiply them by the same factor, e.g., double the dimensions. This is called *geometric* scaling (Sect. 4.2.1). Of course, the volume V grows as the *cubic power* of the length, width, and height. If the linear dimensions belong to a cube, then $V = L^3$ quite literally. Therefore, if you double the sides of the cube, you increase its volume by a factor of eight! As we shall see, this introduces the concept of *power laws* into any discussion of scalability. We shall revisit power law scaling in Chap. 10.

Galileo and Haldane recognized that any volume not only occupies space, it has a mass (since it is made of some kind of material), and that mass has weight (here on earth, anyway). As the volume grows, so does the weight. At some point, the volume will weigh so much that it will literally crush itself! That suggests that there must be some *critical* size that an object can have just prior to crushing itself.

It turns out that a similar notion of critical size applies to scaling up computer systems and the applications they run. In this chapter we introduce a *universal* scaling law (Sect. 4.4) for hardware, and later for software in Chap. 6, which contains within it the notion of critical size, i.e., a critical number of processors or users. This universal scalability law is based on *rational functions*, rather than power laws.

4.2.1 Geometric Scaling

Definition 4.1 (Geometric Growth). *Arithmetic growth can be expressed by a sequence that increases by an additive constant or common difference δ applied to a first term a, i.e., $a, a + \delta, a + 2\delta, a + 3\delta, \ldots$. Geometric growth is represented by a sequence that increases by a multiplicative constant or common ratio ϕ, i.e., $a, a\phi, a\phi^2, a\phi^3, \ldots$.*

A useful method for the subsequent discussion is known as *dimensional analysis*. The three engineering dimensions: mass m, length L, and time t, are chosen as basic because they are easy to measure experimentally. Dimensions are not the same as units. For example, the physical quantity speed may be measured in units of m/s, or miles per hr, but irrespective of the units used, the speed can always be expressed in terms of a fundamental dimension of length L divided fundamental dimension of time t, so we say that the dimensions of speed are L/T. A common notational convention is to write the *dimensions of a quantity* using square brackets [ ], e.g., [speed] $= L/T$.

The surface area A can be expressed of its length dimension as:

$$[A] = L^2, \tag{4.1}$$

and similarly for the volume V:

$$[V] = L^3 \,. \tag{4.2}$$

Alternatively, we can express the volume solely in terms of the area. Starting with (4.2) written as:

$$
\begin{aligned}
V &= A\,L \,, \\
&= A\sqrt{A} \ \text{from (4.1)}\,, \\
&= A^{3/2} \,.
\end{aligned} \tag{4.3}
$$

Equation (4.3) has the general form of a *power law* function:

$$y = a x^b \,. \tag{4.4}$$

Taking the logarithms of both sides produces:

$$\ln(y) = b\ln(x) + \ln(a) \,, \tag{4.5}$$

and substituting $Y = \ln(y)$, $X = \ln(x)$, and $c = \ln(a)$ into (4.5) simplifies to:

$$Y = bX + c \,, \tag{4.6}$$

which is a linear function that can be fitted using the method of *linear least squares* (Levine et al. 1999), as we shall demonstrate in Chap. 5.

4.2.2 Allometric Scaling

Definition 4.2 (Allometric Growth). *Geometric similarity cannot continue indefinitely. When an organism changes shape in response to size changes (i.e., does not maintain geometric similarity), we say that it scales allometrically (allo: different, metric: measure). Allometric scaling is common in nature, both when comparing two animals of different sizes and when comparing the same animal at two different sizes (i.e., growth).*

The *density*:

$$d = \frac{m}{V} \equiv \text{const.} \tag{4.7}$$

is assumed to be a constant, i.e.,

$$[V] \propto m \,. \tag{4.8}$$

We further assume that:

- The weight $m \times g$, where g is terrestrial acceleration due to gravity, is proportional to the volume V. This follows from (4.2). The weight is also called the mechanical *load*.
- Mechanical *strength* is proportional to the cross-sectional area A. In other words, the strength of a rigid body can be measured by the applied pressure P, or force per unit area: $P = m \times g/A$.

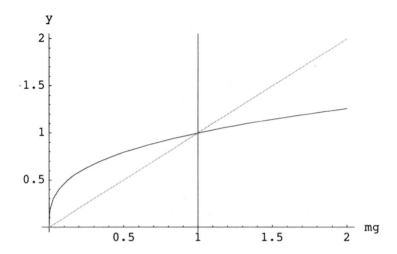

Fig. 4.1. Allometric scaling as a function of weight ($m \times g$). As long as the system strength (*curve*) exceeds its weight (*line*), growth is sustainable. Beyond the critical point, where the two curves cross, the system will collapse

Substituting (4.2) into (4.3) it follows that $m = A^{3/2}$ or , after rearranging:

$$[A] \propto m^{2/3} . \tag{4.9}$$

Using (4.9), the pressure P or load per unit area can be written as:

$$\frac{mg}{A} \propto \frac{m^{3/3}}{m^{2/3}} = m^{1/3} ,$$

or equivalently:

$$[P] \propto m^{1/3} . \tag{4.10}$$

The mechanical strength (4.10) also tells us how the bulk V scales with the surface area A:

$$\left[\frac{V}{A}\right] \propto m^{1/3} . \tag{4.11}$$

The mechanical strength associated with (4.10) appears as a curve in Fig. 4.1, when plotted as a function of m. The total weight $m \times g$, on the other hand, is a linear function of m (since g is constant). At some value of the body's weight the two curves cross, and beyond that *critical point* the body becomes prone to complete collapse due to its weight exceeding its mechanical strength.

4.2.3 Critical Size

If we consider various organisms (including giants), we know that the crushing strength of bone is essentially constant for all of them. Since the pressure

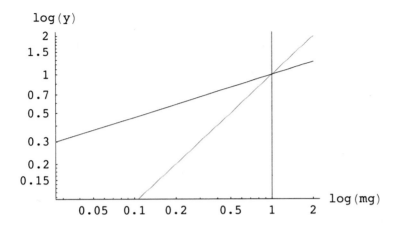

Fig. 4.2. Any allometric curve of the form $y = ax^b$ in Fig. 4.1 becomes a straight line on a log-log plot, and the growth parameter b can be determined from the slope of that line

function given by (4.10) is a monotonically *increasing* function, there must be the critical size for each organism. This becomes particularly apparent if we plot both (4.8) and (4.10) using log-log coordinates like Fig. 4.2.

4.2.4 Sizing Examples

We consider some estimates of critical size.

Example 4.1 (Can Giants Exist?). In his essay "On Being the Right Size," Haldane (1928) takes issue with the notion of giants in such fairy tales as *Jack and the Beanstalk*. One fairy tale has a giant that is ten times as tall an a human and scaled in geometric proportion. If we take the typical human attributes to be:

- height: $L = 1.8$ m
- weight: $w = 90$ kg

The critical weight w_c for bone is assumed to be $10 \times w = 900$ kg. Taking the giant's (geometric) attributes as:

- height: $L_G \equiv 10 \times L = 18$ m
- volume: $V_G = (10L)^3 = 1000 \times V$ m^3
- weight: $w_G \sim 1000 \times w = 90,000$ kg, which is close to 100 US tons!

Clearly, such a humanoid would be crushed under their own weight. The critical size for a human involves more than just weight, e.g., pulmonary capacity, size of capillaries, etc. The Guinness record is held by a man 8 ft 4 in tall (2.54 m), which is less than twice the typical human height. □

Example 4.2 (Beanstalks). In the *Jack and the Beanstalk* story, assume the cloud base is 1000 ft (fairly low), and instead of a beanstalk, consider a tree. Taking the typical tree attributes to be:

- height: $L = 100$ ft
- radius: $R = 1.5$ ft
- weight: $w = 10,000$ lb (approx. 5 US tons)

Treating the tree as a simple cylinder, its volume is given by $V = \pi R^2 \times L$. Scaling the tree geometrically means $L \to 10\,L$ and $R \to 10\,R$, so the volume and therefore the weight increases by a factor of 1000. At 5000 tons, not only is a 1000-ft tree unlikely to be sustainable, a 1000-ft beanstalk is even less likely to be able to bear its own weight, let alone the giant in Example 4.1.

□

Example 4.3 (Space Elevator). Although perhaps not too far removed from the realm of fairy tales, but much more likely than giants and cloud-climbing beanstalks, is the so-called *space elevator* (www.elevator2010.org/site/primer.html). This proposed alternative means of putting payloads into earth orbit will be constructed from a ribbon of carbon nanotubes having the 30 times the tensile strength of steel.

- height: $L_{se} = 62,000$ miles (99,779,328.0 m)
- width: $W_{se} = 3$ ft (1 m)
- weight: $w_{se} = 1000$ tons (907,184.74 kg)

Using (4.7), the density of this new material is:

$$d = \frac{w_{se}}{g \times L_{se} \times W_{se}},$$
$$= \frac{907,184.74}{9.82 \times 1 \times 99,779,328},$$
$$= 0.000925856 \text{ kg}/m^2,$$

or about 1 gm/m², which is close to the density of the plastic-wrap used to preserve food items.   □

To summarize the key points so far, we have seen that scaling is primarily a geometric notion. Conceptually, you can make a system bigger or smaller by merely stretching it equally in every dimension (isometrically). However, it has been documented since the time of Galileo that mechanical and biological systems have inherent limitations to growth (and to shrinkage). As we scale up a physical system, intrinsic overheads (such as weight) begin to dominate and eventually cause the system to fail beyond some critical point. Therefore, scaling is actually allometric (Fig. 4.1).

Remark 4.1. Even something like nanotechnology (the technology of scaling down) suffers from intrinsic limits. That is why a nanoscale version of say, an electric motor, is constructed in a way completely different from the way a terrestrial-scale electric motor is built.

As we shall see in the remainder of this chapter and the rest of this book, computer systems can also be scaled up in terms of their computing capacity. Indeed, they also scale in a monotonically increasing fashion, not unlike the strength curve in Fig. 4.1. But, just like physical systems, they also have intrinsic limits such that the computer system cannot be scaled indefinitely. These limits do not usually lead to catastrophic system failure, but the increasing overhead can degrade system performance (Fig. 4.3) and therefore can also have a significant impact on capacity planning.

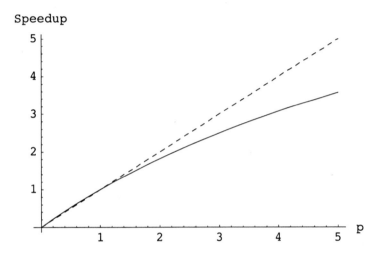

Fig. 4.3. Ideal linear speedup (*dashed*) compared with more realistic nonlinear speedup (*solid*). Unlike Fig. 4.1, however, there is no critical intersection. Instead, speedup shows diminishing returns from the outset at small p-processor configurations.

4.3 Hardware Scalability

It is easiest if we begin our discussion of computer system scalability from the standpoint of hardware scalability, and then extend those concepts to software scalability later. In this chapter we lay down the fundamental concepts and theorems for a *universal law of scalability*, and then show how to apply them in Chap. 5. Our approach is *universal* because it applies to any hardware, including symmetric multiprocessors (SMPs), chip multiprocessors (CMP) or multicores, and clusters. And, as we shall see in Chap. 6, it also applies to the scalability of applications software.

Since, at root, scalability is intimately tied up with the concept of parallel workloads, we start by reviewing the simple notion of ideal parallelism.

4.3.1 Ideal Parallelism

It is useful to begin by distinguishing between the terms *speedup* and *scaleup*. The former term is commonly associated with a measure of parallel numerical performance, while the latter is more appropriate for commercial system workloads. Speedup quantifies the reduction in elapsed time obtained by

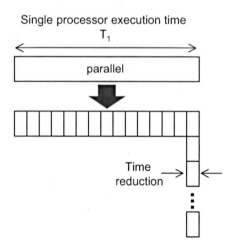

Fig. 4.4. Ideal parallelism. The uniprocessor execution time T_1 is reduced to T_1/p by equipartitioning the workload across p physical processors

executing a fixed amount of work on a successively greater number of processors. This notion underlies the motivation for an aircraft designer to use a supercomputer—she wants the same complex calculations to be executed faster. This is not, however, the reason that commercial businesses invest in additional processing power.

More commonly, a commercial enterprise needs to support more users in such a way that the additional workload does not adversely impact the response times of the current user community. This, in turn, requires that the capacity of the computing system be increased by scaling it up in proportion to the additional load.

Whereas the concept of speedup assumes a fixed size workload with the execution time being scaled down in proportion to the number of processors applied to it, scaleup assumes the converse constraints: maintaining a fixed execution time (or response time) per user while scaling the workload up in proportion to the number of processors applied to it. We shall denote this scaled up capacity $C(p)$, where p is the number of processors in the system. To establish some terminology for our later discussion, we give a formal definition of speedup $S(p)$.

The simplest notion of speedup applies to what might best be described as "naive parallelism" depicted in Fig. 4.4. Naive parallelism assumes that a workload that runs on a uniprocessor in time T_1 can be equally partitioned and executed on p processors in one pth of the uniprocessor execution time, viz., T_1/p. This is tantamount to linear speedup.

4.3.2 Amdahl's Law

It was Gene Amdahl's seminal observation (Amdahl 1967), almost forty years ago, that most workloads cannot be partitioned in this ideal way because there is some portion of the workload that is *sequential* and, therefore, can only be executed on a single processor. We denote this serial portion of the execution time by the parameter σ. The remainder of the workload is said to be *parallelizable*. Fig. 4.5 shows this effect graphically. The execution time for a

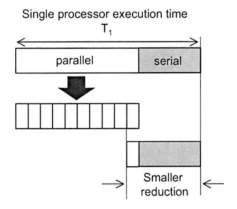

Fig. 4.5. Amdahl's law recognizes that ideal parallelism (Fig. 4.4) cannot be achieved in general because there are certain portions of the workload that can only be executed sequentially (*gray*). That aggregate portion of the total execution time is called the serial fraction

fixed-size workload on a uniprocessor is the same as Fig. 4.4. The uniprocessor time can be split into two portions: a portion that can be made to execute in parallel and a portion that remains sequential or serial.

Definition 4.3 (Serial fraction). *The serial fraction σ of the total execution time is the cumulative time for which the workload executes in purely sequential of serial fashion. The serial fraction takes values in the range:* $0 < \sigma < 1$.

The serial fraction is depicted as the dark segment of Fig. 4.5. Only the remaining portion of the total time $(1 - \sigma)T_1$ can be run in parallel by subdividing that part of the workload into p equal subtasks and executing those subtasks on p physical processors. This is depicted by the divisions on the middle bar of Fig. 4.5.

The reduced execution time to perform the complete computation with p processors is depicted by the shorter bar in the lower right of Fig. 4.5. We see immediately that the ratio of the parallel portion to the serial portion grows as the parallel portion is made smaller (finer granularity). What are the consequences of this effect? Using the above notation, we can write this time reduction as:

$$T_p = \sigma T_1 + \frac{(1 - \sigma)T_1}{p} . \tag{4.12}$$

Definition 4.4 (Speedup). *The speedup:*

$$S(p) = \frac{T_1}{T_p} \tag{4.13}$$

is defined as the ratio of the elapsed time on a uniprocessor T_1 to the elapsed time on a p-way multiprocessor T_p. The smaller the denominator T_p can be made, the greater the speedup that can be achieved.

Substituting (4.12) into (4.13) produces:

$$S(p) = \frac{T_1}{\sigma T_1 + \left(\frac{1-\sigma}{p}\right)T_1} , \tag{4.14}$$

which simplifies to:

$$S(p) = \frac{p}{1 + \sigma(p - 1)} \tag{4.15}$$

after canceling the common factors of T_1 and rearranging terms. Hereafter, we shall refer to (4.15) as Amdahl's law.

Remark 4.2. It is noteworthy that (4.15) does not appear in Gene Amdahl's 1967 paper. In fact, there are no equations at all in that three-page paper. Its content is entirely empirical. Equation (4.15) is usually considered to be due to Ware (1972). One has to admire the skill in having an equation named after you that you never wrote down. But Amdahl did not have it all his own way. A major goal was to convince people that multiprocessors were not cost effective because of the difficulty in achieving parallel performance (see Remark 4.3). On this score he lost badly. Not only are most servers today multiprocessors, but Amdahl's law has its highest citation frequency in the parallel processing literature.

This speedup function has the characteristic curve shown in Fig. 4.6. Similar models have been used to express speedup bounds on various types of parallel platforms, e.g., speedup of vector parallel processors, where p is identified with the ratio of vector to scalar speed, and σ is interpreted as the fraction of time spent in scaler mode. According to (4.15), significant speedup

Speedup

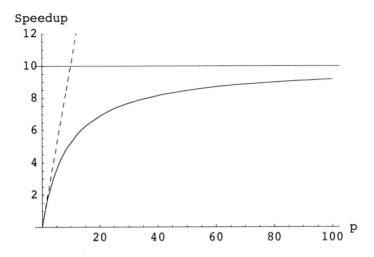

Fig. 4.6. Amdahl speedup (*solid*) compared to linear scalability (*dashed*). The serial fraction $\sigma = 0.010$ corresponds to the asymptotic ceiling at $\sigma^{-1} = 10$

is likely only for a relatively high percentage of vectorization which leads to the ironic conclusion that, to first order, supercomputer performance is determined by its scalar speed rather than its vector speed.

If the seriality parameter vanishes ($\sigma = 0$) then the speedup would follow the ideal linear rising trajectory in Fig. 4.6. The presence of non-zero seriality ($\sigma \neq 0$) in the denominator of (4.15), however, means that as the number of processors is increased to compute the parallel portion of the workload, the scaling curve falls away from linear. The rate at which it diverges is determined by the actual value of σ.

Theorem 4.1 (Amdahl asymptote). *As $p \to \infty$, (4.15) approaches the upper bound σ^{-1} shown in Fig. 4.6*

Proof. Rewrite (4.15) in the form:

$$S(p) = \frac{1}{\frac{1}{p} + \sigma\frac{(p-1)}{p}} \, . \tag{4.16}$$

As $p \to \infty$, the first term in the denominator vanishes and the second term approaches σ. Hence, $S(p) \sim \sigma^{-1}$ for large p. $\qquad\qquad\square$

Note, as the parallel execution time is reduced, the constant serial portion of the workload begins to dominate the speedup ratio. Put another way: the greater the parallelism, the greater the serial proportion. And this phrasing captures the motivation behind Amdahl's original observation. His interest as a mainframe manufacturer was not in understanding the benefits of parallel architectures but to provide a simple, intuitive demonstration that a very fast single processor is likely to be more cost effective than the overhead of orchestrating many slower processors.

Remark 4.3. This conclusion is also consistent with a well-known result in queueing theory (See Gunther 2005a, Chap. 2). When comparing the response time performance of a fast $M/M/1$ queue with an $M/M/m$ queue, where the m-servers have the same total capacity as the single server, the fastest single server is always the best choice! This is the basis for the canonical argument favoring mainframes. See Remark 4.2.

In evaluating parallel systems, another important performance measure is efficiency.

Definition 4.5 (Efficiency). *The efficiency is defined in terms of the speedup $S(p)$ in Definition 4.4 as:*

$$E(p) = \frac{S(p)}{p}, \tag{4.17}$$

which is the average speedup per processor.

Using Definition 4.5 together with (4.15), and assuming the variable p can take on continuous values, Karp and Flatt (1990) point out the following relationship between efficiency and the seriality parameter:

$$\frac{\mathrm{d}}{\mathrm{d}p} E^{-1}(p) = \sigma, \tag{4.18}$$

which provides a useful additional performance metric. The seriality can be viewed as a direct measure of the change in efficiency as the system is scaled up. In the ideal case, E^{-1} increases linearly with p. Any deviation of E^{-1} from linear is a sign of lost parallelism. The value of the seriality can be ascertained from direct measurements of $S(p)$ by virtue of the relationship

$$\sigma = \frac{(p/S) - 1}{p - 1}, \tag{4.19}$$

which is just a rearrangement of (4.15).

4.3.3 Multiuser Scaleup

Database applications represent ideal candidates for parallelism since each transaction is a relatively small, independent task that can be run on separate processors. The capacity function $C(p)$ is defined as the throughput achieved using p processors, X_p, relative to that achieved on a uniprocessor, X_1.

Definition 4.6 (Scaleup). *The scaleup capacity is given by the ratio*

$$C(p) = \frac{X_p}{X_1}, \tag{4.20}$$

which is equivalent to a normalized throughput.

We further assume that each processor is optimized with respect to process concurrency, i.e., enough users or transaction generators are executing to fully utilize the available cycles on each processor without causing an inordinate amount of context switching. Only one transaction generation process runs at a time on a single processor. In general, a processor will not be doing useful work if it has to do other things such as:

- wait for a bus transfer from another processor memory
- wait for a disk or network I/O completion
- serial wait on a database latch

We suppose that a uniprocessor performs compute-intensive operations at 100% utilization (i.e., no significant wait I/O) and completes C_1 transactions with response time T_1. The uniprocessor throughput is given by:

$$X_1 = \frac{C_1}{T_1}. \tag{4.21}$$

The impact of multiuser scaleup on response time is shown in Fig. 4.7.

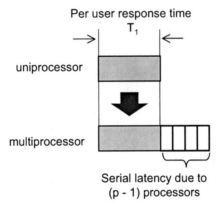

Fig. 4.7. The effect of multiuser scaleup is to stretch the response time in proportion to the number of physical processors

To understand the effect of scaleup on response time, consider the case where the size of the workload is doubled so that twice the number of uniprocessor transactions are completed. The dual processor capacity is expected be twice that of the uniprocessor:

$$C_2 = 2C_1. \tag{4.22}$$

Moreover, the uniprocessor should only take twice as long to complete twice the number of transactions, viz., $2T_1$, because the throughput is already saturated and therefore remains as X_1.

Doubling the compute capacity by adding another processor ($p = 2$), we might expect, naively, that the dual-processor system will complete C_2 transactions with the same response time it takes the uniprocessor to complete C_1 transactions. We know, however, from queueing theory and from measurements on real multiprocessor systems that the dual-processor consistently completes slightly less than $2C_1$ transactions in time T_1.

Referring to Fig. 4.7, and following the notation established in our derivation of speedup (4.15), we suppose that the stretch in user-response time for a dual processor is some fraction σT_1 of the uniprocessor response time:

$$T_2 = T_1 + \sigma T_1 . \tag{4.23}$$

Since the dual processor time T_2 is longer than T_1, the throughput will be somewhat less than expected. To see this in more detail, we use (4.21), (4.22), and (4.23), to derive the explicit dual processor throughput. The steps are:

$$X_2 = \frac{C_2}{T_2} ,$$

$$= \frac{2C_1}{T_1 + \sigma T_1} ,$$

$$= \frac{2}{1 + \sigma} \frac{C_1}{T_1} ,$$

which simplifies to:

$$X_2 = \frac{2X_1}{1 + \sigma} . \tag{4.24}$$

What is the significance of this result? Clearly, for any nonzero value of σ, the dual processor throughput capacity is less than twice that of the uniprocessor system. Suppose, for example, that σ is only 3% of T_1, then the capacity scaleup $C(2) = X_2/X_1$ is only 1.94 times the capacity of the uniprocessor. Consequently, if the uniprocessor is capable of 100 transactions per second (within some specified response time period), the dual processor will achieve only 194 transactions per second; not 200 transactions per second as would be expected on the basis of naive parallelism.

Extending this argument by analogy with (4.23), the three-way multiprocessor response time gains another time increment σT_1:

$$T_3 = T_1 + \sigma T_1 + \sigma T_1 = T_1 + 2\sigma T_1 ,$$

such that the corresponding throughput becomes:

$$X_3 = \frac{3X_1}{1 + 2\sigma} . \tag{4.25}$$

Generalizing this line of argument, the throughput for a p-way multiprocessor is given by:

$$X_p = \frac{p\,C_1}{T_1 + (p-1)\sigma T_1}$$

$$= \frac{pX_1}{1 + \sigma(p-1)}.$$

and from (4.20), the p-way scaleup is:

$$C(p) = \frac{p}{1 + \sigma(p-1)}. \tag{4.26}$$

This result is very surprising. Equation (4.26) for scaleup is *identical* to Amdahl's law (4.15) for speedup, even though we used entirely different logical arguments to arrive at each. How can it be explained?

4.3.4 Serial-Parallel Duality

The reason for the underlying identity between the scalability laws (4.15) and (4.26) is contained in the following theorem.

Theorem 4.2 (Gunther (1998)). *Let (σ, π) be a continuous dual-parameter pair, where σ the serial fraction and π the parallelizable fraction of the workload. Then, the ratio σ/π is invariant under scaling by an integer number of physical processors $p \in \mathbb{N}$.*

Proof. Consider each case separately.

Speedup: Referring to Fig. 4.5, σ corresponds to the shaded region in the top part of the diagram, while $\pi = 1 - \sigma$ corresponds to the white region. In this case, σ is held fixed while π is reduced in integral multiples of p (the meaning of "parallelism"). We can summarize this transformation as:

$$\frac{\sigma}{\pi} \mapsto \frac{\sigma}{\pi'} \equiv \frac{\sigma}{\pi/p} \tag{4.27}$$

Scaleup: Referring to Fig. 4.7, π corresponds to the shaded region in the bottom part of the diagram, while σ corresponds to each accumulated white region. In this case, π is held fixed while σ is expanded in integral multiples of p (the meaning of "scaleup"). We summarize this transformation as:

$$\frac{\sigma}{\pi} \mapsto \frac{\sigma'}{\pi} \equiv \frac{p\sigma}{\pi} \tag{4.28}$$

Since the rescaled ratios in (4.27) and (4.28) are identical, the ratio σ/π remains invariant under configuration transformations.   □

Remark 4.4. In the case of speedup, the elapsed time becomes $\sigma + \pi' = \sigma + \pi/p$, which corresponds to the denominator in (4.14). For scaleup, however, the elapsed time becomes:

$$\pi + \sigma' = \pi + p\sigma$$
$$= (1 - \sigma) + p\sigma$$
$$= 1 + (p\sigma - \sigma)$$

which leads to (4.26).

4.3.5 Scaled Speedup

Another form of scaling that appears in the literature is called scaled speedup [Gustafson 1992] which shall denote here by $C_{ss}(p)$. The form of $C_{ss}(p)$ can easily be derived using Figure 5-4.

The total uniprocessor elapsed time, $T(1)$, can be trivially rewritten as the sum of two terms viz., $T_1 = \sigma T_1 + (1 - \sigma)T_1$. The assumption of a fixed size workload is now replaced by the alternative notion that the parallelizable portion of the workload can be increased to p times the uniprocessor workload. As a consequence, the serial portion no longer dominates the speedup ratio. Rewriting the speedup (4.15) to reflect this workload scaleup gives:

$$C_{ss}(p) = \frac{[\sigma + (1 - \sigma)p] \, T_1}{\left[\sigma + \frac{(1-\sigma)p}{p}\right] T_1}, \tag{4.29}$$

which immediately simplifies to the linear form:

$$C_{ss}(p) = \sigma + (1 - \sigma)p. \tag{4.30}$$

Equation (4.30) suggests that it is possible to beat Amdahl's law (4.26) since capacity now scales linearly with the number of processors; provided the amount of work (single problem size) is also scaled concomitantly. Workloads of this type are referred to as data-parallel and gives rise to the term SPMD (single program multiple data) in contrast to SIMD (single instruction multiple data).

Linear scaling on scientific problems was reported by Sandia National Laboratories in 1998. This kind of quasi-linear speedup is difficult to achieve in reality because communications overhead begins to dominate; a term not accounted for in this simple formulation (See e.g., Gelenbe 1989).

4.4 Universal Scalability Model

We now turn to an assessment of capacity when a parallel architecture is running an online transaction processing workload. As more processors are added, both the speedup $S(p)$ and the multiuser scaleup $C(p)$, respectively, approach the asymptote σ^{-1} as $p \to \infty$. Although both these scaling models include degradation effects due to serialization, neither accounts for the additional overhead due to interprocessor communication (Gunther 1993, 1996, 2000).

Typical sources of multiprocessor overhead include:

- code paths in the operating system
- exchange of shared writable data between processor caches
- data exchange between processors and main memory
- spin lock synchronization (serialization) of shared writable data accesses
- waiting for an I/O or memory access to complete

In database management systems, the server processes may need to communicate with each other via the supervising database process when there are updates to database tables.

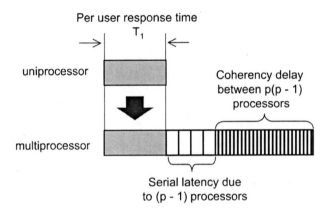

Fig. 4.8. Multiuser scaleup showing the per-user response time growing linearly with the number of processors due to serial delays (cf. Fig. 4.7), and the additional, but smaller, coherency delays increasing quadratically due to point-to-point exchanges between processors

Assuming, for the moment, there is only one database process per physical processor, any process may communicate with up to $(p-1)$ other processes. Figure 4.8 shows that, on average, the interaction between processes will grow like $p(p-1) \simeq p^2$ (quadratically) for a large number of processes.

Definition 4.7 (Coherency). *The magnitude of this additional point-to-point latency is denoted by a new parameter $\kappa \geq 0$.*

Following the same steps we used to derive (4.26), this additional term must appear in the denominator of the capacity formula. The result is:

$$C(p) = \frac{p}{1 + \sigma\,(p-1) + \kappa\,p(p-1)}\,. \tag{4.31}$$

The universal scaleup characteristic is shown in Fig. 4.9 together with Amdahl scaling, which corresponds to $\kappa = 0$. It is a *concave* function. Comparison with Fig. 4.1 shows that although the computer system does not fail beyond $p^* = 25$, its available capacity does degrade significantly.

Remark 4.5 (Previous Versions). Elsewhere, (4.31) is written:

$$C(p) = \frac{p}{1 + \sigma\big[(p-1) + \lambda p(p-1)\big]} . \tag{4.32}$$

and I called it the *super-serial model* in deference to Amdahl's law (Gunther 1993, 1998, 2000). Note the position of the square brackets. They imply a dependency between the coherency λ and the contention σ, viz., if $\sigma = 0$ (no contention) then the value of λ is irrelevant. This is true for the tightly-coupled SMP architectures from which (4.32) was originally derived. In modern loosely-coupled systems it is possible to have coherency latencies independent of contention latencies, e.g., NUMA architectures. To reflect these trends, the two parameters σ and κ are now treated as independent in (4.31), thus making it universal. In terms of the previous super-serial model, $\kappa = \sigma \lambda$.

Definition 4.8 (Rational Function). *Universal scalability as given in (4.31) is defined by a rational function rather than a power law (cf. Sect. 4.2). $R(x)$ is a rational function if it can be expressed as the quotient of two polynomials $P(x)$ and $Q(x)$:*

$$R(x) = \frac{P(x)}{Q(x)} .$$

That this scaling function is associated with certain fundamental aspects of queueing theory (see Appendix A), has some very important implications for physically achievable computer system scalability.

If $\sigma > 0$, then as $\kappa \to 0$ (4.31) reduces to the simpler scaleup equation (4.26). In terms of the effect on elapsed times in Fig. 4.7, the coherency term in (4.31) dilates the multiprocessor elapse time even more, as shown in Fig. 4.8.

Remark 4.6. The term *concave function* is being used here in the mathematical sense. Concave refers to the fact that the function has a bump shape ($\frown$), when viewed from the x-axis, and therefore has a unique maximum (see Figs. 4.9 and 5.14). Conversely, a convex function is bowl shaped ($\smile$), when viewed from the x-axis, and therefore has a unique minimum. For more details, the interested reader should see `mathworld.wolfram.com/ConcaveFunction.html` and `mat.gsia.cmu.edu/QUANT/NOTES/chap2/node6.html`.

4.4.1 The Role of Coherency

Universal scalability in (4.31) incorporates three important effects in the denominator of a single equation:

1. **Concurrency:** The first term in the denominator. If there were no interaction between the processors the capacity function would scale linearly, i.e., $C(p) = p$.

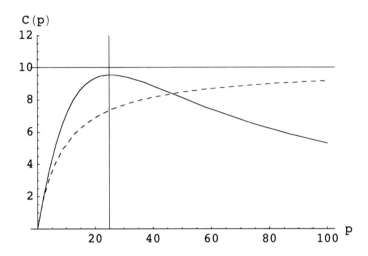

Fig. 4.9. Universal scalability characteristic (*solid*) compared with Amdahl scaling (*dashed*), which corresponds to a coherency value of $\kappa = 0$ in (4.31). A key feature of universal scaling is that a maximum can develop (here located at $p^* = 25$) depending on the values of σ and κ in (4.33). Comparison with Fig. 4.1 shows that although the system does not fail beyond p^*, its available capacity can degrade significantly

2. **Contention:** The second term in the denominator. It represents the degree of serialization on shared writable data and is parameterized by the constant σ.
3. **Coherency:** The third term in the denominator. It represents the penalty incurred for maintaining consistency of shared writable data (see e.g., Hennessy and Patterson 1996, Appendix E) and is parameterized by a separate constant κ. When $\kappa = 0$, the universal model reduces to Amdahl scaling.

These three effects determine the characteristic profile shown in Fig. 4.9.

Example 4.4 (Database Coherency Delays). Consider a hotel reservation system running on an SMP platform. The reservation database application involves shared writebale data. When a room is allocated to a customer, certain database tables have to be updated to reflect the fact that that room is no longer available, and so on. Since the central reservation system supports more than one user terminal or Web browser and typically a single database instance handles more than one hotel location, this is a perfect application for an SMP. Let us track what happens to a particular user process.

- A user process in the system that needs to write into a table, must first contact the database management system (DBMS). Since there are likely other database processes also wanting to access table rows, the DBMS will only grant the DB row lock to one process while all the others wait in a queue for that same DB lock. This is the contention or serialization phase associated with the value of σ in (4.31).

- Finally, our user process is granted the DB lock, but it discovers that it cannot write in the appropriate table. Why not? Even though it has permission from the DBMS (and has possession of the DB lock), there is also considerable likelihood that another process already wrote into the same table entry, but it did so while executing on another CPU. Therefore, the most recent copy of the data now resides in the cache of a different CPU. Our process sees that a flag has been set in its local cache indicating that its copy of the data is "stale." Consequently, our process must continue to wait while its local data instance is made consistent with the most recent copy by fetching it from the other cache.

This last step is responsible for the coherency delay associated with the value of κ in (4.31).   □

Remark 4.7. It does not take much imagination to realize that a similar argument also explains virtual memory thrashing (see e.g., Gunther 2000, Part III). The universal scalability law makes no distinction between fetching a cache line and fetching a set of memory pages, other than through the specific values of the parameters σ and κ. See Sect. F.3 of the Guerrilla Manual.

By definition, the location on the x-axis of the maximum (or minimum) of a function is given by the roots of its derivative, i.e., values of x where the gradient is zero.

Theorem 4.3 (Maximum Capacity). *The location on the p-axis of the maximum in (4.31) is given by*

$$p^* = \left\lfloor \sqrt{\frac{1-\sigma}{\kappa}} \right\rfloor , \qquad (4.33)$$

where $\lfloor \cdot \rfloor$ denotes the floor function. The magnitude of the corresponding capacity maximum is given by $C_{max} = C(p^*)$. (See Fig. 4.9.)

Proof. Let
$$F(p) = 1 + \sigma(p-1) + \kappa p(p-1) , \qquad (4.34)$$

and rewrite (4.31) as
$$C(p) = pF^{-1} .$$

The derivative with respect to p is

$$C'(p) = F^{-1} - [\kappa p(p-1) + \kappa p^2 + \sigma p]F^{-2} .$$

We seek the value of p when the gradient is zero i.e., the location of the maximum in the concave function $C(p)$. Setting $C'(p) = 0$ produces:

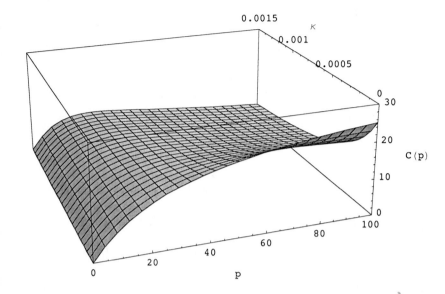

Fig. 4.10. The effect of increasing the coherency parameter from $\kappa = 0$ to $\kappa = 0.0015$ (z-axis). A maximum forms, and the effective capacity decreases as that maximum progressively moves diagonally leftward toward the origin at the *rear of the plot*

$$F = \kappa p(p-1) + \kappa p^2 + \sigma p. \qquad (4.35)$$

Substituting the definition (4.34) into (4.35) and simplifying leads to

$$(1 - \sigma) = \kappa p^2,$$

which has the solution

$$p^* = \pm\sqrt{\frac{1 - \sigma}{\kappa}}.$$

The positive root is equivalent to (4.33).   □

Corollary 4.1. *The following properties of (4.33) control the profile of the universal scalability function (Fig. 4.10):*

(i) $p^* \to 0$ as $\kappa \to \infty$
(ii) $p^* \to \infty$ as $\kappa \to 0$
(iii) $p^* \to \kappa^{-\frac{1}{2}}$ as $\sigma \to 0$
(iv) $p^* \to 0$ as $\sigma \to 1$

As κ increases (with σ held constant), property (i) states that the maximum occurs at progressively lower values of the speedup and simultaneously

p^* moves backwards to the origin. Such behavior is clearly undesirable for scalability.

Property (ii) states that universal scalability in (4.31) reduces to Amdahl's scaleup in (4.26) as κ vanishes. Property (iii) states that a maximum can exist, even in the absence of contention. Conversely, as contention reaches its maximum value (100%), p^* also moves toward the origin because the asymptotic threshold is $\sigma^{-1} = 1$.

Once the scalability curve develops a maximum due to $\kappa \gg 0$, the precise mathematical form of the function beyond the point p^* is usually of little interest because a monotonically *decreasing* function represents severe performance degradation. As the curves in Fig. 4.11 reveal, there is little virtue in having more than two parameters in a scalability model based on rational functions. The more important question is how to improve performance by reducing κ, recognizing that it may be unrealistic to make $\kappa = 0$.

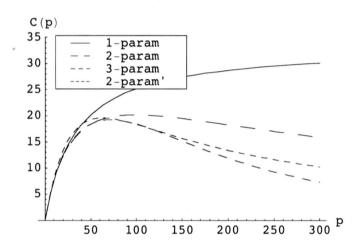

Fig. 4.11. This plot indicates why more than two parameters are superfluous in a scalability model based on rational functions. The third parameter is associated with a cubic term in the denominator of Eqn.(4.31), but offers no significant purchase over an adjusted two-parameter model (*primed*)

Remark 4.8. Since the universal parameters have definite physical meaning, they can employed as a *heuristic* to determine where to make performance improvements. The details of how this can be accomplished are presented in Chap. 5.

4.5 Other Scalability Models

In Sect. 4.4 we showed the advantages of extending Amdahl's law. The introduction of a second parameter (κ) allows us to model capacity degradation due to coherency losses or thrashing-type effects. There are a number of other possible scalability models, and we briefly compare some of them in this section.

4.5.1 Geometric Model

Geometric speedup $S_\phi(p)$ on p processors is defined by:

$$S_\phi(p) = \frac{1 - \phi^p}{1 - \phi}, \tag{4.36}$$

which is the sum of $p - 1$ terms from the geometric sequence in Definition 4.1 with $a = 1$. The parameter ϕ is known as the *MP factor*. Since it refers to the remaining fraction of available processor capacity after various computational overheads have been subtracted out, its value lies in the range $0 < \phi \leq 1$; generally it is closer to one than zero.

Like Amdahl's law, (4.36) is a single-parameter model used by a number of well-known hardware vendors. Its origin is unclear, but that is not too surprising since its form is based on the rather obvious notion of compound interest (Gunther 2004a).

I have discussed this model in great detail in (Gunther 2000, Chap. 14). More recently, however, I discovered that the geometric model of multiprocessor systems is unphysical for large processor configurations in that each processor corresponds to a stage in a Coxian server queueing model (Gunther 2002a). Since the overall residence time is proportional to the number of Coxian stages, larger processor configurations take longer. This is completely counter to the rationale for large-scale multiprocessors.

4.5.2 Quadratic Model

Quadratic speedup $S_\gamma(p)$ on p processors is defined by:

$$S_\gamma(p) = p - \gamma p(p - 1), \tag{4.37}$$

where the *overhead* parameter $0 \leq \gamma < 1$. I developed this single-parameter model in 1991 (Gunther 2000, Chap. 14) because, unlike Amdahl's law, it has a critical point at:

$$p_\gamma^* = \left\lfloor \frac{1 + \gamma}{2\gamma} \right\rfloor. \tag{4.38}$$

One sees immediately the similarity with (4.33) for the universal model in Sect. 4.4. Historically, the quadratic model can be considered as a precursor to universal model.

The unphysical aspect of (4.37) pertains to the negative sign in front of γ. This means that the scalability curve is an inverted parabola (Fig. 4.12), which in turn requires that (4.37) has two roots. The smaller root is always at the origin ($p = 0$), but the existence of a larger positive root ($p = 2p_\gamma^*$) means that there is a definite processor configuration beyond which speedup $S_\gamma(p)$ becomes negative!

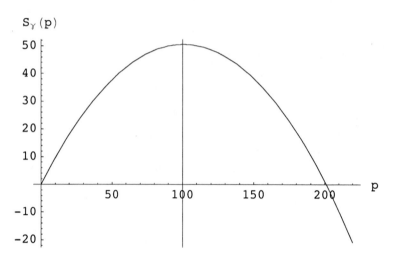

Fig. 4.12. Profile of quadratic scalability from Eqn.(4.37) showing the presence of two roots and the concomitant negative speedup, which makes the model unphysical

4.5.3 Exponential Model

Exponential speedup $S_\alpha(p)$ on p processors is defined by:

$$S_\alpha(p) = p(1 - \alpha)^{(p-1)}, \qquad (4.39)$$

where single parameter α lies in the range $0 \leq \alpha < 1$. Equation (4.39) does exhibit a critical point and is very sensitive to the value of α.

For large processor configurations, (4.39) becomes:

$$\lim_{p \to \infty} S_\alpha(p) = p\,e^{-\alpha(p-1)} \qquad (4.40)$$

It is noteworhty that (4.40) resembles the continuous (large population) model of ALOHA packet-radio throughput (Gunther and Shaw 1990; Gunther 2000; Bertsekas and Gallager 1987). From this we can infer that it represents a single shared-bus model.

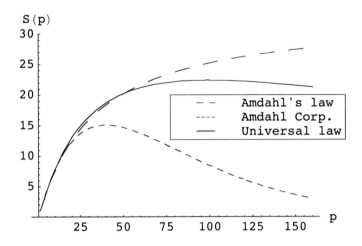

Fig. 4.13. Scaling profile of the Amdahl Corp. model in Eqn.(4.39) compared with Amdahl's law Eqn.(4.15) and the universal scalability model Eqn.(4.31)

Ironically, I first became aware of this model while presenting a training class at Amdahl Corporation in 1999. I was told that performance engineers had been using (4.40) for many years to do internal SMP sizing and capacity planning. In Fig. 4.13, we see that although (4.40) is valid for small-processor configurations, the predicted onset of capacity degradation for large-processor configurations is often too severe.

Table 4.1. Comparative properties of scalability models

Model	Parameters	Critical point	Remark
Amdahl	σ	No	Models contention only
Exponential	α	Yes	Contention and coherency are mixed in parameter α
Geometric	ϕ	No	Inconsistent with Coxian queueing theory
Quadratic	γ	Yes	Second root is unphysical
Universal	σ, κ	Yes	Physical. Contention and coherency are separated

From Definition 4.8 we know that scalability models like Amdahl's law (4.26) and the universal model (4.31) are defined by rational functions.

Conjecture 4.1. Two parameters are necessary and sufficient for scalability models based on rational functions.

The other scalability models in Table 4.1 are not rational functions, and are defined in terms of just one parameter. This makes them simpler to apply, but as we shall discover in Chap. 5, the added degree of difficulty can be handled using statistical methods and the analysis is more revealing.

4.6 Multicores and Clusters

We have implicitly presented the universal scaling model in the context of multiprocessor hardware, but there is nothing specific in the model that restricts (4.31) to multiprocessors. Moreover, there is nothing in (4.31) that tells us anything about the type of hardware being modeled. In particular, it includes no terms representing the kind of interconnect technology between processor nodes e.g., a hypercube or torus topology. Since the universal model has no intrinsic structure, it can be used to model more general computer systems such as multicores and clusters. Figure 4.14 shows how this might be done.

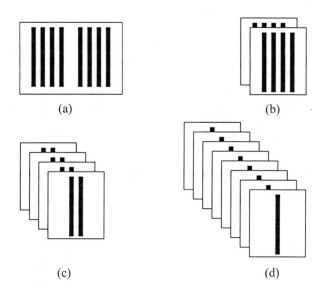

Fig. 4.14. Integer partitioning of $p = 8$ processors (*black stripes*) among (**a**) $n = 1$, (**b**) $n = 2$, (**c**) $n = 4$, and (**d**) $n = 8$ nodes

Definition 4.9 (Cluster Parameters).

- n: *nodes*
- $p_n = p/n$: *processors per node*
- σ_g: *global internode contention*

- κ_g: *global internode coherency*

For $n = 1$, $\sigma_g = 0$ so that (4.41) reduces to (4.31). The partitioning of p processors among n nodes in Fig. 4.14 result from the integer partitions:

n	p_n	p
1	8	8
2	4	8
4	2	8
8	1	8

such that the total number of processors is always given by the product $p = n \times p_n$.

These definitions allow us to write a generalization of (4.31) for predicting universal cluster scalability:

$$C(p, n) = \frac{n\, C(p)}{1 + \sigma_g\,(n-1)\,C(p) + \kappa_g\, n(n-1)\, C^2(p)}, \qquad (4.41)$$

where $C(p)$ is the *intra*node scalability defined by (4.31). In order to apply (4.41), one has to be able to measure both the local and global buses shown in Fig. 4.15 independently. The other important assumption is that the nodes and the processors are *homogeneous*. This assumption is most likely to hold for a multicore system (see Chap. 7), but may not be as appropriate for certain *inhomogeneous* clusters with mixed node types (see Chap. 9).

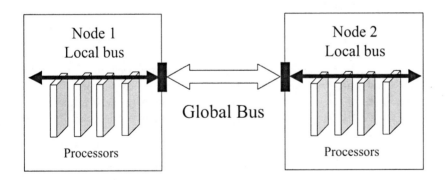

Fig. 4.15. Local bus connecting processors on each node and the global bus connecting each node

One would want to perform this kind of analysis to see where certain configurations match one another in capacity. In Fig. 4.16, these configurations correspond to the points where the scalability curves cross each other.

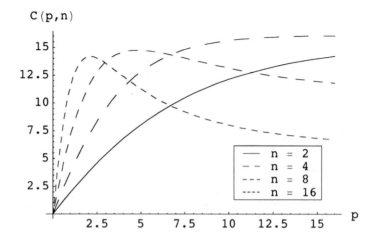

Fig. 4.16. Scalability curves for a cluster partitions with *intra*node parameters $\sigma = 0.03$ and $\kappa = 0.0015$, and *inter*node parameters $\sigma_g = 0.01$, $\kappa_g = 0.001$. Such undesirable parameter values have been chosen merely to demonstrate the ability of (4.41) to display comparative scalability across multiple node configurations

4.7 Summary

In this chapter we started out by examining the general concept of scaling in some detail. We shall make further use of these ideas in Chap. 10. The key idea is that scaling cannot be unbounded. In a physical system, is bounded by a critical point where the weight exceeds the physical capability of the system to support itself.

We showed that a similar idea exists for computer systems. They cannot be scaled indefinitely because certain internal overheads accrue at a critical point where the processing capacity is consumed more by overhead cycles than application cycles. All of this is expressed in the universal scalability model given by (4.31).

The universal scalability model is a two-parameter model defined by a rational function. We conjecture that any scalability model based on rational functions requires no more than two parameters. The model is universal in that it is not restricted to a particular architecture or workload—there are no terms in (4.31) to account for them. Conversely, in the case where performance is considered inferior (the critical capacity maximum sets in too early), it cannot be used in *reverse* to resolve which subsystem needs to be tuned to improve it. However, since the parameters σ and κ do have a definite physical meaning, viz., contention and coherency delay, respectively, we can use them as a heuristic to determine where to make performance improvements (see, e.g., Sect. 6.4).

The burning question becomes, how can the universal scalability model be applied to real computer systems? Moreover, since it is a two-parameter model one might anticipate that its usage would be very difficult because we have to determine two parameters rather than one, as would be the case for Amdahl's law. After all, Gene Amdahl based his conclusions on a tedious analysis of the serial delay in individual test workloads. For a two-parameter model, this looks like a daunting and unpalatable task. But ye of little faith, never fear; mathematical statistics to the rescue!

5

Evaluating Scalability Parameters

With four parameters I can fit an elephant.
With five, I can make his trunk wiggle!

—John von Neumann

5.1 Introduction

In this chapter we are going to take the theoretical discussion of Chap. 4 and show how it can be applied to assessing the scalability of a particular hardware platform running a well-defined workload. Scalability, especially application scalability, is a perennial hot topic. See for example the following Web links discussing the scalability of:

Linux: `lse.sourceforge.net`
P2P: `www.darkridge.com/~jpr5/doc/gnutella.html`
PHP: `www.oreillynet.com/pub/wlg/5155`
Windows: `www.techweb.com/wire/story/TWB19991015S0013`

Yet few authors are able to *quantify* the concept of scalability. The two-parameter universal scalability model

$$C(p) = \frac{p}{1 + \sigma(p - 1) + \kappa p(p - 1)} \, , \tag{5.1}$$

derived in Chap. 4, predicts the relative capacity:

$$C(p) = \frac{X(p)}{X(1)} \, , \tag{5.2}$$

for any workload running on p physical processors.

For the purposes of this chapter, the main points established in Chap. 4 can be summarized as follows. Scalability, as defined quantitatively by (5.1), is a *concave* function. The independent variable is the number of physical processors p belonging to each hardware configuration. It is assumed that there are N *homogeneous processes* executing per processor such that the ratio N/p is held constant across all processor configurations. In other words, each additional processor is assumed to be capable of executing another N processes. The concavity of $C(p)$ is controlled by the parameters σ and κ in

(5.1). The σ parameter is a measure of the level of *contention* in the system, e.g., waiting on a database lock, while the κ parameter is a measure of the *coherency* delay in the system, e.g., fetching a cache line.

Remark 5.1. If $\kappa = 0$, $C(p)$ reduces to Amdahl's law. This is why Amdahl scaling is necessary (to explain contention) but not sufficient (it cannot exhibit a maximum).

In Sect. 5.5 of this chapter, we calculate the universal scalability parameters based on benchmark measurements which span a set of processor configurations up to and including the full complement of processors allowed on the backplane. In Sect. 5.7, we consider how these scalability predictions differ when only a relatively small subset of processor configurations are measured—the latter being the most likely situation in practice. All of the examples are presented using Excel (Levine et al. 1999)).

5.2 Benchmark Measurements

We begin by describing the particulars of the benchmarked system. More details can be found in (Atkison et al. 2000).

5.2.1 The Workload

The ray-tracing benchmark (Atkison et al. 2000) (available from `sourceforge.net/projects/brlcad/`) referred to throughout this chapter consists of computing six reference images from computer aided design (CAD) models (Fig. 5.1). These optical renderings are compared with reference images and verified for correctness. The images consist of 24-bit RGB pixel values (8 bits for each color channel). Images are considered correct if pixel channel values differ by no more than 1 from the reference. This accommodates the variability due to differences in floating-point representation of the various CPU architectures.

The six reference models used represent differing levels of complexity. The first three (*moss, world,* and *star*) represent simple validation of correctness tests. The latter three models (Bldg391, M35, and Sphflake) strongly resemble those used in production analysis. The inclusion of these models assures that there is a strong correlation between performance on the benchmark and performance in actual use.

The benchmark reports the number of ray-geometry intersections performed per second during the ray-tracing phase of the rendering. Time spent reading the model into memory and performing setup operations is not included in the performance evaluation. This gives a more realistic prediction of actual performance, since typical applications spend relatively little time in I/O and setup compared to ray tracing. The amount of time the benchmarks spend doing I/O and setup is about equal to that spent raytracing.

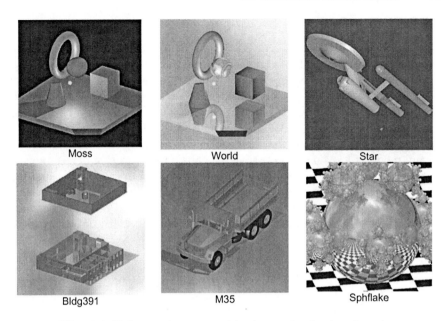

Fig. 5.1. Reference images used in the ray-tracing benchmark

Table 5.1 summarizes the ray tracing benchmark results. It is generally more illuminating to plot these data as shown in Fig. 5.2 in order to reveal the shape of the throughput curve. The homogeneity of the ray-tracing benchmark workload makes it a very useful candidate for analysis using our universal capacity model (5.1). To that end we now present in detail how to evaluate the σ and κ parameters from the data in Table 5.1.

Table 5.1. Ray tracing benchmark results on a NUMA architecture

Processors p	Throughput $X(p)$
1	20
4	78
8	130
12	170
16	190
20	200
24	210
28	230
32	260
48	280
64	310

5.2.2 The Platform

The benchmark platform is an SGI Origin 2000 with 64 R12000 processors running at 300 MHz. The Origin 2000 runs the IRIX operating system—a UNIX-based operating system with SGI-specific extensions[1].

The Origin 2000 is a nonuniform memory architecture (NUMA) architecture in which the memory is partitioned across each processor. These physically separate memory partitions can be addressed as one logically shared address space. This means that any processor can make a memory reference to any memory location. Access time depends on the location of a data word in memory (Hennessy and Patterson 1996). The performance did not increase uniformly with the number of processors. Three of the benchmark codes exhibited a definite ceiling in performance between $p = 10$ and $p = 12$ processors. All of the benchmark codes showed considerable variability in each experimental run.

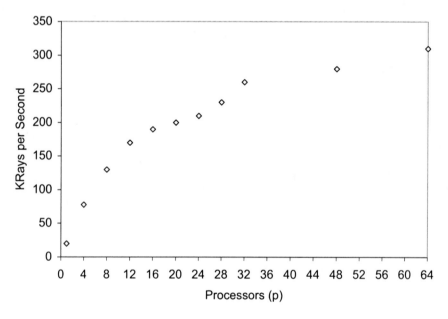

Fig. 5.2. Scatter plot of the benchmark throughput data in Table 5.1

Each processor board contained two CPUs, local memory, and two remote memory access ports. Up to six processors can be interconnected without a router module to the crossbar switch. Up to eight CPUs can be placed in a single backplane. To accommodate more than eight CPUs, multiple backplanes

---

[1] At the time of writing SGI has announced that production of its IRIX/MIPS line will end on 29th December 2006.

are interconnected through their respective memory buses. Accesses from one CPU module to another are satisfied in the order of the bus distance to the CPU module containing the desired data. Thus, when large numbers of CPUs contend for common data, CPUs in the neighborhood of a cluster can starve remote CPUs of access. The great variability of performance in higher numbers of CPUs can be explained by the distribution of the computation across the available nodes of the system. Work appears to be distributed randomly across the available CPUs, but during execution the operating system may reschedule work on different a CPU without any apparent reason.

5.2.3 The Procedure

Below, we summarize the steps to be carried out in the remainder of this chapter for analyzing the scalability of the ray-tracing benchmark. As the following steps are carried out, they can be incorporated into an Excel spreadsheet like that shown in Fig. 5.3.

The procedural steps for the calculation of σ and κ and $C(p)$ are as follows:

1. Measure the throughput $X(p)$ for a set of processor configurations p.
2. Preferably include an $X(1)$ measurement and at least four or five other data points.
3. Calculate the capacity ratio $C(p)$ defined in (5.2) (Sect. 5.4).
4. Calculate the efficiency C/p, and its inverse p/C (Fig. 5.3).
5. Calculate the deviation from linearity (Sect. 5.5.2).
6. Perform regression analysis on this deviation data to calculate the quadratic equation coefficients a, b, c (Sect. 5.5).
7. Use these coefficients a, b, c to calculate the scalability parameters σ, κ (Sect. 5.6.2).
8. Use the values of σ, κ to calculate the processor configuration p^* where the maximum in the predicted scalability occurs—even though it may be a theoretical configuration (Sect. 5.6.3). p^* is defined by (4.33) in Chap. 4.
9. Use σ and κ to predict the complete scalability function $C(p)$ over the full range of p processor configurations (Fig. 5.7).

5.3 Minimal Dataset

In this chapter we are going to use a form of polynomial modeling (Box et al. 1978, p. 482). An nth degree polynomial in the variable x has $n + 1$ terms such that:

$$\hat{y} = \alpha_n x^n + \cdots + \alpha_1 x + \alpha_0 \,. \tag{5.3}$$

The basic idea is to estimate the value of $\hat{y}$ by determining the $n+1$ coefficients on the right-hand side of (5.3).

Measured CPU (p)	KRays/Sec X(p)	RelCap C=X(p)/X(1)	Efficiency C/p	Inverse p/C	Linearity p-1	Deviation (p/C)-1
1	20	1.00	1.00	1.00	0	0.00
4	78	3.90	0.98	1.03	3	0.03
8	130	6.50	0.81	1.23	7	0.23
12	170	8.50	0.71	1.41	11	0.41
16	190	9.50	0.59	1.68	15	0.68
20	200	10.00	0.50	2.00	19	1.00
24	210	10.50	0.44	2.29	23	1.29
28	230	11.50	0.41	2.43	27	1.43
32	260	13.00	0.41	2.46	31	1.46
48	280	14.00	0.29	3.43	47	2.43
64	310	15.50	0.24	4.13	63	3.13

Fig. 5.3. Example spreadsheet including the normalized capacity, efficiency, and linear deviation calculations

Polynomial models are sometimes referred to ambiguously as *linear* or *nonlinear* models. This is because (5.3) is linear with respect to the model coefficients α_1, since the degree of all the parameters is equal to one, but it is nonlinear with respect to the x-variables since there are terms with exponents greater than one. We want to estimate the value of the model coefficients α_1. How many data points do we actually need to estimate the parameters in our universal scalability function? There are two ways to look at this question.

5.3.1 Interpolating Polynomial

One possibility for esimating the parameters in the universal scalability model is to require the polynomial curve to pass through all the data points. The simplest polynomial is a straight line:

$$\hat{y} = \alpha_1 x + \alpha_0 , \tag{5.4}$$

which has one variable (x) and two coefficients. We need at least two data points to unambiguously determine the slope and the y-intercept.

The general rule is that we need at least $n+1$ data points to unambiguously determine an nth-degree polynomial. In Table 5.1 there are eleven data points; therefore we could unambiguously determine a tenth-degree polynomial.

As we shall see in Sect. 5.5.1, our universal scalability model can be associated with a second-degree polynomial or a quadratic equation. From the standpoint of unambiguously determining the interpolating polynomial, we should only need three data points. However, because the measured throughputs involved systematic and statistical errors (see Chap. 3), we cannot expect those data to lie exactly on the curve corresponding to the universal scalability model. For this, we need regression analysis.

5.3.2 Regression Polynomial

Regression analysis is a technique for estimating the values of the coefficients in (5.3) based on statistical techniques to be described in Sect. 5.6. In general, we more than the three data points required to determine a simple interpolating polynomial.

On the other hand, you do not necessarily require a data set as complete that in Table 5.1. In Sect. 5.7, we discuss how to perform scalability analysis with fewer measured configurations. In any event, it is advisable to have at least four data points to be statistically meaningful. This is to offset the fact that it is always possible to fit a parabola through three arbitrary points. Hence, four data points should be considered to be the *minimal* set.

5.4 Capacity Ratios

Having collected all the benchmark throughput measurements in one place, let us now turn to the second step in the procedure outlined in Sect. 5.2. Referring to the benchmark data in Table 5.1, we first calculate the relative capacity $C(p)$ for each of the measured configurations. The single-processor throughput is at $X(1) = 20$ kRays/s. Therefore, that capacity ratio (5.2) is:

$$C(1) = \frac{X(1)}{X(1)} = \frac{20}{20} = 1.0.$$

Similarly, with $p = 64$ processors:

$$C(64) = \frac{X(64)}{X(1)} = \frac{310}{20} = 15.50.$$

All intermediate values of $C(p)$ can be calculated in the same way.

Remark 5.2. This result already informs us that the fully loaded 64-way platform produces less than one quarter of the throughput expected on the basis of purely linear scaling.

Additionally, we can compute the efficiency C/p and the inverse efficiency p/C for each of the measured configurations. The results are summarized in Table 5.2. We are now in a position to prepare the benchmark data in Excel for *nonlinear regression analysis* (Levine et al. 1999) of the type referred to in Sect. 1.4.

5.5 Transforming the Scalability Equation

Unfortunately, since (5.1) is a rational function (see Definition 4.8), we cannot perform regression analysis directly using Excel. As shall see in Sect. 5.5, Excel does not have a option for this kind of rational function in its dialog box (Fig. 5.5). We can, however, perform regression on a *transformed* version of (5.1). The appropriate transformation is described in the following sections.

Table 5.2. Relative capacity, efficiency, and inverse efficiency

p	C	C/p	p/C
1	1.00	1.00	1.00
4	3.90	0.98	1.03
8	6.50	0.81	1.23
12	8.50	0.71	1.41
16	9.50	0.59	1.68
20	10.00	0.50	2.00
24	10.50	0.44	2.29
28	11.50	0.41	2.43
32	13.00	0.41	2.46
48	14.00	0.29	3.43
64	15.50	0.24	4.13

5.5.1 Efficiency

As a first step, we divide both sides of (5.1) by p to give:

$$\frac{C(p)}{p} = \frac{1}{1 + \sigma(p - 1) + \kappa p(p - 1)} . \tag{5.5}$$

This is equivalent to an expression for the processor efficiency (cf. Definition 4.5 in Chap. 4).

5.5.2 Deviation From Linearity

Second, we simply invert both sides of (5.5) to produce:

$$\frac{p}{C(p)} = 1 + \sigma(p - 1) + \kappa p(p - 1) . \tag{5.6}$$

This form is more useful because the right-hand side of (5.6) is now a simple second-degree polynomial in the p variable. Overall, (5.6) is a *quadratic* equation having the general form:

$$y = ax^2 + bx + c \tag{5.7}$$

defined in terms of the coefficients: a, b, and c. The shape of this function is associated with a *parabolic* curve (see, e.g., www-groups.dcs.st-and.ac.uk/~history/Curves/Parabola.html). The general shape of the parabola is controlled by the coefficients in the following way:

- The sign of a determines whether (5.7) has a maximum ($a > 0$) or a minimum ($a < 0$).
- The location of the maximum or minimum on the x-axis is determined by $-b/2a$.

- c determines where the parabola intersects the y-axis.

Equation (5.7) is the nonlinear part of the regression referred to in Sect. 5.4. Excel, as well as most other statistical packages, can easily fit data to such a parabolic equation.

5.5.3 Transformation of Variables

Finally, we need to establish a connection between the polynomial coefficients a, b, c in (5.7) and the parameters σ, κ of the universal model (5.1). Note, however, that we have more coefficients than parameters. In other words, we have more degrees of freedom in the fitting equation than the universal model allows. Since we are not simply undertaking a "curve-fitting" exercise, we need to constrain the regression in such a way that:

- There are only two scaling parameters: σ, κ.
- Their values are always positive: $\sigma, \kappa \geq 0$.

This can most easily be accomplished by reorganizing the inverted equation (5.6) by defining the new variables:

$$Y = \frac{p}{C(p)} - 1,\qquad(5.8)$$

and

$$X = p - 1,\qquad(5.9)$$

so that (5.6) becomes:

$$Y = \kappa X^2 + (\sigma + \kappa)X\qquad(5.10)$$

Notice that (5.10) now resembles (5.7) with $c = 0$, which means that the y-intercept occurs at the origin (see Fig. 5.4). Eliminating c is the necessary constraint that matches the number of regression coefficients to the two parameters in (5.1).

> This change of variables, (5.8) and (5.9), is only necessary if you do the regression analysis in Excel since it does not offer rational functions as a modeling option. The transformed variables can be interpreted physically as providing a measure of the deviation from ideal linear scaling discussed in Sect. 5.5.2. Table 5.3 shows some example values for the ray-tracing benchmark described in Sect. 5.2.

The parabolic shape of the regression curve (5.10) can be seen clearly in Figs. 5.10 and 5.13. It is not so apparent in Fig. 5.7 because the overall deviation from linearity is milder and the regression curve is therefore very close to a straight line. This is explained further in Sect. 5.5.4.

Theorem 5.1. *In order for the scalability function (5.1) to be a concave function, the deviation from linearity (5.7) must be a convex function, viz., a parabola (Fig. 5.4).*

Proof. Equation (5.7) is the inverse of (5.1). See the discussion in Sect. 5.5.2.

Theorem 5.2. *The relationship between the universal model parameters* σ, κ *and the nonzero quadratic coefficients* a, b *is given by:*

$$\kappa = a,\tag{5.11}$$

and

$$\sigma = b - a.\tag{5.12}$$

Proof. Equate coefficients between (5.7) and (5.10):

$$a = \kappa,\tag{5.13}$$

which is identical to (5.11), and

$$b = \sigma + \kappa.\tag{5.14}$$

Substituting (5.13) into (5.14) produces (5.12). The c coefficient plays no role in determining σ and κ because its value was set to zero.   □

In Chap. 4 we derived (4.33) to calculate the location p^* of the maximum in the scalability function $C(p)$. We can also use (5.13) and (5.14) to write it explicitly in terms of the regression coefficients, viz.

$$p^* = \left\lfloor \sqrt{\frac{1 + a - b}{a}} \right\rfloor,\tag{5.15}$$

which can be useful as an independent validation in spreadsheet calculations.

5.5.4 Properties of the Regression Curve

It is important that both of the scalability parameters, σ and κ, are always positive in order that the physical interpretation presented in Sect. 4.4.1 be valid. The positivity of these parameters is tied to the values of the regression coefficients a and b, which in turn depend very sensitively on the values of the transformed variables X and Y associated with the measured data. In particular, the requirements:

(i) $a, b \geq 0$
(ii) $b > a$

ensure that σ, κ cannot be negative. They are requirements in the sense that they cannot be guaranteed by the regression analysis. They must be checked in each case. If either of the regression coefficients is negative, in violation of requirement (i), the analysis has to be reviewed to find the source of the error. Similarly, requirement (ii) means that the magnitude of the linear regression coefficient b always exceeds that of the curvature coefficient a.

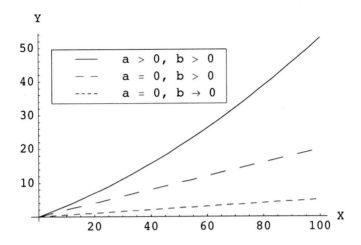

Fig. 5.4. Schematic representation of the allowed regression curves (5.10) for the deviation from linearity Y defined by (5.8) versus X defined by (5.9). The *upper curve* corresponds to the most general case of universal scalability ($\sigma, \kappa > 0$) with regression coefficients $a, b > 0$ in (5.7), viz., a parabola. The *middle curve* corresponds to Amdahl scaling ($\kappa = 0$) with regression coefficients $a = 0$, $b > 0$ (*straight line*). The *bottom curve* represents the approach to ideal linear scalability with regression coefficients $a = 0$ and $b \to 0$ (*horizontal line*).

Corollary 5.1. *It follows from Theorem 5.2, together with requirement (ii) (b > a) and the Definition 4.3 of seriality ($\sigma < 1$), that*

$$a \leq b < a + 1. \tag{5.16}$$

Theoretically, the regression coefficient $a > 0$ can have an arbitrary value on $\mathbb{R}^+$, but in practice $a \ll 1$ and is often close to zero.

Figure 5.4 depicts the allowed regression curves for (5.10). It shows why the above requirements must hold. The upper curve is a parabola which meets requirement (i) and corresponds to the most general case of universal scalability. The middle curve is a straight line corresponding to universal scalability with $\kappa = 0$, or equivalently, regression coefficients $a = 0$, $b > 0$. This regression curve belongs to Amdahl's law discussed previously in Sect. 4.3.2. The bottom curve is a nearly horizontal line with regression coefficients $a = 0$ and $b \to 0$ representing the approach to ideal linear scalability previously discussed in Sect. 4.3.1.

Another way to understand the above requirements is to read Fig. 5.4 as though there was a clock-hand moving in the anticlockwise direction starting at the X-axis. As the clock-hand moves upward from the X-axis, it starts to sweep out an area underneath it. This movement corresponds to the regression coefficient b starting to increase from zero while the a coefficient remains zero-valued. As the b clock-hand reaches the middle inclined straight line, imagine another clock-hand (belonging to a) starting in that position. At that position, the area swept out by the b clock-hand is greater than the area sweep out by the a clock-hand, since the latter has only started moving. Hence, requirement (ii) is met. As we continue in an anticlockwise direction, the two clock-hands move together but start to bend in Daliesque fashion to produce the upper curve in Fig. 5.4.

Having established the connection between the regression coefficients and the universal scalability parameters, we now apply this nonlinear regression method to the ray-tracing benchmark data of Sect. 5.2.

Table 5.3. Deviations from linearity based on the data in Table 5.2

$X = p - 1$	$Y = (p/C) - 1$
0	0.00
3	0.03
7	0.23
11	0.41
15	0.68
19	1.00
23	1.29
27	1.43
31	1.46
47	2.43
63	3.13

5.6 Regression Analysis

The simplest way to perform the regression fit in Excel is to make a scatter plot of the transformed data in Table 5.3. Once you have made the scatter plot, go to the *Chart* menu item in Excel and choose *Add Trendline*. This choice will present you with a dialog box (Fig. 5.5) containing two tabs labeled *Type* and *Options*.

5.6.1 Quadratic Polynomial

The *Type* tab allows you to select the regression equation against which you would like to fit the data. Usually, there is a certain subjective choice in this step, but not in our case. We are not seeking just any equation to fit the data; rather we have a very specific physical model in mind, viz., our universal scalability model. Therefore, according to Sect. 5.5.3, we select a *Polynomial* and ratchet the *Degree* setting until it equals 2. This choice corresponds to the quadratic equation (5.10) in the regressor variable X.

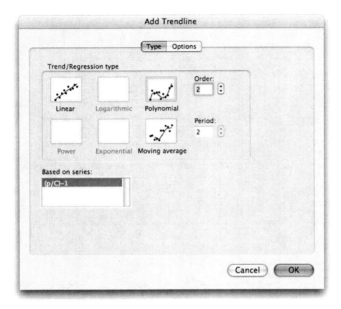

Fig. 5.5. Type dialog box for the Excel Trendline

Next, select the *Options* tab, as shown in Fig. 5.5. The corresponding dialog box for this choice is shown in Fig. 5.6. Select each of the checkboxes as follows:

- Set intercept $= 0$ (this numerical value may have to be typed in)
- Display equation on chart
- Display R-squared value on chart

The first checkbox forces the c coefficient in (5.7) to be zero, as required by the discussion in Sect. 5.5.3. Checking the second box causes the numerical values of the regression coefficients calculated by Excel to be displayed as part of the quadratic equation in the resulting chart (see Fig. 5.7). Checking the third box causes the corresponding numerical value of R^2 to be displayed in the chart as well.

Remark 5.3. The quantity R^2 is known to statisticians as the *coefficient of determination* (See e.g., Levine et al. 1999). It is the square of the correlation coefficient, and is interpreted as the percentage of variability in the data that is accounted for by (5.10) and, by inference, the universal seriality model. Values in the range $0.7 < R^2 \leq 1.0$ are generally considered to indicate a good fit.

5.6.2 Parameter Mapping

The result of this Trendline fit in Excel is shown in Fig. 5.7. The Excel chart shows the transformed data from Table 5.3 along with the fitted quadratic

Table 5.4. Regression coefficients as reported by Excel in Fig. 5.7 for the deviation from linearity

Coefficient	Value
a	5×10^{-6}
b	0.0500
c	0.0000
R^2	0.9904

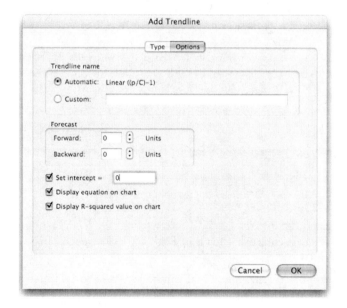

Fig. 5.6. Options dialog box for the Excel Trendline

curve (dashed curve) as well as the calculated quadratic equation and the R^2 value. The calculated a, b coefficients are summarized in Table 5.4. We see that $R^2 = 0.9904$, which tells us that better than 99% of the variability in the benchmark data is explained by our scalability model.

The scalability parameters σ and κ can be calculated by simply substituting the values from Table 5.4 into (5.11) and (5.12). The results are summarized in Table 5.5. This ends the regression analysis, but we still need to generate the complete theoretical scaling curve using (5.1) and interpret the significance of the σ and κ values for these benchmark data.

Remark 5.4 (Excel Precision Problems). The values computed by Excel in Table 5.5 suffer from some serious precision problems. You are advised to read Appendix B carefully for more details about this issue. This raises a dilemma. It is important from a GCaP standpoint that you learn to perform quantitative scalability analysis as presented in this chapter, and Excel provides a

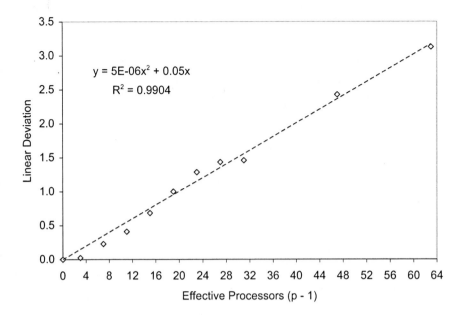

Fig. 5.7. Regression curve (*dashed line*) for deviation from linearity based on all measured configurations. The exceedingly small value of the x^2 coefficient $a = 5 \times 10^{-6}$ indicates that the deviation is very slight and the regression curve is only weakly parabolic

Table 5.5. Universal scalability parameters calculated by substituting the regression coefficients of Table 5.4 into Eqns. (5.11), (5.12), and (5.15)

Parameter	Value
σ	0.0500
κ	5×10^{-6}
p^*	435

very accessible tool for doing that. However, because of its potential precision limitations, known to Microsoft (`support.microsoft.com/kb/78113/`), you should always consider validating its numerical results against those calculated by other high-precision tools, such as *Mathematica*, R, S-PLUS or Minitab.

5.6.3 Interpreting the Scalability Parameters

The resulting scalability curve is compared to the original measurements in Fig. 5.8. Several remarks can be made.

Table 5.6 shows that the largest discrepancy between the model and measurement is 10% at $p = 4$ processors. The contention parameter σ at 5% is relatively large, as we saw in our discussion of Amdahl's law in Chap. 4. It was later determined that this high contention factor was due to efficiencies in the NUMA bus architecture and certain compiler issues. The coherency parameter κ, on the other hand, is relatively small. This suggests that there are likely to be few cache misses, very little memory paging, and so on.

The maximum in the scalability curve is predicted by (5.15) to occur at $p^* = 435$ processors. Clearly, this is a purely theoretical value, since it is almost seven times greater than the maximum number of physical processors that can be accommodated on the system backplane.

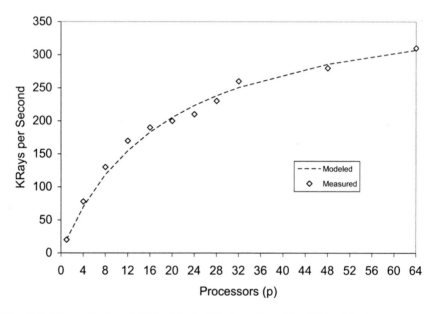

Fig. 5.8. Theoretical scalability (*dashed line*) predicted by (5.1) with the parameter values in Table 5.5. It is a concave function. As expected, very few data points actually lie on the curve. Inferior performance of configurations in the range $16 < p < 32$ suggests significant performance improvements may be possible

5.6.4 Error Reporting

Because the theoretical scalability function in Fig. 5.8 is monotonically increasing, it is preferable to use the absolute errors in Table 5.6 rather than the relative or percentage errors described in Chap. 3. The largest absolute error occurs at $p = 12$, whereas the last two columns in Table 5.6 shows, that largest relative error occurs at $p = 4$ with the relative errors for larger configurations monotonically decreasing.

Example 5.1. Consider a small p-configuration that has a measured throughput of, say, 4 units and a deviation between the measured and modeled value of 1 unit. This will produce a percentage error of 25%. At larger p-configurations where the measured throughput is, say, 100 units, the same deviation only produces a percentage error of only 1%. □

The absolute errors or residuals in Table 5.6 provide a point estimate for the error. Error reporting can be improved even further by repeating multiple throughput measurements at each p-configuration. Then, a complete set of statistics can be generated using *analysis of variance* (ANOVA) in Excel (Levine et al. 1999). We did not have repeated measurements in this case. The F-test indicates the significance of the overall regression (Box et al. 1978). The larger the F-value, the more significant the regression. Statistical p-values from an ANOVA table in Excel provides a significance test of the parameter regression. We take up this ANOVA procedure in more detail in Chap. 8.

Table 5.6. Error reporting for the scalability data in Fig. 5.8

| Processor | Estimated | Measured | Absolute | | Relative | |
p	$X(p)$	$X(p)$	Error	Residual	Error	Error%
1	20.00	20.00	0.00	0.00	0.00	0.00
4	69.56	78.00	8.44	8.44	0.12	12.13
8	118.50	130.00	11.50	11.50	0.10	9.71
12	154.78	170.00	15.22	15.22	0.10	9.83
16	182.74	190.00	7.26	7.26	0.04	3.97
20	204.94	200.00	4.94	−4.94	0.02	2.41
24	222.98	210.00	12.98	−12.98	0.06	5.82
28	237.93	230.00	7.93	−7.93	0.03	3.33
32	250.51	260.00	9.49	9.49	0.04	3.79
48	285.63	280.00	5.63	−5.63	0.02	1.97
64	306.97	310.00	3.03	3.03	0.01	0.99

5.7 Less Than a Full Deck

You may be thinking that the universal scalability model worked well in the previous example because the measured data set spans intermediate processor configurations up to a fully loaded system containing 64 processors. How well does this regression method work when there is less data? We consider the following typical cases:

(a) A sparse subset of data that is *evenly* spaced.
(b) A sparse subset of data that is *unevenly* spaced.
(c) The $X(1)$ datum (used for normalization) is absent.

Keep in mind that one of the advantages of this regression procedure is that it can be applied to sparse data, and, what is more important, sparse data from small-processor configurations.

A significant virtue of applying regression analysis to the universal scalability model is that it can make scalability projections based on a limited number of measurements. Modeling projections can be more cost-effective than actual measurements. Remember that there are always significant errors in measured performance data. (See Chap. 3) In particular, setting up and performing measurements on small platform configurations are usually much less expensive than large platform configurations.

5.7.1 Sparse Even Data

Suppose we only had a subset of the benchmark measurements on the four processor configurations shown in Table 5.7. Note that the corresponding scatter plot appears in Fig. 5.9

Table 5.7. Benchmark measurements on four evenly spaced small-processor configurations

Processors p	Throughput $X(p)$
1	20
4	78
8	130
12	170

These data should correspond to a low-load or low-contention region in the scalability curve. Recall from Sect. 5.3 that four data points is the minimum requirement for meaningful regression (see Fig. 5.10). The projected scalability in Fig. 5.11 is strikingly different from Fig. 5.8. The estimated σ value is only one fifth of the original regression analysis in Table 5.5, whereas the estimated κ value is one thousand times higher!

Table 5.8. Regression coefficients and scalability parameters for the evenly spaced small-processor configurations in Table 5.7

Regression		Scalability	
Coefficient	Value	Parameter	Value
a	0.0023	σ	0.0103
b	0.0126	κ	0.0023
R^2	0.9823	p^*	20

However, $R^2 = 0.9823$ suggests that the regression fit is very good. The σ value implies that serial contention is not an issue. Rather, it is the extremely high value of κ which suggests that some kind of thrashing effect at play—presumably in the memory architecture—is responsible for pulling the throughput maximum down by a factor of twenty-five.

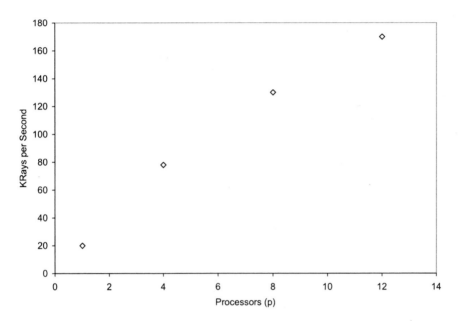

Fig. 5.9. Scatter plot of benchmark throughput data for the uniformly spaced configurations in Table 5.7

Another interpretation of Fig. 5.11 is that scalability is being prematurely throttled around $p = 16$ processors, but it then displays a tendency to begin recovering above $p = 32$ processors, which lies outside the measurement range in the scenario we are considering here. Referring to the platform architecture described in Sect. 5.2.2, $p = 16$ processors implies the existence of two interconnect buses. The temporary adverse impact on scalability observed in the data could be a result of coherency delays to memory references across these multiple buses.

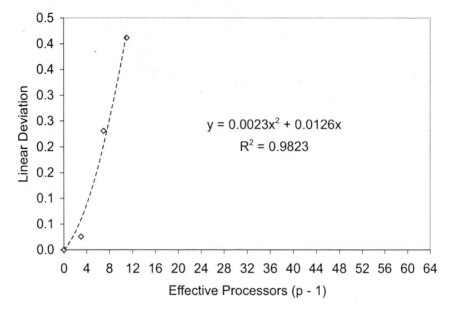

Fig. 5.10. Linear deviation for the benchmark data in Fig. 5.9

This is precisely how it should be. Predictions based on the universal scalability model depend significantly in the amount of data provided as input to parameterize the model. As with all models, providing either additional data values or new values for previously measured configurations can heavily influence the modeling projections. This is another reason that error reporting (Sect. 5.6.4) is so important.

5.7.2 Sparse Uneven Data

Next, suppose we have the subset of four nonuniformly spaced data points in Table 5.9 and Fig. 5.12. What effect does this spacing have on the scalability predictions?

The fitted deviation from linearity is shown in Fig. 5.13. Again, these data are expected to correspond to a low-contention region in the scalability curve. The projected scalability in Fig. 5.14 now appears to be more intermediate in shape between that of Fig. 5.11 and Fig. 5.8. However, $R^2 = 0.9979$ indicates that the regression fit is still very good.

The estimated σ value in Table 5.10 is now increased to approximately twice the value in Table 5.8. On the other hand, the estimated value of κ is reduced by more than one third of the value in Table 5.8. As a consequence, the maximum in the scalability curve has moved upward to $p = 28$ processors.

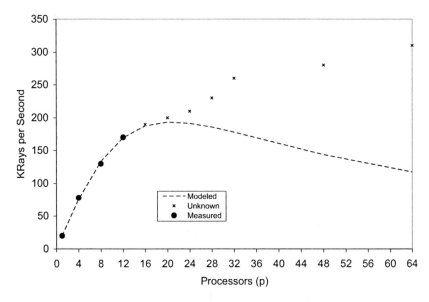

Fig. 5.11. Predicted scalability for the limited benchmark data in Table 5.7 (*black dots*) compared with the complete dataset (*crosses*) in Table 5.1, which is assumed to be unknown in this example. Clearly, the predicted scalability depends quite sensitively on what is known and what is unknown. This is exactly how it should be

Table 5.9. Benchmark measurements on four small-processor configurations spanning nonuniform intervals

Processors p	Throughput $X(P)$
1	20
4	78
8	130
28	230

The reason for this impact on the regression analysis derives from the fact that we have more information about the system throughput at larger processor configurations. The fourth data point in Table 5.9 carries information about the slight recovery from memory thrashing noted in Sect. 5.7.1.

5.7.3 Missing $X(1)$ Datum

The procedure described in this chapter is based on normalizing the benchmark throughput measurements to $X(1)$ the single processor throughput value. Unless the performance measurements are planned with the universal scalability model in mind, it is not uncommon for $X(1)$ to be absent, thus

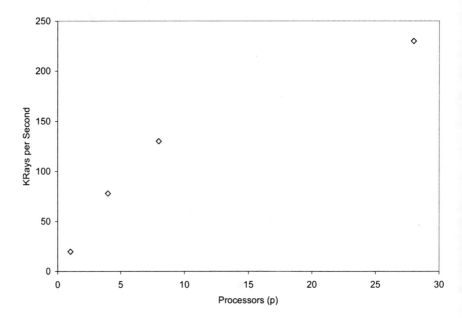

Fig. 5.12. Scatter plot of benchmark throughput data for the nonuniformly spaced configurations in Table 5.9

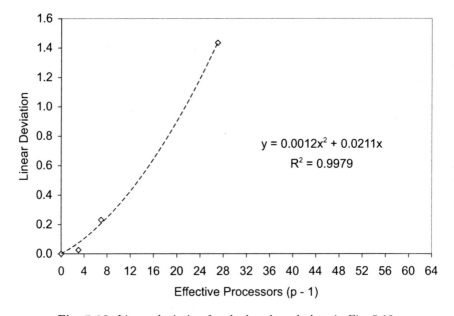

Fig. 5.13. Linear deviation for the benchmark data in Fig. 5.12

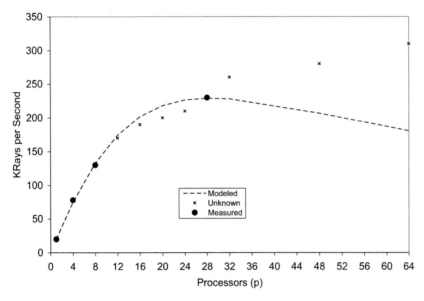

Fig. 5.14. Predicted scalability for the limited benchmark data in Fig. 5.12 (*black dots*) compared with the complete dataset (*crosses*) in Table 5.1 which is assumed to be unknown in this example. Clearly, the predicted scalability depends quite sensitively on what is known and what is unknown. This is exactly how it should be

Table 5.10. Regression coefficients and scalability parameters for the small-processor unevenly spaced configurations in Table 5.9

Regression		Scalability	
Coefficient	Value	Parameter	Value
a	0.0012	σ	0.0199
b	0.0211	κ	0.0012
R^2	0.9979	p^*	28

rendering this form of regression analysis unusable. Is there any way around this problem?

There are two answers to this question. First, having read this far, you should make every effort to make universal scalability analysis part of your future Guerrilla capacity planning. Second, you can do a form of regression analysis on the raw data without normalizing it, but this may involve more trial and error than described in this chapter.

A simpler rule of thumb is to simply estimate $X(1)$ by taking the first measured throughput value, say $X(p_0)$, and dividing by that processor configuration p_0:

$$\hat{X}(1) = \frac{X(p_0)}{p_0}.\tag{5.17}$$

This estimate for the $p = 1$ datum is likely to be too low because it is tantamount to assuming linear scalability in the range $p = 1$ to $p = p_0$. Worse yet, (5.17) may cause the regression parabola to develop a negative curvature, i.e., $a < 0$ in (5.7) in violation of requirement (i) in Sect. 5.5.4 If this situation arises, it can be corrected by manually adjusting (5.17) upward with some usually small amount Δ, so that the corrected estimate becomes:

$$\hat{X}(1) = \frac{X(p_0)}{p_0} + \Delta.$$

Example 5.2. Suppose the $X(1)$ datum was missing from the benchmark data in Table 5.1. We can estimate it using the first available value $X(4) = 78$. Using (5.17):

$$\hat{X}(1) = \frac{X(4)}{4} = 19.50. \tag{5.18}$$

In this case $\Delta = 0.5$, so it makes no appreciable difference to the regression analysis in Excel. $\hat{X}(1)$ and $X(1)$ are the same number, to 2-sigdigs (see Chap. 3). □

Finally, it is worth remarking that this kind of estimation scheme may be more applicable for the assessment of software-based scalability where a single-user load measurement may have its own peculiar set of challenges. We take up this point in Chap. 6.

5.8 Summary

In this chapter we have applied our universal scalability model (5.1) to a ray-tracing benchmark executing on a distributed-memory NUMA architecture, despite the lack of any terms in the equation which account for that architecture. How is that possible?

Conjecture 4.1 states that the two parameters in the universal model are necessary and sufficient: $\sigma > 0$ means that $C(p)$ becomes sublinear, while $\sigma, \kappa > 0$ means it becomes retrograde. A capacity maximum is not evident in the ray-tracing benchmark data, although one is predicted to occur out of range at $p = 435$ processors.

Moreover, (5.1) does not contain any explicit terms representing the interconnect, type of processors, cache size, operating system, application software, etc. All that information is contained in the respective regression values of σ and κ. It is in this sense that (5.1) is universal, and therefore must contain NUMA as an architectural subset. As validation, in Sect. 5.6.3 we uncovered bus-contention in our analysis that suggested potential performance improvements which indeed were implemented.

The procedural steps for applying regression analysis in Excel to estimate the scalability parameters was described in Sect. 5.2.3. Rather than requiring three or more parameters, the physical nature of the universal model constrains the number of regression coefficients to just two; thus avoiding von Neumann's criticism.

We now move on to examine how these quantitative scalability concepts can be applied to software applications.

6

Software Scalability

Program testing can be used to show the presence of bugs, but never to show their absence!

—Edsger Dijkstra

6.1 Introduction

In this chapter we demonstrate how to apply the universal law of computational scaling, developed in Chaps. 4 and 5, to *software* scalability testing.

Section A: 180 lines

```
class JackNet:
    """ Constructor for the queueing ne
    def __init__(self, netname, debugFl
        """ Globals should be contained
        self.name = netname
        self.debugging = debugFlag
        self.arrivRate = 0.50
        self.work = "Traffic"
        self.router = ["Router1", "Route
        self.servTime = [1.0, 2.0, 1.0]
        self.routeP =[ # Table of routir
        [0.0, 0.5, 0.5],
        [0.0, 0.0, 0.8],
        [0.2, 0.0, 0.0]
        ]
        self.visitRatio = []
        self.GetVisitRatios()
        self.totalMsgs = 0
    def GetVisitRatios(self):
        """ Compute visit ratios from th
        # Traffic equations
        lambda0 = self.arrivRate
        lambda3 = (1 + self.routeP[1][2]
            / (1 - (1 + self.routeP[1][2]
        lambda1 = lambda0 + (0.2 * lambc
        lambda2 = 0.5 * lambda1
        # Visit ratios
        self.visitRatio.append(lambda1 /
        self.visitRatio.append(lambda2 /
        self.visitRatio.append(lambda3 /
        if self.debugging:
            dbstr0 = "GetVisitRatios(self
            dbstr1 = "Probs:  %5.4f %5.4f
            (self.routeP[0][1], self.r
            dbstr2 = "Lambdas: %5.4f %5.4
            lambda2, lambda3, lambda0)
            dbstr3 = "Visits: %5.4f %5.4f
            self.visitRatio[1], self.v
        ShowState ("Dialacalculate" t
```

Section B: 20 lines

```
class JackNet:
    debugging = 0
    arrivRate = 0.50

def SetVisits():
    routeP =[
        [0.0, 0.5, 0.5],
        [0.0, 0.0, 0.8],
        [0.2, 0.0, 0.0]
        ]

    lambda0 = JackNet.arrivRate
    lambda3 = (1 + routeP[1][2]) * route
            / (1 - (1 + routeP[1][2]) *
    if JackNet.debugging:
        print "Check computed traffic var
        print "Probs:   %5.4f %5.4f %5.4f"
        print "Visits: %5.4f %5.4f %5.4f"
        (JackNet.visitRatio[0], JackNet.vis
        sys.exit()
```

Consider the two code segments shown above, which together represent a program consisting of 200 lines of code. For our purposes, the actual code and what is does is unimportant. What matters is that section A comprises 180 lines (not all of which are displayed here), while section B consists of just 20 lines. Suppose the objective is to improve the run-time performance of the entire program. Since section A represents 90% of the program, and section A represents only of 10% of the program, should we try to optimize section A or section B?

The obvious choice is to look for opportunities in the largest body of code. For example, we would expect a significant improvement if we could make section A run 90 times faster than the current implementation. But suppose we also determine that section A only executes 10% of the time, while section B accounts for 90% of the current runtime T. What performance improvement can be expected under these circumstances?

One way to assess the performance improvement is to consider the ratio of the unimproved runtime $T = T_A + T_B$ to the improved runtime $(T_A/90) + T_B$. We also know that $T_A = 0.10\,T$ and $T_B = 0.90\,T$, so the overall runtime performance improvement is given by:

$$\frac{T}{\frac{1}{90}T_A + T_B} = \frac{1}{\frac{1}{90}(0.10) + 0.90} = 1.11\,. \tag{6.1}$$

In other words, a very significant reduction in the execution time of section A (assuming we can achieve it) will only produce slightly better than a 10% improvement over the current application performance.

On the other hand, if we were able to reduce the execution time of section B by just a factor of 10, then the overall run-time performance improvement would be:

$$\frac{T}{T_A + \frac{1}{10}T_B} = \frac{1}{0.10 + \left(\frac{1}{10}\right)0.90} = 5.26\,. \tag{6.2}$$

So, reducing the execution time of section B by a smaller factor than we assumed for section A produces better than 500% improvement in overall application runtime. This win follows from the fact that section B is executed nine times more often than section A.

For many readers, this will be the most likely application of the universal scalability law. Moreover, since some virtual-user loads lie beyond those available on the real platform, either because the hardware configurations cannot support heavier loads or the number of virtual users is restricted by licensing costs, we can think of this approach as being like a *virtual load-testing* environment.

6.2 Amdahl's Law for Software

Following Sect. 4.3.4, we denote by π that portion of the run time we are interested in reducing, and denote the fractional time reduction by ϕ. Section B corresponds to $\pi = 0.90$ such that T_A and T_B can be replaced by $T_A = (1 - \pi)\,T$ and $T_B = \pi\,T$. The desired time reduction is $\phi = 1/10$, hence (6.2) can be written more generally as:

$$S_{sw} = \frac{1}{(1 - \pi) + \phi \pi} . \tag{6.3}$$

Theorem 6.1. *Software speedup as defined by (6.3), and used in the analysis of in Sect. 6.1, is identical to Amdahl's law in Chap. 4.*

Proof. Assume that π can be broken into N smaller tasks. Replace ϕ by $1/N$ and $(1 - \pi)$ by σ in (6.3) to produce:

$$S_{sw} = \frac{1}{\sigma + \frac{1}{N}(1 - \sigma)},$$
$$= \frac{N}{\sigma N + (1 - \sigma)}.$$

Rearranging terms in the denominator gives:

$$S_{sw} = \frac{N}{1 + \sigma(N - 1)} . \tag{6.4}$$

Equation (6.4) has the same form as (4.15), and is identical to it if we assume that each task is assigned to its own processor, i.e., $N = p$. □

Remark 6.1. Some readers might recognize (6.3) from the following version of Amdahl's law:

$$\text{Speedup}_{\text{overall}} = \frac{1}{\left(1 - \text{Fraction}_{\text{enhanced}}\right) + \frac{\text{Fraction}_{\text{enhanced}}}{\text{Speedup}_{\text{enhanced}}}} \tag{6.5}$$

appearing in (Hennessy and Patterson 1996, p. 30). Quite apart from the utter clumsiness of writing Amdahl's law in this wordy way, those wordy terms are ambiguous. Subsituting

$$\text{Fraction}_{\text{enhanced}} \equiv \pi$$
$$\text{Speedup}_{\text{enhanced}} \equiv \phi^{-1}$$

into (6.5), produces (6.3).

To understand why Theorem 6.1 works, recall the rationale provided in Sect. 4.3.2 and compare it with Fig. 6.1. In Sect. 4.3.2, the longest portion of the run time was associated with code that could be equipartitioned into N smaller pieces and executed on $N = p$ physical processors. In the software case, the longest portion of the run time π is reduced by a fraction $\phi = 1/N$. As Fig. 6.1 shows, the formal result is the same.

Corollary 6.1. *From (6.3) it follows that $S_{sw} \to (1 - \pi)^{-1}$ as $\phi \to 0$. Since $(1 - \pi) \equiv \sigma$ (see proof of Theorem 6.1), this is equivalent to $S_{sw} \to \sigma^{-1}$, in agreement with the Amdahl asymptote of Theorem 4.1 in Chap. 4.*

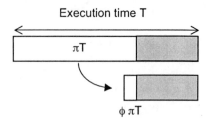

Fig. 6.1. The software execution time associated with the largest run-time portion π is reduced by a fraction $\phi = 1/N$. Clearly, as $N \to \infty$ the fraction $\phi \to 0$, and the run time approaches the irreducible execution $\sigma = 1 - \pi$. This is precisely the meaning of Amdahl's law

A more formal derivation of (6.4) can be given which is based on a particular queue-theoretic model of a multiprocessor known as the *repairman* model (See Gunther 2005a, Sect. 2.8).

Theorem 6.2 (Gunther (2002a)). *Amdahl's law as given by (6.4) is equivalent to the synchronous relative throughput bound of the repairman queueing model with mean uptime Z and service time S.*

Proof. The proof hinges in part on the identity

$$\sigma = \frac{S}{S + Z} \tag{6.6}$$

between the serial fraction σ and the queueing model variables Z and S. See Appendix A and Gunther (2002a, 2004b, 2005b) for details.   □

Recall from Chap. 4 that scalability is a function. The effective capacity function $C(\cdot)$ is defined in terms of the normalized throughput. Amdahl's Law corresponds to the extreme case where all N requests are either executing on $N = p$ processors ("up" in repairman terminology) or serialized for service ("down" in repairman terminology). In this sense Amdahl scalability, expressed as $S_{sw} \equiv C(N)$, reflects synchronous queueing in an application.

6.3 Universal Software Scalability

We can now generalize the analysis of Sect. 6.2. We already know that the universal scalability law of Chap. 4 contains Amdahl's law (for hardware) as a special case. Since we also know that Amdahl's law can be applied to software, we can also safely assume that that version of Amdahl's law is also subsumed by a software version of the universal scalability law:

$$C_{sw}(N) = \frac{N}{1 + \alpha(N-1) + \beta N(N-1)}. \qquad (6.7)$$

Here, the scalability function $C(N)$ is expressed in terms of the number of active user processes N or load generators in a benchmark environment. We also replace the parameters σ and κ by α and β, just to remind ourselves that we are considering software scalability rather than hardware scalability. Otherwise, their interpretation remains the same as in Chaps. 4 and 5.

The procedural steps for the calculation of α, β and $C(N)$ are as follows:

1. Measure the throughput $X(N)$ for a set of user loads N.
2. Preferably include an $X(1)$ measurement and at least four or five other data points.
3. Calculate the capacity ratio $C(N)$ defined in (6.7).
4. Calculate the efficiency C/N, and its inverse N/C.
5. Calculate the deviation from linearity. (cf. Sect. 5.5.2).
6. Perform regression analysis on this deviation data to calculate the quadratic equation coefficients a, b, c. (cf. Sect. 5.5).
7. Use these coefficients a, b, c to calculate the scalability parameters α, β. (see Sect. 5.6.2).
8. Use the values of α, β to calculate the user load N^* where the theoretical maximum in the predicted scalability occurs.
9. Use α and β to predict the complete scalability function $C(N)$ over the full range of N users.

When following this procedure, it is very important to keep the following assumptions in mind:

Hardware Measurements: In Chap. 5 we measured $C(p)$ as a function of the number of physical processors p; the latter is the independent variable. The underlying assumption is that the number of processes N executing on each processor remains constant across all measured configurations. In other words, the ratio N/p is determined on a single processor (e.g., $N = 10$) and remains fixed so that at $p = 4$ processors, the configuration is assumed to be capable of running $N = 40$ processes in aggregate.

Software Measurements: In this case, we measure $C(N)$ as a function of the user load N; the latter being the independent variable. The underlying assumption is that the platform processor configuration remains fixed for all measured load points N.

Finally, you may be wondering if there is also a queueing model representation of (6.7), similar the repairman model for Amdahl's law? Indeed, there is. It is the repairman model (Appendix A), but with a load-dependent server. The details would take us well outside the scope of this book, but the interested reader can find a related example in Gunther (2005a, Chap. 10).

6.4 Concurrent Programming and Coherency

In a paper entitled, "The Free Lunch Is Over: A Fundamental Turn Toward Concurrency in Software," Herb Sutter (2005) of Microsoft, points out that the shift towards multicores (Sect.4.6) will demand an increased focus on issues related to software concurrency. Associated presentations are available online:

Paper: www.gotw.ca/publications/concurrency-ddj.htm
Slides: gotw.ca/publications/SoftwareAndConcurrencyPARC.pdf
Talk: www.parc.com/cms/get_article.php?id=533

Sutter's thesis is largely qualitative, so it is of interest to see if some of his points can be related to the quantitative perspective on software scalability presented in this chapter.

The main thrust of his argument can be summarized as follows. Application programmers have come to expect the continuing exponential growth in processor cycles identified with Moore's law. As a side effect of this expectation, they have tended to write programs using simpler sequential code constructs, with little or no attention paid to achieving significant concurrency. Because of recent changes in the way microprocessors are now being produced, however, that exponential growth in processor power (the "free lunch") has come to an end. Therefore, the habit of writing sequential code will now have to be changed (I would say, reversed), but this change will be relatively difficult because the available programming-language constructs for implementing concurrency control are difficult to apply. We are likely to have to live with Hoare-style monitors and locks to control synchonization in a concurrent environment (see, "Guidlines for Making Multiprocessor Applications Symmetric," Gunther 2000, Appendix C). Ultimatley, Sutter concludes that concurrency-oriented programming will supercede the current paradigm of object-oriented (OO) programming.

Why have we fallen off the Moore's law curve? Sutter does not explain that, but part of the reason has to do with the thermal barrier that accompanies high clock frequencies in CMOS. To first order, the dynamic power dissipated by CMOS circuitry is given by:

$$P = CV^2 f, \tag{6.8}$$

where P is the power, C is the effective switch capacitance, V is the supply voltage, and f is the frequency of operation (closely associated with the system clock frequency). The power dissipation occurs from charging and discharging of nodal capacitances found on the output of every logic gate in the circuit. Each logic transition in the CMOS circuit incurs a voltage change, which draws energy from the power supply.

What is worse than (6.8), is the power per unit area (P/A) or power density. As microprocessor geometries continue to shrink, A becomes smaller and increases the power density that has to be dissipated in the form of heat. Combine that with increasing clock frequency in (6.8) and heat dissipation quickly becomes a very serious problem—especially in the personal computer and laptop marketplace. To ameliorate this problem, microprocessor manufacturers have decided to place more, lower speed, and therefore lower power, processor cores on the same die, viz., multicores (see Sect.4.6).

Whether or not you agree with the details of Sutter's thesis, from the standpoint of (6.7) and Sect. 4.4.1, it is likely to be substantially correct because his observations are not entirely new. Similar issues are well-known in the context of concurrent programming on symmetric multiprocessors (SMPs). The major difference between multiprocessors and multicores is one of *scale*. Instead of having multiple processors in a single box, we are beginning to see multiple processors on a single silicon die.

Experience with SMP platforms, both historically (e.g., porting database management applications to SMPs during the 1990s) and theoretically (e.g., Chap. 4), tells us that when it comes to shared data in general, and shared-writable data in particular, not only is minimizing contention (α) important, but minimizing the coherency delay (β) is vital. The only way these values can be known is by system measurement, as we show in the following sections.

6.5 UNIX Multitasking Application

As a first application of (6.7), we consider a controlled workload from the SPEC System Development Multitasking (SDM) benchmark suite (www.spec.org/osg/sdm91/), which is currently part of the Open Systems Group (OSG) working group within the SPEC organization. The data for the subsequent scalability analysis is derived from the *SDET* component of the SDM suite. The analytic method is the same as that described in Chap. 5, viz., regression analysis.

6.5.1 The Workload

The SDET workload simulates a group of UNIX software developers doing compiles, edits, as well as exercising other shell commands. These multiuser activities are emulated by concurrently running multiple copies of scripts containing the shell commands. The relevant performance metric is the *throughput* measured in *scripts per hour*.

Remark 6.2. An historical account of the development of the SDET benchmark by Steve Gaede, the benchmark's author, can be found online at www.spec.org/osg/sdm91/sdet/SDETPerspectives.html.

A very important distinguishing feature of the benchmark is that it does not rely on a single metric (as does CPU2000, www.spec.org/osg/cpu2000/, for example). Rather, a graph showing the complete throughput characteristic must be reported. There are run rules for SPEC SDM that indicate how this throughput data must be collected and presented.

6.5.2 The Platform

The results I will use in the subsequent analysis come from SPEC SDET data reported in June 1995 for a 16-way Sun SPARCcenter 2000. You can download the full report from `www.spec.org/osg/sdm91/results/res9506/`.

Table 6.1. SPEC SDET Benchmark on a 16-way Sun SC2000

Concurrent generators	Throughput scripts/h	Normalized throughput
0	0.00	0.00
1	64.90	1.00
18	995.90	15.35
36	1652.40	25.46
72	1853.20	28.55
108	1828.90	28.18
144	1775.00	27.35
216	1702.20	26.23

Table 6.1 and Fig. 6.2 summarize those data. The most significant features of this benchmark from the SPEC SDM standpoint are:

1. The full throughput profile has to be reported.
2. The peak throughput is 1853.20 scripts/hour.
3. It occurs at 72 generators or virtual users.
4. Beyond the peak, the throughput becomes retrograde .

Remark 6.3. In an ironic twist of fate, the measurements in Table 6.1 were carried out at Amdahl Corporation in Sunnyvale, California; the company founded by Gene Amdahl!

6.5.3 Regression Analysis

As already mentioned, the regression analysis can be carried out using an Excel spreadsheet (see Chap. 5). The relationship between the regression co-efficients in Table 6.2 and the universal scalability parameters is given by the equations:

$$\alpha = b - a. \tag{6.9}$$

$$\beta = a. \tag{6.10}$$

$$N^* = \left\lfloor \sqrt{\frac{1 - \alpha}{\beta}} \right\rfloor. \tag{6.11}$$

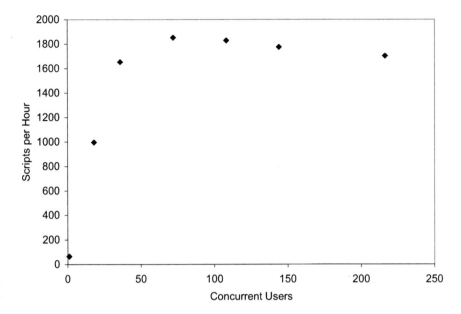

Fig. 6.2. SPEC SDET graph of data in Table 6.1

These equations are the same as (5.11), (5.12) and (5.15).

Table 6.2. Regression coefficients for the data in Table 6.1

Coefficient	Value
a	8×10^{-5}
b	0.0171
c	0.0000
R^2	0.9961

Clearly, the maximum *measured* throughput is 1853.20 scripts/hour. The SC2000 benchmark platform was configured and tuned to generate this maximum value (that is what the SPEC benchmarking is about). Moreover, part of the tuning effort is to make the system CPU-bound, not memory-bound or I/O-bound. So, we can presume the SPARC processor was a dominant bottleneck governing throughput performance.

Contrast this with the regression analysis in Table 6.3. The maximum throughput is predicted to occur at $N = 110$ virtual users. Using (6.7) together with $X(1) = 64.90$ from Table 6.1, the corresponding throughput in Fig. 6.3 can be calculated as:

Table 6.3. Universal scalability parameters corresponding to the regression coefficients in Table 6.2

Parameter	Value
α	0.0170
β	0.0001
N^*	110

$$X_{sw}(110) = \frac{110 \times 64.90}{1 + (0.0170 \times 109) + (0.0001 \times 110 \times 109)} = 1761.85\,.$$

This difference is accounted for by keeping mind that the actual benchmark is aimed at finding the peak throughput, whereas the application of regression analysis using the universal scalability model tries to smooth out such peaks in favor of predicting a more average profile.

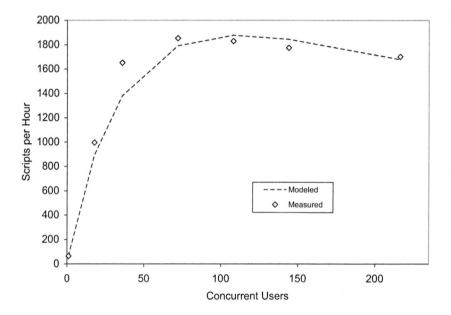

Fig. 6.3. Universal scalability model (*dashed line*) of SPEC SDET data in Table 6.1

If we ignore the relatively small value of β, the dominance of the contention parameter α can be understood from the standpoint of Amdahl's law. The Amdahl bound represents a worst-case scenario where all the users issue their requests simultaneously (see Appendix A). Consequently, all N requests get piled up at the CPU. Moreover, all the users have to wait until all the requests have been serviced and returned to their respective owners before any further "thinking" can be done. This is an all-or-nothing situation; all users who have requests are either waiting in the run-queue or thinking. Both these phases represent relatively low throughput. The proportion of time spent all thinking to all waiting during some measurement period is what determines the actual value of σ.

Remark 6.4. As I suggest to students in my classes (`www.perfdynamics.com/Classes/schedule.html`), if the SPEC SDM multiuser benchmark looks relevant for your capacity planning needs, you might consider purchasing a copy of the benchmark code from SPEC `www.spec.org/cgi-bin/osgorder` but use it merely as a harness for your own workload scripts. This Guerrilla-style approach could be a lot more cost-effective than purchasing more expensive commercial load-testing tools.

6.6 Windows-Based Applications

In this section we apply the our universal scalability law (6.7) to a Microsoft Windows application—the SQL Server relational database management system. The regression analysis, used to determine the α, β parameters, is identical to that presented in Chap. 5.

The reader should keep in mind that our purpose here is to understand how to apply the universal scalability law to software applications, and not to determine which platform or application combination has the best performance. To demonstrate the point, we have deliberately chosen to analyze older versions of both Microsoft Windows and the Microsoft SQL Server relational database management system. Those data and a comparative analysis with Windows 2000 and later versions of SQL Server are discussed by Bass (2000).

Although SQL Server 6.5 provides an excellent departmental database, many users are aware that the software is not scalable to the enterprise level. SQL Server 7.0 dramatically changes that situation. Microsoft has refreshed the product from the ground up. Numerous architectural enhancements have boosted the scalability of SQL Server 7.0 into the enterprise arena. As a result, Enterprise Resource Planning (ERP) vendors have readily adopted SQL Server 7.0.

6.6.1 The Workload

To stress the server configurations adequately, a CPU-intensive benchmark based on the *Benchmark Factory for Databases* from Quest Software (`www.quest.com/benchmark_factory`) was used. Benchmark Factory simulates real database application workloads by generating loads using industry standard benchmarks, e.g., TPC-B, TPC-C, TPC-D. It enables users to evaluate scalability of databases, test hardware, and configurations. Standard benchmarks provide a more valid comparison between different environments, database platforms, and hardware.

6.6.2 The Platform

The platform was a Dell *PowerEdge 8450* with the *Profusion* architecture chipset based on 400 MHz Pentium *Xeon* processors[1]. Baseline measurements were taken on both the Windows NT 4.0 Enterprise Edition with Service Pack 6 and Windows 2000 Advanced Server operating systems. The SPEC CINT2000 benchmark CPU ratings are available at www.spec.org/cpu2000/results/res2001q2/cpu2000-20010424-00592.pdf.

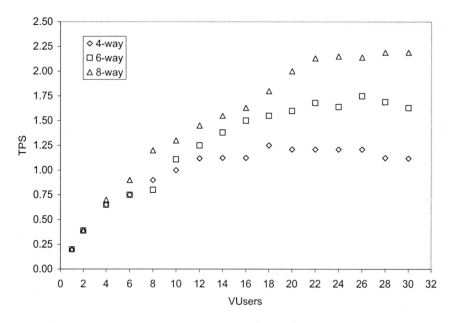

Fig. 6.4. Throughput measurements of SQLServer transactions per second (TPS) as a function of 1 to 30 VUsers on a Windows NT platform with $p = 4, 6, 8$-way hardware configurations

The throughput measurements are shown in Fig. 6.4. Prima facie, we can see a distinct drop in throughput beyond $N = 25$ virtual users (VUsers) for both the 4-way and the 6-way processor configurations. This is similar to the retrograde throughput analyzed in the SPEC SDM benchmark in Sect. 6.5. Even the 8-way throughput appears to have saturated at the same VUser load. As we shall see in the next section, appearances can be deceiving.

---

[1] The reader is reminded that most scalability data is kept confidential, especially when it comes to the lastest system performance. Our analysis methods, however, are valid for any system speeds.

6.6.3 Regression Analysis

These data can be inserted into the same spreadsheet layout as shown in
Fig. 5.3. The coefficients that result from performing regression on the appro-
priately transformed data are summarized in Table 6.4. Notice also that each
of the R^2 values is better than 95%.

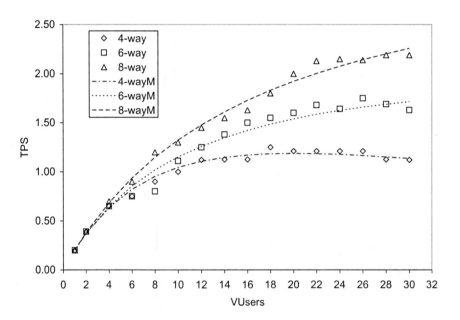

Fig. 6.5. Universal scalability models (*dashed lines*) for the data in Fig. 6.4

Table 6.4. Regression coefficients for the data in Fig. 6.4

Coefficient	4-Way	6-Way	8-Way
a	2.3×10^{-3}	2×10^{-4}	2×10^{-5}
b	0.0813	0.0804	0.0566
c	0.0000	0.0000	0.0000
R^2	0.9948	0.9628	0.9853

Applying the relations (6.9)–(6.11) we determine the universal scaling parameters as summarized in Table 6.5. Now, we can perceive a deeper explanation of the throughput measurements. The degree of contention (represented by the α parameter) is almost the same for both 4-way and the

6-way platforms. The coherency delay (represented by the β parameter), however, is larger in the 4-way system by an order of magnitude. This explains why its throughput becomes severely retrograde in the 4-way above $N^* = 20$ VUsers. On the other hand, the 6-way throughput would reach its maximum at $N^* = 67$ VUsers—beyond the current set of measurements.

Table 6.5. Universal scalability parameters corresponding to the regression coefficients in Table 6.4

Parameter	4-Way	6-Way	8-Way
α	0.0790	0.0802	0.0566
β	0.0023	0.0002	0.0000
N^*	20	67	217

Contrary to initial impressions, the 8-way platform has the least contention and coherency delay of the three platforms, and therefore does not reach its theoretical maximum throughput until $N^* = 217$ VUsers. In other words, the saturation effect seen in the data beyond 25 VUsers is really a false alarm.

Without the perspective offered by the universal scalability model, the question of possibly extending the load beyond 30 VUsers, simply would not arise. Alternatively, one can take the view that these data are sufficient and the projections obtained from the universal scalability model are to be accepted as part of the virtual load-testing methodology.

6.7 Multitier Architectures

Many of today's production applications, such as e-commerce or other Web-based services, run on multitier architectures like that shown in Fig. 6.6. Application scalability is a perennial issue (Williams and Smith 2004), and the usual tool for assessing it is a load-test environment that spans a distributed platform involving:

1. PC front-end drivers.
2. multiple Web servers.
3. application servers or clusters.
4. back-end database server with attached storage.

Each tier is connected via a network, such as 1000Base-T switched Ethernet. Testing up through thousands of potential users is expensive both in terms of licensing fees and the amount of hardware needed to support such intense workloads, and very time consuming. The question naturally arises, Can the universal scaling model be applied in the sense of providing the *virtual load-test environment* described in Chap. 1 to reduce the number of physical test configurations?

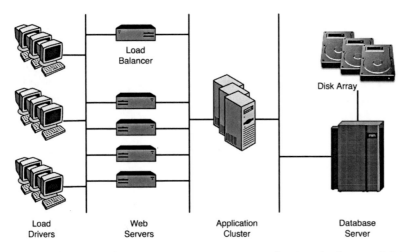

Fig. 6.6. Multitier performance testing environment showing the front-end drivers (typically PCs) that run the load-test scripts, multiple Web servers running HTTP daemons, application servers (e.g., WebLogic or WebSphere) and the database back end

In this section we draw on scalability data reported in Buch and Pentkovski (2001) for a 3-tier e-business application tested using Microsoft's Web Application Stress (WAS) tool, which can be downloaded from `www.microsoft.com/technet/` at URL `archive/itsolutions/intranet/ downloads/webstres.mspx`. These results demonstrate clearly how the universal scaling model can be applied to more complex multitier systems and applications.

6.7.1 The Workload

The flow of an application transaction can be understood with reference to Fig. 6.6. The load-driver client sends an Web request (e.g., an HTTPGet) to the Web server tier. A script (e.g. ASP or JSP) or Java servlet runs on the Web server and communicates with a business object (e.g., using COM, EJB) on the application server tier (e.g., WebLogic or WebSphere). The business object uses a database connection (e.g., ODBC or JDBC) to send a query to the database server. The database server responds with the result of the query. The business object processes the result and sends the response back to the Web server tier. The Web server formats this response and sends it back to the client—in the case of the performance-testing environment—the load drivers. The overall response time of the transaction is also measured.

6.7.2 The Platform

The measurement platform employed middleware at the application layer. Middleware technologies, e.g., WebLogic, are commonly used to separate business process logic from the front-end presentation layer and enterprise data access at the back end (See Gunther 2005a, Chap. 9).

Table 6.6. Combined measurement and modeling results for the three-tier platform depicted in Fig. 6.6. Both throughput and response time data are shown

Concurrent WAS threads	Measured HTTPGets/s	Modeled throughput	Measured delay (s)	Modeled delay
1	24	24.00	0.039	0.042
2	48	44.32	0.039	0.045
4	85	74.19	0.044	0.054
7	100	97.50	0.067	0.072
10	99	104.94	0.099	0.095
20	94	93.35	0.210	0.214

The load-test results for throughput (i.e., HTTPGets per second) and response times (i.e., time to receipt of last byte) are summarized in Table 6.6. The Intel-based hardware configuration remains fixed throughout, with one each of a web server, an application server running the middleware, and a single database server, while the number of concurrent Web Application Stress tool threads executing on the load drivers acts as the independent variable in the range from $N = 1$ to $N = 20$. Unfortunately, these authors have only measured the minimal number of data points needed for statistically meaningful regression analysis, but it is sufficient.

Table 6.7. Excel regression coefficients corresponding to the data in Table 6.6

Coefficient	Value
a	7.5×10^{-3}
b	0.0755
c	0.0000
R^2	0.9956

6.7.3 Regression Analysis

Performing the by now familiar regression analysis described in Chap. 5, we determine the parameters for the *deviation from linearity* shown in Table 6.7. Coincidentally, we note that a and b happen to be numerically equal.

We note from Table 6.8 that the coherency delay parameter $\beta = 0.1103$ is almost twice as large as the contention parameter $\alpha = 0.0680$, so we expect to see some retrograde behavior in the throughput data, and indeed Fig. 6.7 confirms it.

Table 6.8. Universal scalability parameters corresponding to the regression coefficients in Table 6.7

Parameter	Value
α	0.0680
β	0.1103
N^*	10

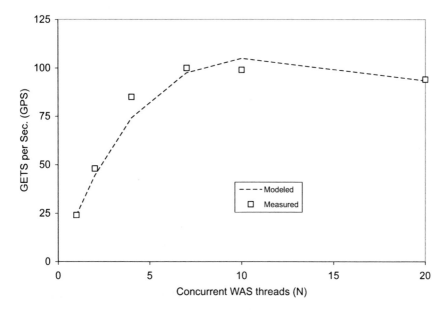

Fig. 6.7. Comparison of the multitier load-test throughput measurements and the universal scaling model (*dashed line*) using the parameter values in Table 6.8

Since the measurements were taken in steady-state (see Gunther 2005a, Chap. 8), and there are a finite number of e-business transactions executing during steady state, we can apply the so-called *interactive response time law*:

$$R(N) = \frac{N}{X(N)} - Z,\qquad(6.12)$$

for a closed queueing system. See (A.2) and the discussion in Appendix A. The underlying queueing model (the so-called *Repairman* model) is discussed in (Gunther 2005a, Chap. 2). Substituting the modeled values for the throughput from Table 6.6 into $X(N)$ in (6.12), we see from Fig. 6.8 that it provides very good agreement with the response times measured by the WAS tool. The interested reader can find an alternative queue-theoretic treatment of this same example using a *load-dependent* PDQ queueing model in (Gunther 2005a, Chap. 10).

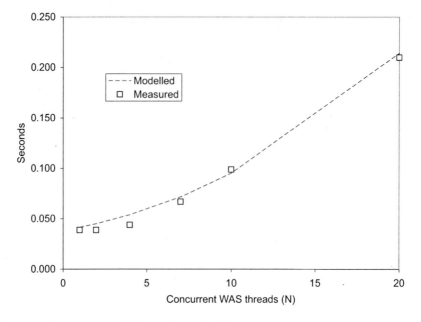

Fig. 6.8. Comparison of the multitier load-test response time measurements and the universal scaling model (*dashed line*)

6.7.4 Why It Works

So, why does the universal scalability model work for multitier architectures? First, performance metrics like the throughput and response time are measured at the system level. The aggregate transactions are measured, not the individual subtransactions. In addition, the test platform configuration is treated like a black box and kept constant throughout the measurement process. Second, as noted in Sect. 4.6, the universal scaling model (6.7) is independent of any particular choice of interconnect topology.

The key assumption that facilitates the use of (6.7) for multitier architectures is *homogeneity*. Homogeneity means we assume that the test platform:

1. executes a homogeneous workload, rather than multiple classes of work or subtransactions
2. maintains a homogeneous configuration of fixed hardware components as the user-load N is varied

Under these assumptions, the multitier architecture in Fig. 6.6 can be treated purely as a set of subsystems operating on the same workload. This is the same set of assumptions we used when analyzing more tightly-coupled platforms in Chaps. 4 and 5. There also, we were not aware of the performance of individual subsystems, e.g., processors, memory, disk, and networking. The system was treated holistically.

The interested reader should compare this simpler holistic approach with the more detailed measurements required to apply queueing models. For example, the PDQ queueing model presented in (Gunther 2005a, Chap. 10) demonstrates that the first-tier Web server is load-dependent and therefore responsible for the retrograde behavior of the throughput characteristic. We could have reached a similar conclusion using (6.7), by noting that the κ value was larger than expected. However, because of the homogeneity assumption, we would not be able to single out the first-tier Web server as the cause, without deeper investigation.

6.8 Classification by Workload

It might help software engineers and application developers to relate more easily to the universal scaling law (6.7) if they can approach it from the standpoint of the software applications they develop (S. Jenkin, private communication, 2005). To this end, I have collected a set of typical applications in Table 6.9 and arranged them according to their expected α and β values.

Table 6.9. Classification of software applications and systems according to their predominant values of the universal scaling parameters, N (concurrency), α (contention), and β (coherency)

Class A Ideal concurrency $(\alpha, \beta = 0)$	Class B Contention-only $(\alpha > 0, \beta = 0)$
Shared-nothing platform	Message-based queueing (e.g., MQSeries)
Google text search	Message Passing Interface (MPI) applications
Lexus–Nexus search	Transaction monitors (e.g., Tuxedo)
Read-only queries	Polling service (e.g., VMWare) See Chap. 7
	Peer-to-peer (e.g., Skype) See Chap. 9
Class C Incoherent-only $(\alpha = 0, \beta > 0)$	**Class D** Worst case $(\alpha, \beta > 0)$
Scientific HPC computations	Anything with shared writes
Online analytic processing (OLAP)	Hotel reservation system
Data mining	Banking online transaction processing (OLTP)
Decision support software (DSS),	Java database connectivity (JDBC)
etc., (See Gunther 2000, Chap. 6)	

Example 6.1 (Google). Depending on who you talk to, Google.com is considered to operate the world's largest commercial Linux cluster comprising with anywhere between 10,000 and 80,000 blades. (see, e.g., www.computerworld.com.au/index.php/id;1306281842;fp;16;fpid;0). It also depends on how you count. There are at least two mirrors on opposite coasts of the USA for disaster recovery. More important, from a scalability point of view, the underlying reason why Google can scale to anything like these proportions is

because their workload is of the Class A type in Table 6.9. This kind of scalability is eminently achievable with indexed text processing. □

Example 6.2 (OLTP Workloads). When a user process in a database system needs to write into a table, it must first be granted the lock by the database manager. Since there are likely other database processes also wanting to access tables, the database manager will only grant permission to certain processes while all the others must wait for the lock. This is the contention or serialization phase quantified by σ. Eventually, the user process is granted the DB lock, but it cannot always execute because there is a considerable likelihood that another process already updated the same table entry while executing on another processor. The user process must continue to wait until its local cache is made consistent with the cache that has the most recent entry. This is the coherency phase associated with the value of κ. Since σ and κ are both nonzero, this is a Class-D workload in Table 6.9. □

6.9 Summary

In this chapter we have demonstrated that the universal scalability law, originally developed in the context of hardware capacity planning in Chaps. 4 and 5, is also applicable to software capacity planning. This is by no means obvious and a more formal queue-theoretic argument is presented in Appendix A. We applied the software version of the universal scalability law (6.7) to measurements based on the SPEC SDM benchmark on a UNIX platform, a database benchmark measured on a Windows NT platform, and the analysis of a multitier application.

For many readers, this version of the universal scalability law will most likely be the typical application. We termed this a virtual load-testing environment. In particular, some user loads of interest will lie beyond those achievable on the real test platform, either because the hardware configurations cannot be confiigured or the number of generators is limited by licensing costs.

We have examined the connection between concurrent programming, contention α and coherency delays β. Sect. 6.4 considered the thesis that the advent of multicore processors has brought concurrent programming back into the foreground for application development on multicores. We emphasized that this view can be made more quantitative in terms of (6.7) for concurrent-programming scalability.

7

Fundamentals of Virtualization

Reality is merely an illusion, albeit a very persistent one.

—Albert Einstein

7.1 Introduction

This chapter is about *illusions*, the illusion of the *virtual*. In particular, modern computer systems are now sufficiently powerful to present users with the illusion that one physical machine is really multiple virtual machines, each one running a separate instances of a different operating system (OS). This is one reason for the resurgence of interest in virtualization technologies. The idea of creating virtual resources, like software emulators and virtual memory, is not new (See `www.kernelthread.com/publications/virtualization/` and references therein). Virtualization is a hot topic from a capacity planning standpoint because of the opacity of modern virtual implementations to conventional performance measurement tools.

This chapter attempts to provide a more unified picture of modern virtualization by recognizing that many of the apparently disparate forms of virtual machines (VMs) can be considered to lie on a discrete spectrum—the *virtual machine spectrum* or *VM-spectrum*—comprised of three principal regions:

Microlevel VMs: Represented by the *hyperthreaded* processors.
Mesolevel VMs: Represented by *hypervisors* and *virtual machine monitors*.
Macrolevel VMs: Represented by the *GRID services* and *peer-to-peer* (P2P) architectures.

The inclusion of GRIDs and P2P under the umbrella of virtualization is an unconventional step, but the idea is to use the VM-spectrum both as a classification scheme, and as a quantitative framework for explaining some well-known performance anomalies in a variety of VM systems. Macrolevel VMs are discussed in more detail in Chap. 9.

The tendency has been to organize VM capacity planning issues according to whether they are implemented in *hardware* or *software* (See e.g., Johnson 2003; Ding et al. 2003; Brady 2005; Fernando 2005). Macrolevel VMs have not featured in such discussions, as far as I am aware. Consequently, anomalous capacity planning with hyperthreaded hardware and software hypervisors, have been presented as distinct effects. The VM-spectrum paradigm, however, views these effects as arising from a single architectural feature that is common to both hardware and software implementations; a form of scheduling which we define in Sect. 7.2.2 as *proportional polling*. In particular, proportional polling provides a simple explanation for the observed *Missing MIPS* problem reported by those using hyperthreaded processors (see Sect. 7.3.3). The VM-spectrum also leads to the notion that performance management of modern VMs is a function of the time and distance scales on which their respective polling mechanisms operate.

7.2 The Spectrum of Virtual Machines

In this section, we consider the notion of a VM spectrum in more detail. Throughout this chapter, VM means *virtual machine*, while VMM stands for *virtual machine monitor*.

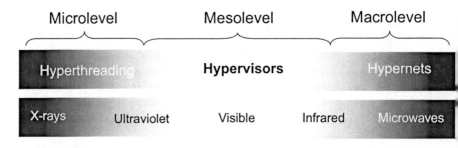

Fig. 7.1. Finite virtual machine spectrum constructed by analogy with the continuous electromagentic spectrum. Hypervisors are arguably more "visible" from the capacity planning viewpoint than either hyperthreads or hypernets

7.2.1 VM Spectroscopy

Just as the electromagnetic spectrum or EM-spectrum can be grouped into the ultra-violet (UV), visible and infra-red (IR) regions, the VM-spectrum can be similarly grouped into the micro-VM, meso-VM, and macro-VM spectral regions depicted in Fig. 7.1. The EM-spectrum is, of course, a *continuous* function of the frequency (or wavelength) of the electromagnetic radiation. The VM-spectrum is a discontinuous or *discrete* function of the respective VM polling rate or VM frequency shown in Table 7.1. It is this polling frequency that determines the relative position of each VM in the spectrum.

The so-called *visible* region on the EM-spectrum is an anthropocentric term. Certain snakes, for example, can see IR radiation (detect heat) and bees can see UV light. In a similar way, only meso-VMs are "visible" to the capacity planner via conventional performance tools, in the sense of providing an immediate view of performance and thereby some level of potential control. Conversely, micro-VMs and macro-VMs tend to be invisible to those same tools, so they remain largely beyond our capacity management control.

Table 7.1. VM-spectrum length and time scales associated with Fig. 7.1

Spectral region	Size scale (m)	Polling	
		Period	Frequency
Macro	10^2 to 10^6	min to day	mHz to μHz
Meso	10^0 to 10^2	ms to min	kHz to mHz
Micro	10^{-6} to 10^{-3}	ns to μs	GHz to MHz

From this standpoint, the distinction between VMs according to whether they are implemented in hardware or software, seems artificial—as artificial as the distinction between heat and light. Recognizing each as different manifestations of the same spectrum can lead to important insights. As we reveal in the remainder of this chapter, the VM-spectrum classification is more than mere whimsy.

7.2.2 Polling Rates and Frequency Scales

A key observation of this chapter is that relative position of each VM sub-type on the VM-spectrum (Fig. 7.1) is determined by the rate at which polling is carried out by the underlying scheduling subsystem. To make this statement more quantitative, we refer to a case where the polling periods are well documented: meso-VM scheduling (see Sect. 7.4.2). The polling period T_p, for the scheduler to associate physical resource consumption with a each active OS instance (software VM), is once every 4000 ms or $T_p = 4$ s. The frequency is therefore $f = 1/T_p = 0.25$ cycles per second or 250 mHz.

We assume (because it is not documented) that the micro-VM polling period lies in the range of ns (the processor GHz clock frequency) to μs (MHz frequency). Macro-VMs can take minutes or days to detect active peer horizons. These frequencies are key VM performance determinants. For those who prefer to think in terms of size, a distance scale d (in meters) can be loosely related to the period T_p by $d = vT_p$ where v is the phase velocity of the communication signal. Typically, $v = c$, where c is the speed of light. All these scales are summarized in Table 7.1.

7.3 Microlevel Virtual Machines: Hyperthreading

We begin a detailed analysis of VMs starting with the highest frequency (smallest size) scale on the bottom of the VM-spectrum in Fig. 7.1; virtualization of physical processing resources. Intel, for example, refers to this form of processor virtualization as *hyper-threading technology* (HTT)) or *multithreading* (MT) on its Xeon and Pentium 4 product lines. The rationale is to maximize throughput performance by utilizing idle cycles. Part of the current confusion over hyperthreading performance stems from two possible views of what HTT offers.

Definition 7.1 ($1 + \epsilon$ Model). *This is the* hardware *perspective where ϵ is a small fractional quantity. Since there is a only one execution unit—which is often under-utilized—by simply duplicating a small number of registers, it becomes possible to have another thread ready to utilize any idle cycles. Intel quotes typical performance gains ranging from $\epsilon = 0.1$ to 0.3.*

Definition 7.2 ($2 - \delta$ Model). *This is the* software *perspective as seen by the OS and thus, performance management tools. An HTT-enabled processor presents itself to the OS as two logical or virtual processors (VPUs). The OS literally detects the number of VPUs (amongst other things) by interrogating Architecture State (AS) registers EAX and EBX on the chip (Fig. 7.2) using the APIC (Advanced Programmable Interrupt Controller) and CPUID IA-32 instructions. Ideally, one might expect $\delta \to 0$, but in reality $0 \ll \delta < 1$ so compute cycles appear to be lost viz., the "Missing MIPS" problem.*

The relationship between these two views can be summarized simply as: $\delta = 1 - \epsilon$. We take the $(2 - \delta)$ view because it best represents the source of confusion for many performance analysts and capacity planners. As we shall see, the starting point is closer to $\delta = \epsilon = 0.5$ for best case cpu-intensive workloads in both controlled benchmarks and some production workloads. More typically, since $\epsilon \ll 0.5$ it follows that $\delta \gg 0.5$ which results in a virtual capacity of $(2 - \delta) \ll 1.5$ VPUs. This already tells us that part of the Missing MIPS problem is an illusion.

Hyperthreading can also be combined with *multicore* technology (Kumar et al. 2005), where multiple physical CPUs are interconnected (like an SMP) on the same VLSI die. Sun Microsystems refers to this as a *chip multiprocessor* (CMP) and offers it with the UltraSPARC T1 processor comprising 8 cores with 4 threads per core for a total of 32-way VPUs. All the measurements presented in this section, however, were made on Intel processors with HTT capability.

To further disambiguate physical CPUs from virtual VPUs in the subsequent discussion, we employ the simple mnemonic of a generic *polling system* (Gunther 2005a) in which multiple queues or buffers are multiplexed onto a common server or execution unit (Fig. 7.3). In the case of HTT processors there are just two queues corresponding to single-entry thread buffers viz., the AS state registers in Fig. 7.2. It is the state of these buffers that are monitored by the OS scheduler. Threads are taken off the run-queue and placed in the next empty AS buffer. On chip, each thread buffer is serviced by the single execution unit in some order e.g., round-robin for "fairness" (cf. Sect. 7.4.1),

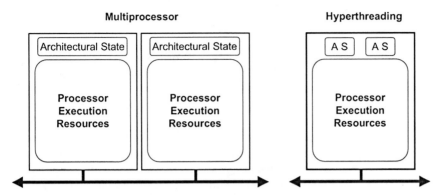

Fig. 7.2. Simple block diagram comparing a 2-way SMP (*left*) with an HTT-capable Intel processor (*right*). The two blocks labeled AS (Architectural State) are registers which present themselves to the OS as two VPUs

although the exact protocol may be quite complex and undocumented as part of micro-VM opacity. In this chapter, CPU shall refer to the execution unit or core processor, while VPU shall refer to the two AS registers or thread buffers. The polling model has not been widely recognized in this context and differs from the tandem-queue model presented in (Ding et al. 2003). The reader should note we are not suggesting that a constant polling delay (on the order of nanoseconds in Table 7.1) is responsible for the measured variation in HTT performance. That extension to the polling model is developed next.

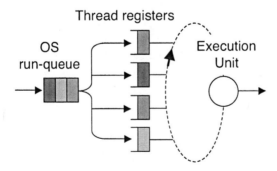

Fig. 7.3. Simple polling model of a generic hyperthreaded processor with one execution unit servicing four thread registers or single-entry buffers (e.g. UltraSPARC T1). The AS registers in Fig. 7.2 correspond to two thread buffers (e.g. Intel Xeon)

7.3.1 Micro-VM Polling

Polling systems are not new e.g., token-ring networks use this principle, and are in common use for high-speed data network switches and routers. The performance characteristics of network polling systems are notoriously difficult to solve analytically (Gunther et al. 2003).

Careful measurements of hyperthreaded processors indicate that execution times can depend significantly on the type of applications being run (Sect. 7.3.2). Tools like Intel's VTune (`www.intel.com/cd/software/products/asmo-na/eng/vtune/vpa/219898.htm`) and thread analysis tools (`www.intel.com/.../eng/threading/index.htm`) can be helpful here. While hyperthreading improves performance in many instances, some tests suggest that thread processing times are dependent on the load being borne by the thread-scheduler. Moreover, there are internal complexities such as how context switching is handled, whether L1 caches are shared as in Intel processors or independent L1 caches per core as in Sun's T1, so on. These invisible contributions to variability in processing times can lead to erroneous capacity forecasting without an appropriate performance model (See e.g., Fernando 2005; Brady 2005; Ding et al. 2003; Johnson 2003).

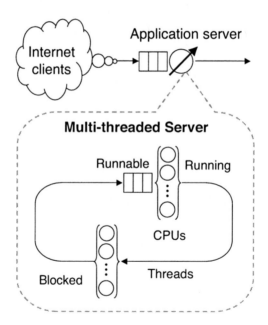

Fig. 7.4. Extended PDQ model of a threaded web-application showing the load-dependent thread server

An $M/G/1$ queue can be used to represent the performance of polling systems, but that requires rarely measured first and second moments of the service time (Gunther et al. 2003; Gunther 2005a). Instead, we accommodate thread-state variability in Fig. 7.4 by aggregating the thread-buffers with the execution unit into separate load-dependent servers. Taken together with the OS run-queue this composite model more closely resembles an $M/M/m$ queue with a non-constant mean service time ($M/M/2$ for HTT).

7.3.2 Thread Execution Analysis

We apply the composite PDQ model of Sect. 7.3.1 to measurements of micro-VMs. Sect. 7.3.2 compares a multithreaded test workload with HTT enabled and disabled. Sect. 7.3.4 is based on measurements of a production application with HTT enabled.

Johnson (2003) constructed a test program to consume all available CPU cycles by configuring the number of executing threads. The test platform comprised a dual-processor HP-Compaq ML530 equipped with 2.4GHz Intel Xeon processors running Microsoft Windows 2000. A BIOS utility provided the ability to enable and disable HTT. Elapsed time was measured at 1 s resolution using the `time` function. System and user processing time were measured using `GetProcessTimes` at 100 ns resolution which included the activity of all process threads.

Table 7.2. Throughputs Calculated from (Johnson 2003)

m	X_{off}	$X_{\text{off}}^{\text{PDQ}}$	X_{on}	$X_{\text{on}}^{\text{PDQ}}$
1	0.004739	0.0046989	0.004975	0.004698
2	0.009302	0.0093970	0.009434	0.009397
3	0.009288	0.0093970	0.012000	0.014096
4	0.009346	0.0093970	0.014493	0.018794
8	0.009346	0.0093970	0.014546	0.018794
16	0.009373	0.0093970	0.014599	0.018794

Throughputs in Table 7.2 were calculated from the data reported in (Johnson 2003) using the definition:

$$X = m/T_m , \tag{7.1}$$

where m is the number of active threads and T_m the test program elapsed time. X_{on} denotes HTT enabled and conversely for X_{off}. Fig. 7.5 compares these calculated throughputs with those predicted by a polling model in PDQ (Gunther 2005a). With HTT disabled (lower curve), measurement and prediction are almost identical and a knee occurs at $m = 2$ (or 2 CPUs). With HTT enabled (4 VPUs), the knee occurs earlier than $m = 4$ and prevents predicted throughput from being achieved. This is the "Missing MIPS" problem referred to in Sect. 11.1. The explanation is provided by analyzing the runtimes.

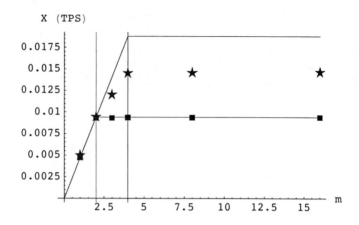

Fig. 7.5. Predicted throughput (*solid curves*) and measurements for a test program exercising $m = 1, 2, \ldots, 16$ threads on a 2-way Intel platform with HTT disabled (*squares*) and enabled (*stars*). The "Missing MIPS" are quite apparent in the latter case

7.3.3 Missing MIPS Explained

Fig. 7.6 compares runtime data with polling model predictions. With HTT disabled (2 CPUs), the data fall on the upper curve with the expected knee occurring at $m = 2$. With HTT enabled (4 VPUs), the data points lie *above* the predicted lower curve by about 30%. The predicted curves in Fig. 7.6 assume a constant mean service time per thread S_0. For a processor-intensive workload with a finite number of threads active during each measurement, the predicted runtime curve should increase *linearly* above saturation ($m = 2$ or 4) because it is a *closed* queueing system (cf. Ding et al. 2003). But these data are *super-linear* relative to the lower curve.

We can equate runtime measured by the OS to residence time R at the VPU. In Fig. 7.6 the residence time:

$$R_0(m \le 4) = S_0 \ , \tag{7.2}$$

is simply the constant service time S_0 at the foot of the "hockey stick", signifying a processor is always available to service threads and no waiting time is incurred. When $m > 4$, however, all processors become saturated and threads begin to queue in the buffers of Fig. 7.3. For a saturated closed queueing model, $X(m) = 1/S_0$ and the residence time above $m = 4$ is:

$$R_0(m > 4) = mS_0 - Z \ , \tag{7.3}$$

which is linear rising in m (cf. Fig. 7.7). For these data, the thinktime $Z = 0$ so that processors are 100% busy during the tests. Previous authors have speculated that increased wait time (mS_0) may be responsible for the observed

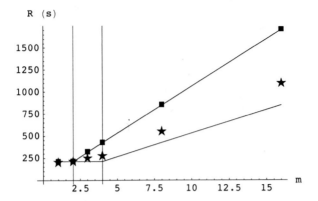

Fig. 7.6. Predicted elapsed times and measurements for Fig. 7.5. Without HTT the data (*squares*) match PDQ predictions (*upper curve*) very closely with the knee occurring at $m = 2$ (i.e., 2 CPUs), but the expected improvement with HTT enabled (*lower curve*) is not fully realized for $m \geq 4$ (*stars*)

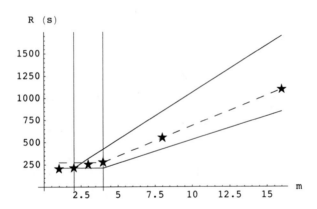

Fig. 7.7. The longer elapsed times under HTT can be accounted for by increasing the service time in the PDQ model by 20% (*dashed line*). The service times are constant but a transition to a longer service time begins at $m = 3$

increase in R (See e.g., Johnson 2003; Ding et al. 2003; Fernando 2005), but with a fixed number of threads, how can the thread-wait time increase *super-linearly*? The answer is, S_0 has increased to a new value $S_b > S_0$. In other words, (7.3) has now become:

$$R_b(m > 4) = mS_b , \qquad (7.4)$$

such that R_b is still linear rising (dashed curve in Fig. 7.7), but at a increased angle relative to R_0. Of the 30% increase in R_b, PDQ reveals that 20% is due to a sudden increase in the thread-*service* time. It seems reasonable to conclude that this increase $(S_b - S_0)$ is associated with the extra time needed for internal state management, as described in Sect. 7.3.1, when the number of thread requests exceeds the number of VPUs (empty buffers in Fig. 7.3).

Using the terminology of Fig. 7.2, the dual-core HP-Compaq ML530 has two independent sets of AS buffers denoted 1a0, 1a1 belonging to core 1, and 2a0, 2a1 on core 2. In Fig. 7.7, the elapsed times start out on the lower hockey stick because threads are likely being assigned to available VPUs (empty thread buffers) in the order 1a0, 2a0 i.e., one thread per core. The third thread has to be assigned to a core that is already busy (probably 1a1). Notice that the elapsed time for $m = 3$ in Fig. 7.7 appears to "lift off" the lower hockey stick, reflecting the extra time needed for internal management of the micro-VM registers and caches. The fourth thread is then assigned to buffer 2a1 on already busy core 2, whereupon the transition to the upper hockey stick (dashed curve) in complete. The increase in service times is reflected in OS measurements as prolonged execution times.

The foregoing analysis was based on the controlled cpu-intensive workload in (Johnson 2003). IO-intensive workloads would likely show a different elapsed time profile but our expectation is that that they too can be analyzed using the same or a similar PDQ model (See e.g., Sect. 7.4.4).

7.3.4 Windows 2000 Production Server

Missing MIPS are also seen in production workloads. (Fernando 2005) discusses performance measurements analyzed with BMC Perform/Predict. The production system is a dual-core Dell 2650 platform with HTT enabled and running Microsoft Windows 2000. The puzzle is to account for web application "CPU-wait" in spite of available processor capacity (cf. Brady 2005). Specifically, high-priority CPU busy never exceeds 85% during peak demand, and Perform/Predict also indicates that CPU time is the major component of response time, rather then disk IO or memory accesses.

Drill-down analysis shows that the system was configured with 4 VPUs, since HTT was enabled, and the available processing capacity was therefore reported by Perform/Predict as 400%. Of this, $323.26 \pm 5\%$ was being utilized by the web application, with an average of 80.82% per VPU. From Sect. 7.3, we can write $(2 - \delta) = 1.62$ VPUs per core or $\epsilon = 0.62$. Even allowing for 5% measurement error, this corresponds to excellent HTT efficiency so, we can assume that each physical execution unit is actually running at 100% busy with no idle cycles remaining. In other words, there are no more processor cycles available to do real work.

The paradox is resolved by noting that each processor is being reported as 81% busy (up to 85% at peak) by the performance management software, but that utilization is calculated incorrectly on the basis of VPUs. From Sect. 7.3 we know that the implied under-utilization is a misdirection. On the other hand, because of the aforementioned micro-VM opacity, performance management tools have nothing else to go on.

7.3.5 Guerrilla Capacity Planning

Micro-VMs, in the form of VPUs, should not be regarded on the same footing as physical CPUs. They are more properly regarded as sophisticated polling systems, polled at rates in the GHz to kHz range, with the number of VPUs corresponding to the number of single-entry thread buffers. Internal state management in these micro-VMs introduces an intrinsic and often variable overhead.

The preceding performance analysis shows that the perceived $(2 - \delta)$ missing MIPS problem is really an illusion due to not recognizing that the number of VPUs is actually $1 + \epsilon$ where $\epsilon = 1 - \delta$. The sudden prolongation of elapsed times can be explained by the prompt increase in service time required for internal micro-VM management when the VPU buffers are fully occupied. This overhead is invisible to the OS and cannot be tuned; only disabled on Intel CMPs.

The value of ϵ is also likely to vary between CMP releases from the *same* vendor, as well as across CMPs from *different* vendors. Because of the aforementioned lack of visibility on the VM-spectrum, qualifying micro-VMs, possibly using some of the methods in Sects. 7.3.2 and 7.3.4, should become a part of your GCaP practice during hardware procurement and software acceptance testing.

7.4 Mesolevel Virtual Machines: Hypervisors

VMWare (`www.vmware.com`) and Xen (`www.xensource.com`) are two examples of software-based VMs which offer a useful of array of new capabilities such as server consolidation, co-located hosting, distributed web services, isolation, secure computing platforms and application mobility. If the VMs are likened to musicians in an orchestra, the conductor is called the *hypervisor* or *virtual machine monitor* (VMM).

The partitioning resources in a physical machine to support the concurrent execution of multiple VMs poses several challenges (Fig. 7.8). First, the VMs must be truly isolated from one another. It is unacceptable for the execution of one VM to adversely affect the performance of another. This is particularly true when virtual machines are owned by mutually untrusting users. Second, it is necessary to support a variety of different OS instances to accommodate the heterogeneity of popular applications. Third, and most importantly from a capacity planning standpoint, the performance overhead introduced by VMMs should be small.

Most VMM implementations rely on something called a *fair-share scheduler*, as opposed to the more common time-share scheduler.

Definition 7.3 (Time-share Scheduling). *Time-share (TS) scheduling gives every user the illusion that they are the only active user on the system. All the*

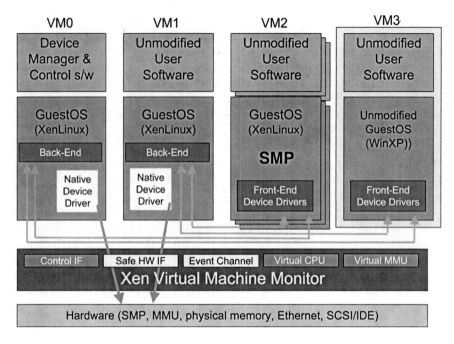

Fig. 7.8. Xen 3.0 hypervisor is aimed at supporting Linux, Linux SMP, and Windows XP meso-VMs

thousands of lines of code in the operating system, which support time-slicing, priority queues, etc., are there merely to provide that illusion.

Definition 7.4 (Fair-share Scheduling). *Fair-share (FS) scheduling gives every user the illusion that each of them or each user group has their own private CPU whose service time is reduced in proportion to their share entitlement.*

Whereas TS scheduling provides each user with the illusion that she is the only user of the physical processor, FS scheduling provides each user (or group of users) with the illusion that she possesses an entire platform—a virtual machine—whose performance is scaled according to her resource entitlement. Entitlement ($\mathcal{E}$ in Table 7.4) is awarded by the system administrator through the allocation of *shares* (like owning shares in a corporation).

The Xen hypervisor uses a form of FSS called *borrowed virtual time* (BVT) as the default scheduler (Fig. 7.8). Other OS options include real-time scheduling (Barham et al. 2003). BVT provides proportional FSS for processor scheduling based on weights. Each runnable domain receives a share of the processor in proportion to its weight. A single processor VMWare guest OS gets 1000 shares by default (VMware 2005). The impact of share allocation on performance is discussed in Sect. 7.4.3.

7.4.1 Fair-Share Scheduling

Enterprise UNIX platforms have taken leaf out of the mainframe management book by providing for more automated control over the consumption of server capacity. Some of the latest implementations of commercial UNIX to offer this level of capacity management on enterprise servers include AIX Workload Manager (WLM), HP-UX Process Resource Manager (PRM), and Solaris Resource Manager (SRM).

The ability to manage server capacity is achieved by making significant modifications to the standard operating system so that processes are inherently tied to specific users. Those users, in turn, are granted only a certain entitlement to system resources. Resource usage is automatically monitored by the system and compared with each users entitlement to gauge how the assigned consumption constraints are being met. This mechanism is called a fair-share (FS) scheduler (Kay and Lauder 1988).

Shared system resources that can be managed in this way include processors, memory, and mass storage. Prima facie, this appears to be exactly what is needed for the system administrator to do rational capacity planning. State-of-the-art resource management, however, is only equivalent to that which has been provided on mainframes more than a decade ago, but UNIX resource management had to start somewhere.

In the context of computer resources, the word fair is meant to imply equity, not equality in resource consumption. In other words, the FS scheduler is equitable but not egalitarian. This distinction becomes clearer if we consider shares in a publicly owned corporation. Executives usually hold more equity in a company than other employees. Accordingly, the executive shareholders are entitled to a greater percentage of company profits. And so it is under the FS scheduler. The more equity you hold in terms of the number of allocated resource shares, the greater the percentage of server resources you are entitled to at run time. The entitlement is the number of the shares belonging to a particular user relative to the share pool.

Definition 7.5 (Entitlement). *The entitlement of user i is defined as:*

$$\mathcal{E}_i = \frac{\mathcal{S}_i}{\sum_k \mathcal{S}_k}, \tag{7.5}$$

where $\mathcal{S}_i$ is the number of shares granted to user i and $\sum \mathcal{S}_k$ is the total number of shares in the pool.

The actual number of shares you own is statically allocated by the system administrator. This share allocation scheme seems straightforward. However, under the FS scheduler there are some significant differences from the way corporate shares work. Although the shares allocated to you is a fixed number, the proportion of resources you receive may vary dynamically because your entitlement is calculated as a function of the total number of active shares, not the total pool of shares.

Definition 7.6 (Fair-Share Goal). *For each pair of users with entitlements* E_i *and* E_j *such that* $i \neq j$, *the goal of the FS scheduler can be stated as:*

$$\lim_{t \to \infty} \frac{\rho_i}{\rho_j} = \frac{\mathcal{E}_i}{\mathcal{E}_j}, \tag{7.6}$$

where ρ_i *and* ρ_j *are the CPU utilizations due to each pair of users.*

In other words, the FS goal is to try and match the sampled ratio of utilizations to the ratio of their entitlements, in the long run.

Suppose you are entitled to receive 10% of processing resources by virtue of being allocated 10 out of a possible 100 system wide processor shares. In other words, your processing entitlement would be 10%.

Further suppose you are the only user on the system. Should you be entitled to access 100% of the processing resources? Most system administrators believe it makes sense (and is fair) to use all of the resources rather than have a 90% idle server. But can you access 100% of the processing resources if you only have 10 shares? You can if the FS scheduler only uses active shares to calculate your entitlement. As the only user active on the system, owning 10 shares out of 10 active shares is tantamount to a 100% processing entitlement.

This natural inclination to make use of otherwise idle processing resources really rests on two assumptions:

1. You are not being charged for the consumption of processing resources. If your manager only has a budget to pay for a maximum of 10% processing on a shared server, then it would be fiscally undesirable to exceed that limit.
2. You are unconcerned about service targets. Its a law of nature that users complain about perceived changes in response time. If there are operational periods where response time is significantly better than at other times, those periods will define the future service target.

There can, however, be potential problems due to user-perceived changes in performance. Consider the following example based on the analogy of capacity planning for a wedding reception.

Example 7.1 (Reception Room). Suppose you decide to throw a big party or reception in a hotel. You invite 200 guests and purchase 2 reception rooms with catering from the hotel for $2000. Each reception room is designed to hold 100 people comfortably.

Capping Enabled: It turns out that 220 guests actually show up, so things are a little cramped in the 200 room occupancy (Fig. 7.9(a)), but you are getting what you paid for. It would not have been wise to purchase an extra room for such a small overflow. This situation is analogous to FS scheduling with capping enabled.

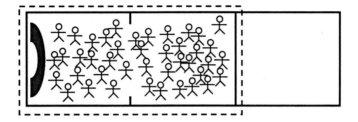

(a) 220 guests occupy the 2 purchased reception rooms intended to hold 100 people each. *Dashed line* represents the least upper bound

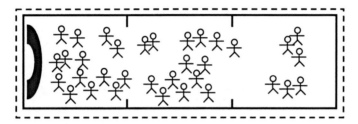

(b) 220 guests temporarily occupy 3 rooms intended for 100 people each until the other party arrives. The uncomfortable congestion upon regrouping into 2 rooms will be noticed by the guests. *Dashed line* represents the greatest upper bound

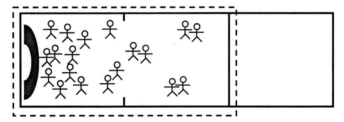

(c) Only 100 guests show up and although they occupy both purchased rooms, they tend to congregate near the buffet table on the left. The purchased room capacity is underutilized

Fig. 7.9. Reception room analog of fair-share capping

Capping Disabled: The hotel grants you permission to occupy the third reception room (Fig. 7.9(b)) until the other party, who have purchased that room, actually arrives. This eases your congestion temporarily until other party does arrive. Then, your guests are going to feel uncomfortable dealing with the congestion of regrouping back into your two rooms.

This situation is analogous to FS scheduling with capping disabled or not implemented.

Capping Inactive: Another possibility is that only 100 guests show up to your party (Fig. 7.9(c)). You have now purchased more capacity than you actually needed but your guests are comfortable. This is analogous to TS scheduling, since the capping boundary is not exercised.

The state of entitlement capping can have a critical impact on the observed performance of applications running under FS control.   □

In Example 7.1, if capping depends on the number of *active* shares in the total pool (as opposed to the total allocated pool), then Fig. 7.9(a) corresponds to the *least upper bound* on capacity, while Fig. 7.9(b) corresponds to the *greatest upper bound*. Such dynamically changing capacity can have detrimental consequences for both performance perceived by the users, and the overall capacity allocation strategy.

One logical consequence of such dynamic resource allocation is the inevitable loss of control over resource consumption altogether. If users perceive that their performance could be better sometimes, they may ultimately try to achieve that performance all the time. This could be accomplished by purchasing more shares and having the corresponding capacity written into the next cycle of service level agreement (SLA) discussions. In which case, the system administrator may as well spare themselves the effort of migrating to a FS scheduler in the first place.

If the enterprise is one where chargeback and service targets are important, then your entitlement may need to be clamped at 10%. This is achieved through an additional capping parameter. Not all FS implementations offer this control parameter. The constraints of chargeback and service level objectives have not been a part of traditional system administration, but are becoming more important with the advent of application consolidation, and the administration of large-scale server configurations (e.g., major Web sites). The capping option can be very important for enterprise capacity planning.

7.4.2 Meso-VM Polling

The most important attribute of FSS for this discussion is that it employs a polling mechanism to govern resource sharing at runtime. Fig. 7.10 shows a PDQ model of TSS with three different process classes (N_r, N_g, N_b) each of which is in one of three possible states: runnable (waiting in the run-queue), running (on a processor) or suspended (in the upper part of the diagram). If a request has not completed execution when the time-quantum expires (e.g., 10 ms or 50 ms in VMWare) it is returned to the tail of the run-queue. Processes waiting for other resources (e.g., I/O requests) are suspended.

The PDQ model of FSS in Fig. 7.11 shows the (N_r, N_g, N_b) user-process of the TSS model having been allocated their own VM whose service time is scaled by their respective share entitlements $\mathcal{E}_g$ running under the supervision

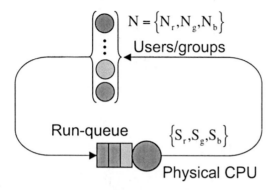

$$N = \{N_r, N_g, N_b\}$$
Users/groups

Run-queue $\{S_r, S_g, S_b\}$

Physical CPU

Fig. 7.10. Time-share scheduler model

of the VMM. Consequently, the actual service time S_g for guest instance g becomes the *virtual* service time

$$S_g^{VM} = \frac{S_g}{\mathcal{E}_g}, \tag{7.7}$$

as indicated by the runtimes in Table 7.4. Each guest virtual server (VM) is polled by the VMM on behalf of the processors in the physical platform. The polling rate operates at a frequency of around 250 mHz (Table 7.1). Note the similarity with Fig. 7.3.

FSS introduces a scheduling superstructure above conventional TSS to connect processes with users and their resource entitlements as represented in the following, highly simplified, pseudocode (Gunther 1999):

VM Share Scheduling: Polls every 4000 ms ($f = 250$ mHz) to compare physical processor usage per user entitlement (Fig. 7.11).

```
for(i = 0; i < USERS; i++) {
    usage[i] *= decayUsage;
    usage[i] += cost[i];
    cost[i] = 0;
}
```

VM Priority Adjustment: Polls every 1000 ms ($f = 1$ Hz) and decays internal FSS process priority values (Fig. 7.11).

```
priDecay = Real number in the range [0..1];
for(k = 0; k < PROCS; k++) {
    sharepri[k] *= priDecay;
}
priDecay = a * p_nice[k] + b;
```

Time Share Scheduling: Polls every physical processor tick ($f = 100$ MHz) to adjust process priorities (Fig. 7.10).

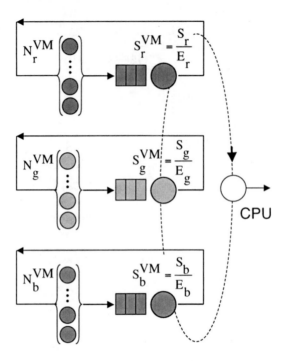

Fig. 7.11. Fair-share scheduler polling model of a meso-VM like Fig. 7.8. The hardware platform has the same logical association to the guest VMs as the physical CPU does to the VPUs in Fig. 7.3

```
for(i=0; i<USERS; i++) {
    sharepri[i] += usage[i] * p_active[i];
}
```

Process-level polling is essentially the same as standard TSS, while VM-share polling controls process-level capacity consumption.

7.4.3 VMWare Share Allocation Analysis

In this section we analyze examples of meso-VM performance based on reported benchmarks for the VMware ESX Server (VMware 2005), and a WebLogic production application.

VMware ESX Server 2.5.1 provides a middleware layer that enables users to create multiple independent VMs on the same physical server. Benchmark experiments employed processor-intensive workloads which consumed 100 percent of available processing resources. A single application called 164.gzip from the SPEC CPU2000 benchmark suite (www.spec.org), was used as the workload. The SPEC version of the GZIP data compression code does not perform any file I/O other than reading the input, and all compression/decompression is performed in memory. More importantly, the workload runs in user-space and therefore induces very little overhead between guest OS kernel and the VMM. See Sect. 7.4.6 for more on these limitations.

With the in mind, this VMWare study is nonetheless useful from the standpoint of quantifying the potential impact of different share allocation choices on meso-VM performance. Such data are otherwise often difficult to come by. The benchmark tests were conducted on an 4-way HP ProLiant DL580 server employing 2.2GHz Intel Xeon processors with HTT disabled. Although the SPEC `gzip` benchmark does not represent a very realistic workload, we note that (Brady 2005) has reported performance anomalies for a production tar/gzip file-compression application running on a system with IBM z/VM as the hypervisor.

Table 7.3. ESX 2 Benchmark Measurements (VMware 2005)

Active VMs		Shares per VM		Runtime (s)	
VM_{hi}	VM_{lo}	$\$_{hi}$	$\$_{lo}$	R_{hi}	R_{lo}
1	7	2000	1000	1296	2352
1	7	2333	1000	1157	2357
1	7	2000	857	1153	2350
2	6	2000	1000	1470	2363
2	6	3000	1000	1159	2359
3	5	5000	1000	1159	2360

Table 7.3 summarizes the benchmark results with different share allocations for the 8 VMs where between 1 and 3 VMS are executed at high priority i.e., a larger proportion of the share pool. Table 7.4 summarizes the corresponding performance prediction using a PDQ model based on Fig. 7.11. The runtimes (R_{hi}) for the high-priority VMs are in very close agreement with the measurements. The increasing divergence between the predicted and measured values of R_{lo} is easily explained by noting that the tests allowed each instance of the SPEC gzip code to run to completion, whereas PDQ assumes the tests are run in steady state. In the tests, when a high-priority VM completed those processor cycles became available to the high-priority VMs, allowing then to complete in near constant time.

7.4.4 J2EE WebLogic Production Application

Missing MIPS are also observed in production meso-VM applications. Fig. 7.12 shows transaction per second (TPS) measurements for a J2EE/WebLogic application accessing a Sybase database. Measurements were conducted on an isolated Dell PowerEdge 1750 server with dual 3.06 GHz Xeon processors. HTT was enabled under Windows Server 2003 Enterprise Edition. LoadRunner generated a controlled workload with $N = 1, 2, \ldots, 30$ virtual users and the maximum achieved throughput was 100 TPS. JXInsight provided traces

Table 7.4. PDQ Model Predictions for Table 7.3

Active VMs		Entitlements		Runtime (s)	
VM_{hi}	VM_{lo}	$\mathcal{E}_{hi}$	$\mathcal{E}_{lo}$	R_{hi}	R_{lo}
1	7	0.2222	0.7778	1296.00	2592.00
1	7	0.2500	0.7500	1152.12	2687.90
1	7	0.2500	0.7500	1151.86	2688.11
2	6	0.4000	0.6000	1440.00	2880.00
2	6	0.5000	0.5000	1152.00	3456.00
3	5	0.7500	0.2500	1152.00	5760.00

from which PDQ service times were extracted as well as revealing that Sybase was not the bottleneck.

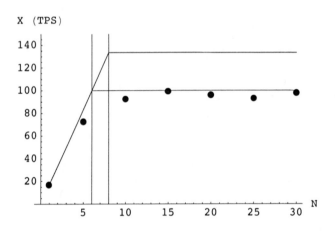

Fig. 7.12. Predicted throughput (*solid curves*) and measurements (*dots*) on a WebLogic J2EE production application. The PDQ model exposes the missing MIPS

Each WebLogic server (or VM) has a single execute queue supported by 25 threads. If all 25 WebLogic threads could do real work, PDQ predicts a maximum application throughput of 415 TPS starting at $N = 25$ vusers. In fact, Fig. 7.12 shows that we only observe 100 TPS or about one quarter of the expected throughput. The explanation is as follows. With HTT enabled, we have 2-way $\times$ 2 = 4 VPUs virtual capacity from Sect. 7.3. The WebLogic architecture involves *listen threads* (not to be confused with the TCP/IP listen queue) that gate work onto the execute queue. WebLogic assigns 2 listen threads per processor which, from the viewpoint of WebLogic/Windows OS on this HTT-enabled platform, translates to initiating 4 VPUs $\times$ 2 = 8 listen threads. The knee in the throughput profile is therefore more properly expected at $N = 8$ vusers, corresponding to a system throughput of 133 TPS (upper curve in Fig. 7.12). The observed throughput, however, exhibits

a premature knee at $N = 6$ or about 75% of the assumed VPU capacity (cf.
Fig. 7.5). From Sect. 7.3, we recognize that there are only 2-way $\times$ 1.5 = 3
VPUs or 6 active WebLogic listen-threads running concurrently, hence the
knee at $N = 6$ and the observed maximum throughput of only 100 TPs. Despite having a pool of 25 threads available to service the WebLogic execute
queue, these six listen threads are the performance limiter. With HTT disabled, the expected maximum throughput would be only 67 TPS at $N = 4$
vusers i.e., 2-way $\times$ 2 = 4 listen threads.

7.4.5 VMWare Scalability Analysis

In the preceding example, a meso-VM is running on a micro-VM such that
the results might be confounded by possible interactions between VM levels.
To separate these effects out, Fig. 7.13 shows measured VMWare throughput
as a function of active VMs together with with HTT separately enabled and
disabled.

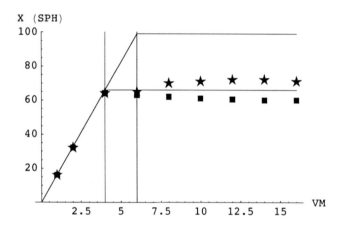

Fig. 7.13. VMWare throughput measured in scripts/hr as function of active guests
with HTT disabled (*squares*) and enabled (*stars*)

With HTT disabled, the 4-way ProLiant DL580 exhibits no missing MIPS.
Besides a moderate decline of about 5 SPH (scripts per hour), possibly due to
increasing VMM overhead, the throughput ceiling of 66 SPH commences at
4 VMs or guests. With HTT enabled, the 4-way HP ProLiant DL580 server
presents 4-way $\times$ 2 = 8 VPUs to VMWare and should therefore exhibit a
knee at 8 VMs. Recalling Sect. 7.3 however, it is more realistic to expect the
actual virtual capacity to be closer to 4-way $\times$ 1.5 = 6 VPUs. Fig. 7.13 reveals
that even this expectation is not met when the micro-VM and meso-VM levels
interacting. Presumably the loss in throughput is due to overheads in VMWare

in this case. Without additional instrumentation, this level of detail remains opaque.

7.4.6 Guerrilla Capacity Planning

Meso-VMs are also implemented as polling systems operating at rates in the kHz to mHz range. Proportional shares are used to create software VPUs in which the service rate is scaled by share-based entitlements according eqn.(7.7). Proper share allocation can be critical for capacity management Gunther (1999) and controlled measurements like those in Sect. 7.4.4 should be considered essential for proper capacity planning.

All meso-VM measurements should be made in *steady state* i.e., where the difference between the average number of requests and the average number of completions becomes vanishingly small (Gunther 2005a). This would exclude potentially misleading side-effects, like early completions benefiting late completions in Table 7.3.

In contrast to the limited perspective offered by the SPEC gzip workload in Sect. 7.4.3, the interested reader can find a more encompassing set of benchmark data in (Barham et al. 2003). These data show that both Xen and VMWare may exhibit significant performance degradation relative to CPU-bound workloads due to VM overhead. For example, the SPEC WEB99 benchmark shows 70% degradation relative to SPEC CPU2000, while an OLTP workload shows as much as 90% relative degradation. Unfortunately, these results were not measured relative to share allocations, which was the purpose in Sects. 7.4.3 and 7.4.5.

Moreover, exercising more realistic workloads in no way detracts from the usefulness of our PDQ models because the service time S_g in (7.7) is the sum of user-time and kernel-time, and both contributions are measured as part of the system response to the workload. If this were not true, then the analysis of the production system in Sect. 7.4.4, which involves network interactions with the Sybase database, could not be validated.

7.5 Macrolevel Virtual Machines: Hypernets

In this section we consider virtualization associated with large-scale macro-VMs such as GRIDs and peer-to-peer (P2P) hypernet networks. The latter include Gnutella (Fig. 7.14), Napster, Freenet, Limewire, Kazaa, SETI@Home, BitTorrent, Skype (see Chap. 9), instant messaging, WiFi, PDAs and even cellphones. They have progressed from simple one-off file transfers to a scalable means for distribution of applications such as games, movies, and even operating systems.

Although P2P networks and GRIDs share the common focus of harnessing resources across multiple administrative domains, they can be distinguished as follows. GRIDs support a variety of applications with a focus on providing

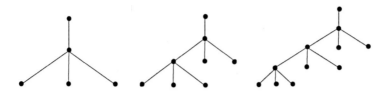

Fig. 7.14. Cayley trees with degree-4 vertices similar to those used in P2P networks like Gnutella and Napster

infrastructure with quality-of-service to moderate-sized, homogeneous, and partially trusted communities (Foster 2005). P2P supports intermittent participation in vertically integrated applications for much larger communities of untrusted, anonymous individuals. P2P systems provide protocols for sharing and exchanging data among nodes. The network architecture tends to be more decentralized, and dynamics requiring resource discovery.

GRID computing has focused on scientific and engineering applications where it attempts to provide diverse resources that interoperate (Gilbert et al. 2005). The concept behind the GRID is analogous to the electrical power grid. When you throw the switch, you expect the light to come on. GRID computing is most often discussed within the context of scientific and engineering applications because they are generally very CPU-intensive. ASCI BlueMountain, part of ASCI-Grid with 6144 processors, employs FSS job scheduling (Kleban and Clearwater 2003). The interested reader should see (Strong 2005) for an overview of the potential application of GRIDs in the commercial enterprise.

These technologies are not mutually exclusive. P2P technologies could be used to implement GRID systems that avoid or alleviate performance bottlenecks (Talia and Trunfio 2004). Although these technologies are still rapidly evolving, applications are becoming more robust (it's not just about music files anymore), so capacity planners should prepare themselves for the occasion when these macro-VMs connect into your data center.

7.5.1 Macro-VM Polling

Polling protocols are employed by macro-VMs in at least two ways: maintaining connectivity between peers, and security on the network. Each type of polling protocol has important ramifications for network performance and capacity. Although generally more nebulous and system specific than micro-VM or meso-VM polling mechanisms, the particular case of wireless networks (see IEEE 802.11 standard) provides an illustrative example of their potential performance impact.

When carrying both voice and data, VoIP packets require contentionless periods in the transmission protocol, whereas data packets can tolerate contention (simple retry). Wireless access points poll, regardless of whether data is available for transmission or not. When the number of stations in the service set grows, the polling overhead is known to become large. Without some kind of service differentiation, performance degrades. One enhancement that has been considered to increase network capacity is a polling list where idle nodes are dynamically deleted or active ones are added. This helps to increase the number of contentionless periods thereby improving WLAN capacity by about 20%.

Polling to maintain P2P network security is employed in the sense of collecting opinions or votes. Providing security for distributed content sharing in P2P networks is an important challenge due to vulnerabilities in many protocols for sharing the "reputations" of peers. Certain polling protocols are subject to attacks which can alter the results of any voting procedure. Securing macro-VM networks has capacity planning implications.

The goal of macro-VMs is to enable scalable virtual organizations to provide a set of well-defined services. Key to performance is the network topology and its associated bandwidth. To assess the scalability of network bandwidth, this section draws on performance bounding techniques described in (Gunther 2005a, Chap. 5).

7.5.2 Bandwidth Scalability Analysis

The main results are summarized in Table 7.5 which shows each of the topologies ranked by their relative bandwidth. The 20-dimensional hypercube outranks all other contenders on the basis of query throughput. For an horizon containing 2 million peers, each servant must maintain 20 open connections, on average. This is well within the capacity limits of most TCP/IP implementations. The 10-dimensional hypertorus is comparable to the 20-hypercube in bandwidth up to an horizon of 1 million peers but falls off by almost 10% at 2 million peers.

Table 7.5. P2P hypernet topologies ranked by maximal relative bandwidth (BW), showing connections per peer (C/N), average number of network hops (H), and the number of supported peers (N) in millions

Hypernet Topology	C/N	H	$N \times 10^6$	BW
20-Cube	20	10	2.1	100
10-Torus	20	11	2.1	93
20-Cayley	20	6	2.8	16
8-Cayley (Napster)	8	8	1.1	13
4-Cayley (Gnutella)	4	13	1.1	8

The 20-valent Cayley tree is included since the number of connections per peer is the same as that for the 20-cube and the 10-torus. An horizon of 6 hops was used for comparison because the peer population is only 144,801 nodes at 5 hops. Similarly for 8-Cayley, a 9 hop horizon would contain 7.7 million peers. These large increments are a direct consequence of the high vertex degree per node. The 4-Cayley (early Gnutella network in Fig. 7.14) and 8-Cayley (Napster network) show relatively poor scalability at 1 million peers (Ritter 2002). Even doubling the number of connections per peer produces slightly better than 50% improvement in throughput.

Because bandwidth in these topologies grows in proportion to added nodes or peers (Fig. 7.15), no throughput ceiling of the type appearing in Figs. 7.5, 7.12 and 7.13 is observed. *BitTorrent* is a P2P file-sharing protocol which effectively implements higher-order topologies dynamically in software. Every client downloading a file from the network usually donates part of its own bandwidth, making it much faster than earlier P2P technologies like Gnutella or Kazaa.

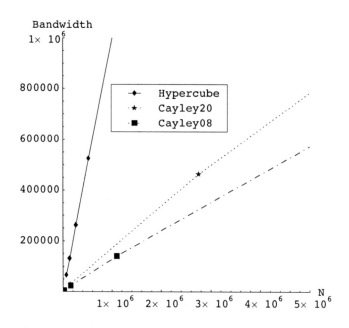

Fig. 7.15. Predicted bandwidth as a function of peers (N) for different hypernet topologies in Table 7.5

7.5.3 Remote Polling Rates

Though BitTorrent is a good protocol for broadband, it is less effective for dial-up, where dropped connections are common. On the other hand, many HTTP servers drop connections over several hours, while many torrents exist long enough to complete a multiday download often required for large files.

An uploading client is flagged as snubbed if the downloading client has not received any data from it in over 60 seconds.

Some BitTorrent clients also report the *share ratio*, a number relating the amount of data uploaded to the amount downloaded. A share ratio of 1.0 means that a user has uploaded as much data as they have downloaded. Some networks, for example, prevent access to new torrents for the first 24–48 hours (i.e., up to 1.7×10^5 seconds in Table 7.1) that the torrent is active to people with overall ratios of less than 1.0 and a certain amount of data uploaded.

7.5.4 Guerrilla Capacity Planning

It is more difficult to make many practical recommendations for meso-VMs because they are still emerging technologies. Sun Microsystems CEO Jonathan Schwartz, a major proponent of enterprise GRID computing, recently stated:

> *"Behind the corporate firewall, the transformation toward multitenant grids has been slower. Frankly, it's been tough to convince the largest enterprises that a public grid represents an attractive future. But things are changing."*

Nonetheless, from a GCaP standpoint, it would be advisable to regard GRIDs and P2P as legitimate compenents of the VM-spectrum (Fig. 7.1).

Two important points for capacity planners. First, adding nodes in macro-VMs adds bandwidth, so the throughput ceilings seen in Figs. 7.5, 7.13 and 7.12 are not expected to appear. Second, macro-VMs are mostly invisible to standard performance management tools, but some of the same performance analysis techniques discussed in Sects. 7.3.5 and 7.4.6 should be applicable as these technologies begin to connect to your data center.

7.6 Summary

Modern computing systems that abstract virtual resources from physical resources have surpassed the measurement paradigms of most performance management tools, thus they remain largely opaque to the performance analyst and capacity planner.

In this chapter, we introduced the spectrum of virtualization that spans microlevel VMs, e.g., hyperthreaded processors, through mesolevel hypervisors to macrolevel networked applications, e.g., GRIDs. Each of these regions has an identifiable proportional polling algorithm, and the polling frequency sets the location on the VM-spectrum. We used this framework to assess various performance case studies reported in the literature. It is clear from these studies that a lot of work remains to be done to better integrate VM performance instrumentation with current capacity management tools.

8
Web Site Planning

> *So schaff' ich am sausenden Webstuhl der Zeit,*
> *Und wirke der Gottheit lebendiges Kleid.*
>
> —J. W. von Goethe, *Faust*

8.1 Introduction

Today's websites are configured as a networked collection of MS Windows, UNIX and Linux servers. The culture that belongs to these mid-range server environments typically has never embraced the concept of capacity planning (for reasons similar to those presented in Chap. 1). Moreover, many of the larger commercial websites are large because they are success disasters. The original business model was implemented in a somewhat ad hoc fashion, but was later discovered to be far more attractive to users than the Web site architects had originally envisaged. Ultimately, the Web site was faced with growing levels of user traffic, and it was concern over the volume of resources being consumed by the high traffic volume that pushed capacity planning into the forefront. Many established Web sites, e.g., Amazon.com and eBay.com, are examples of success disasters that have now evolved and adopted capacity planning methods.

Web site capacity planning inevitably has an impact on application scalability (Chap. 6), but one often sees two extreme approaches to trying to ensure Web site scalability:

1. Overengineer the Web site so that no planning is required
2. Add capacity only when it is seen to be required

The fallacy in item 1 is that it cannot accommodate performance limitations in software, e.g., single-threaded processing. This was discussed in Chap. 1. The fallacy in item 2 is that procurement of new servers requires that you look further ahead than current performance measurements. Additional server capacity has to be foreseen in order that it be procured well in advance of when it is actually needed. Otherwise, by the time the new servers arrive, traffic will have grown to the point where the additional capacity will be immediately absorbed with no advantage gained from the significant fiscal outlay.

This chapter presents Guerrilla capacity planning techniques developed by the author for one of the world's hottest Web sites (which must remain nameless for reasons of confidentiality). In accordance with Chap. 1, a notable attribute is that the performance models used for planning are lightweight and flexible to match the fast-paced growth of this environment. The key topics covered in this chapter include: the effect of time zones on Web traffic patterns, extracting the effective demand on server capacity from measured server utilization, forecasting capacity consumption, and determining the procurement cycle. The centerpiece of this chapter falls into two parts. Section 8.6 presents the short-term analysis of daily performance statistics, while Sect. 8.7 uses summary statistics from the short-term phase to project long-term server growth. The new metric introduced for expressing capacity consumption is the *doubling time*, which sets the pace for the hardware procurement schedule.

In the subsequent analysis, we focus on the bottleneck resource, which turns out to be the back-end database server, not a Web server. Every Web site has multiple bottlenecks, each in different network segments. The network segment that contained the database server was the highest ranking bottleneck at this website. Since any complex networked environment can be decomposed into smaller networked subsystems, the techniques presented in this chapter are completely general. The reader should also keep in mind the *Law of Bottlenecks*: You never remove a bottleneck, you merely move it around (or change its rank). More general Web site capacity planning and performance modeling techniques are discussed in Gunther (2005a, Chap. 10)

8.2 Analysis of Daily Traffic

Because the revenues per user tend to be rather marginal for Web sites, when compared to more traditional business models, success is usually measured in terms of a website's ability to attract high volumes of Internet traffic. The assumption is that financial growth is associated with growth in user traffic to the website. But as many e-commerce websites have discovered (perhaps to the chagrin of Wall Street), connections per second and dollars per connection are not always correlated. Nonetheless, it is vital for successful capacity planning to have a quantitative understanding of Web site traffic profile, which we look at in this section.

One of the most striking features of e-commerce traffic is the unusual variance in its intensity during the day. Mainframe capacity planners are already familiar with the bimodal behavior of conventional commercial workloads due to user activity on a centralized server. This bimodality is sometimes referred to as the *Camel Curve*.

8.2.1 The Camel and the Dromedary

The "camel" designation in Fig. 8.1 refers to the dominant twin peaks in server utilization occurring around 9–10 am and 2–3 pm (local time) within

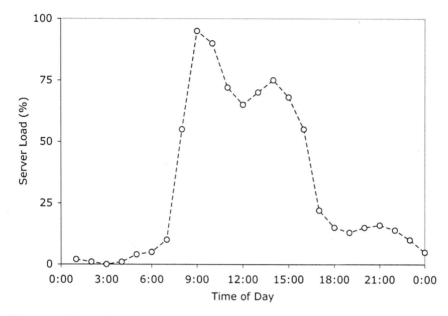

Fig. 8.1. Classic daily loading profile for a mainframe showing the two main peaks around 9 am and 2pm, which are responsible for the name "camel curve"

each day shift. There are two peaks because of the lunchtime slump in system activity around midday.

On the web, however, the day shift can last for 24 hours, across 37 time zones (Fig. 8.2), and together with randomized traffic, it becomes unclear what the characteristic traffic profile looks like. It turns out that worldwide access 24 hours a day, 7 days a week, across all time zones would produce a traffic profile that was very broad without any discernible peaks. On the contrary, measurements from many high-volume Web sites shows there is always a dominant peak around 2:00 hr UTC (Coordinated Universal Time). The single "dromedary" peak in Fig. 8.3 also shows up consistently in the measured processor utilization of in situ Web site servers as well as the measurements of packets inbound to the website. Moreover, this traffic characteristic seems to be quite universal for many heavily trafficed Web sites. The reason for its existence can be understood as follows.

North American Web traffic can be thought of as being comprised of two major contributions: one from the east coast and the other from the west coast. This naive partitioning corresponds to the two major population regions in the USA. If we further assume the traffic intensities (expressed as a percentage) are identical but otherwise phase-shifted by the three hours separating the respective time zones, Figure 8.3 shows how these two traffic profiles combine to produce the dominant peak. As the west coast contribution peaks at

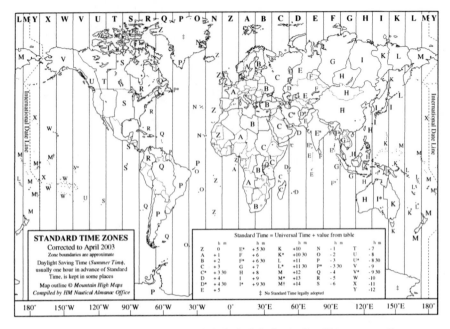

Fig. 8.2. World time zones labeled alphabetically (J is not used)

100% around 4:00 hours UTC, the east coast contribution is already in rapid decline because of the later local time (7:00 hours actual UTC). Therefore, the aggregate traffic peak occurs at about 2:00 hours UTC.

Figure 8.3 show the measured daily traffic intensity at a USA site (circles). The single dominant peak (solid line) at 2 am UTC is the sum of contributions from the east coast (dotted line) and the west coast (dashed line) phase-shifted by 3 hours for the respective time zones. As the western contribution is peaking, the eastern contribution is declining rapidly because of the later local time. A benign bimodal character can be seen in the aggregate data of Fig. 8.3 with a small hump occurring around 16:30 hours UTC. This corresponds to a much more distinct bimodality in both component traffic profiles and is reminiscent of the bimodal mainframe traffic characteristic mentioned earlier but now reversed and shifted in time.

8.2.2 Unimodal but Bicoastal

Another important conclusion can be drawn from this simple, Guerrilla-style traffic analysis. There is no significant traffic coming from time zones in Europe, Asia, Australia, or the Pacific. If these regions were contributing, even at a relatively lower intensity, they would tend to broaden the dromedary peak significantly. Hence, the bimodal profile so familiar in the mainframe context can be understood as belonging to very localized usage where most users are

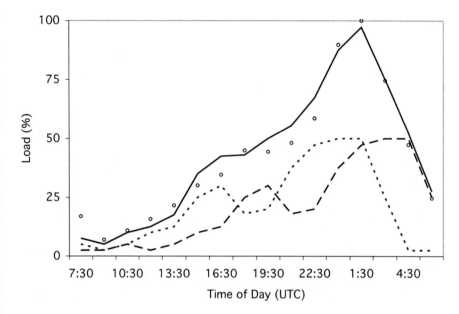

Fig. 8.3. Daily loading profile data (*circles*) for a typical web site. In contrast to the bimodal curve in Fig. 8.3, the data is multimodal (due to access in multiple time zones) but exhibits a dominant peak around 1:30 UTC. These data can be explained in terms of the superposition (*solid line*) of two component component curves (*dashed lines*) that are identical but phase-shifted by three hours

connected to a centralized server (mainframe or otherwise) by terminals or workstations which are active in the same local time zone. Although Web traffic is delocalized into multiple time zones, it is still confined mostly to North America and within that continent, it is dominated by the activity of the coastal populations (Fig. 8.4).

A couple of corollaries follow from these observations about such traffic patterns. If the dromedary curve appears in measurements of daily traffic profiles, we can confidently assume we are looking primarily at North American users. This activity is also usually reflected in the consumption of other Web site resources such as processor utilization across supporting servers and inbound network bandwidth. Secondly, we can use the dromedary curve as a quick validation of any capacity planning predictions

In the subsequent sections, we shall focus entirely on back-end server capacity rather than network capacity. The site in this study had plenty of OC12 bandwidth to handle inbound and outbound packets, so network capacity never caused any performance limitations. Since the measured server utilization is bounded above by 100% busy, a peak in server utilization caused by the characteristic traffic profile discussed above would remain obscured. One

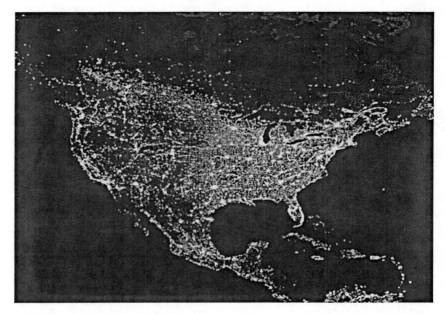

Fig. 8.4. Composite satellite image of the North American continent at night reveals the bicoastal population distribution in the United States. Image credit: NASA Visible Earth (`http://visibleearth.nasa.gov`)

of the objectives in this study was to reproduce a server utilization profile that included the daily dromedary peaks. To this end we now introduce the concept of effective server demand.

8.3 Effective Demand

Effective demand is a measure of the work that is being serviced as well as the work that could be serviced if more capacity was available. It is similar to the mainframe notion of *latent demand* (Forst 1997). This metric is dimensionless in the same way that CPU-busy is dimensionless. However, unlike CPU-busy, which is bounded above by 100%, the effective demand can be expressed as an unbounded percentage.

For example, an effective demand of 167% means that the application workload could have been serviced by one and two-thirds servers, even though only one completely saturated server was physically available to accommodate the workload. Once a server becomes saturated, the run-queue necessarily begins to grow, and this can have an adverse impact on user-perceived response time (Gunther 2005a, Chap. 3). Although user-based response time measurements are possible, they are by no means simple to carry out in the context of a website. In general, it requires a combination of external and internal measurements together with some additional statistical analysis. Even then, such quantification does not provide much insight into the qualitative perceptions of the user.

8.3.1 Modeling Assumptions

As we shall describe in Sect. 8.6, the effective demand metric can be calculated using statistical regression analysis. The predictor is the effective demand (expressed as a percentage), and appropriate regressor variables can be determined from a factorial design of experiment. (See e.g., (Box et al. 1978), (Jain 1990, Chaps. 16–23), and (Lilja 2000, Chap. 9) for a fuller discussion of this technique.) Typical regressors might include CPU clock frequency, the number of user submitting work to the system, the run-queue length, I/O rates, etc. One performance metric that cannot be used is the measured CPU utilization itself, since that is the variable we are trying to predict (Forst 1997).

As with any statistical forecasting, we assume that the workload is CPU-intensive and will remain that way for the duration of the capacity forecast as more work is added. This is an assumption because it could turn out that adding more capacity to the CPU subsystem removes the CPU bottleneck alright, but only to bring disk or memory bottlenecks into play as the new scalability inhibitor.

8.3.2 Statistical Approach

Statistical forecasting projects trends based on current data. The current data cannot, by definition, contain information about future bottlenecks as the workload increases. This is one of the limitations of statistical data modeling. One way to forecast unseen bottlenecks is with the aid of multiclass queueing models Gunther (2005a). The downside to using queueing models is that they require the construction of an underlying system abstraction which embodies all significant bottleneck resources. This is a very time-consuming process and demands more sophisticated measurements than than are generally available to parameterize the queueing model. So, for complex systems where planning time is limited, statistical models can offer a powerful approach, as long as the underlying assumptions are kept in mind.

In this case, about ten weeks of performance data collected from the back-end database server and containing some 200–300 metrics were reviewed for numerical stability. During that period, many upgrades were performed on the server, including: faster CPUs, larger caches, more recent version of the database, and modifying the application software across the entire website. Consequently, only an eight-week subset of the reviewed performance data was found to be stable enough for use in statistical forecasting.

8.4 Selecting Statistical Tools

As mentioned in Sect. 8.3.1, it was decided to undertake statistical regression analysis of these raw server performance data to derive the daily effective demand. Since these data represent a time series, the type of regression which can take into account time-dependent correlations is called *autoregression* or AR analysis (Box et al. 1978). This allows one to pick out seasonal effects and so on. Since we are only going to be analyzing a few weeks of server data, we do not expect to see such seasonal effects. Therefore, resorting to ordinary (time-independent) regression analysis is legitimate.

Having elected to apply statistical analysis, the next issue is to select the statistical tools to use for the analysis and, in particular, whether to purchase statistical software or build a custom application integrated into the current environment. This step in the Guerrilla capacity planning process was discussed in Chap. 1. The methods discussed here, however, had not been used previously by the author and this meant that some prototyping was inevitable. It was also not clear at the outset which statistical functions would be required in carrying out the regression analysis. For example, implementing a set of statistical regression functions in C code (Press et al. 1988) or Perl scripts (Gunther 2005a) is one option, but it would also be more time consuming than using an environment where a reasonably complete set of statistical functions was already available.

8.4.1 Spreadsheet Programming

The choice became obvious once it was realized that almost every desktop at the Web site (including all the management offices) had a PC running Microsoft Office and thereby had Excel readily available. What is not generally appreciated is that Excel is not just a spreadsheet (Levine et al. 1999); it is a programming environment with Visual Basic for Applications (VBA) as the programming language. VBA is a quite a reasonable prototyping language because it is object-oriented, comes with an integrated debugger, and contains a macro recording facility. Excel also comes with a considerable amount of embedded Help documentation, and is quite a good source for basic instruction in statistical analysis.

8.4.2 Online Support

There are several Internet news groups, such as: `comp.apps.spreadsheet` and `microsoft.public.excel.programming`, devoted to spreadsheets and VBA programming where expert-level help is readily available for the most obscure VBA programming problems. In addition, there is Microsoft's own website `http://office.microsoft.com/en-us/FX010858001033.aspx`. As we shall see later, data importing and data filtering are also very useful capabilities integrated into Excel. Plotting is also integrated into Excel and can also be accessed via VBA. A broad set of standard statistical analysis functions (e.g., regression, ANOVA, moving average) are available by default. Excel, as packaged with Microsoft Office, does not include the more sophisticated analysis tools for time-series analysis, but these can often be found on the Internet or as commercial add-on packages. Finally, there is an option to publish spreadsheets as HTML pages.

8.5 Planning for Data Collection

Generally, operations and capacity planning are distinct functions. The former is focused on the tactical monitoring, while the latter is focused on the strategic planning. But modern economics demands a leaner infrastructure to the point where these two traditional functions become merged. Data center operations understands the need to collect performance data and many operations managers are prepared to spend hundreds of thousands of dollars on performance management software. What is often overlooked is the purpose for which the performance data is being collected. In each case it is very different.

8.5.1 Commercial Collectors: Use It or Lose It

Commercial data collection products have a set of default time boundaries across which they aggregate the collected data into coarser time intervals. This is primarily done to conserve disk space.

For example, performance data might be sampled every few minutes, but after 12 hours all those sampled statistics (e.g., CPU utilization) are averaged over the entire 12-hour period and thereby reduced to a single number. This is good for data storage and it does not impede performance monitoring, but it is no so good for capacity planning. Such averaged performance data is likely far too coarse for meaningful statistical analysis. Some commercial products offer separate databases for storing monitoring and modeling data. Either the default aggregation boundaries should be reset, or operations management needs to be prescient about saving capacity planning data prior to the aggregation boundaries. In either case, data collection and data modeling may need to be scheduled differently and well in advance of any data aggregation. This idea is foreign to many Web site managers and administrators.

8.5.2 Brewing in the Background

And so it was with the Web site described here. Fortunately, alternative data were available because the platform vendor had installed their own non-commercial data collection tools on the back-end server. It was called *SE Percolator* (Cockcroft and Pettit 1998) (See also Chap. 11). Thankfully, SE

Percolator was sufficiently unsophisticated that it retained 2-minute samples of more than 200 Solaris performance metrics. These data were used in our subsequent statistical modeling.

8.6 Short-Term Capacity Planning

As discussed in Sect. 8.3, the effective server demand is calculated using statistical regression techniques. We new present that technique in more detail using Excel, but the reader should be aware that it can also be calculated using other statistical tools like those mentioned in Chap. 1, e.g., R (Venables and Ripley 2002; Faraway 2004).

8.6.1 Multivariate Regression of Daily Data

Because of a prior succession of changes that were made to the system configuration, only five weeks of data were stable enough to show consistent trending information. An Excel macro was used to analyze the raw metric samples and predict the effective demand using a multivariate linear regression model

$$U_{\text{eff}} = \alpha_1 X_1 + \alpha_2 X_2 + \cdots + \alpha_6 X_6 + \beta, \qquad (8.1)$$

where each of the X's is a regressor variable, and the α's and β are the coefficients determined by an ANOVA analysis of the raw performance data. Here, U_{eff} is the estimated effective utilization of the server and it can exceed 100%. Multivariate regression is also known as *multiple* regression.

The random variables $X_1, X_2, \ldots$ in (8.1) are identified with the half dozen collected performance metrics appearing in columns C through H of Fig. 8.5, i.e., the dispersion measures of the utilization U and the run-queue length Q.

Example 8.1. If we were to carry out the regression procedure manually in Excel, it would unfold as follows:

1. All the data in Fig. 8.5, except *AvgU*, are used to determine the regression coefficients $\alpha_1, \alpha_2, \ldots, \beta$ as described in Fig. 8.6.
2. The coefficient values for our example are shown in Fig. 8.7.
3. The effective utilization U_{eff} is calculated for each row of the spreadsheet in Fig. 8.5 using (8.1) using the evaluated coefficients and the values for each of the performance metrics in that row.
4. The resulting value of U_{eff} for each row would generate a new column in the spreadsheet.

Section 8.6.2 explains how this process can be automated within Excel. □

It is important to make sure you have the *Analysis Tools Pack* loaded into Excel. The Regression application is invoked from the Tools menu as *Tools>Data Analysis* ... which brings up a dialog box from which you choose

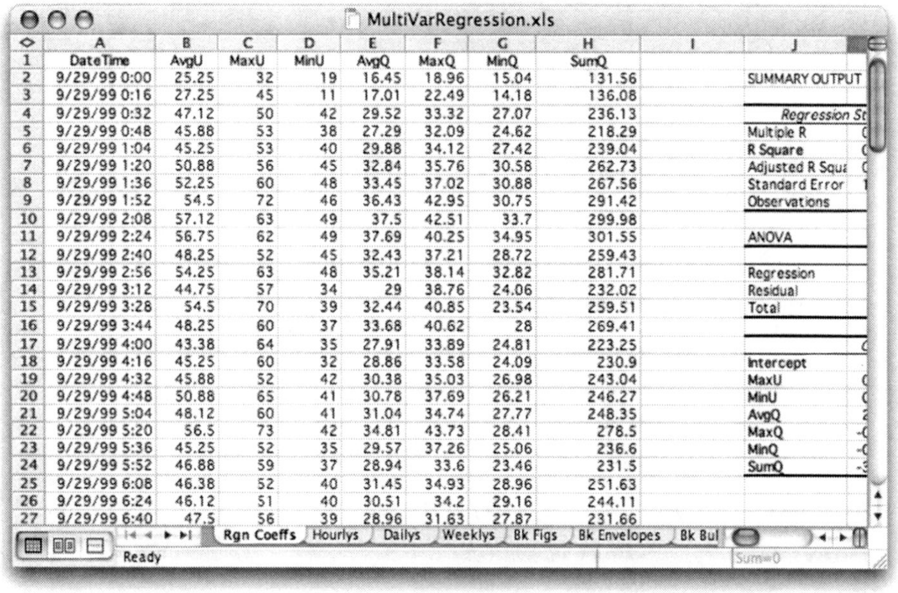

	A	B	C	D	E	F	G	H	I	J
1	DateTime	AvgU	MaxU	MinU	AvgQ	MaxQ	MinQ	SumQ		
2	9/29/99 0:00	25.25	32	19	16.45	18.96	15.04	131.56		SUMMARY OUTPUT
3	9/29/99 0:16	27.25	45	11	17.01	22.49	14.18	136.08		
4	9/29/99 0:32	47.12	50	42	29.52	33.32	27.07	236.13		*Regression St*
5	9/29/99 0:48	45.88	53	38	27.29	32.09	24.62	218.29		Multiple R
6	9/29/99 1:04	45.25	53	40	29.88	34.12	27.42	239.04		R Square
7	9/29/99 1:20	50.88	56	45	32.84	35.76	30.58	262.73		Adjusted R Squa
8	9/29/99 1:36	52.25	60	48	33.45	37.02	30.88	267.56		Standard Error
9	9/29/99 1:52	54.5	72	46	36.43	42.95	30.75	291.42		Observations
10	9/29/99 2:08	57.12	63	49	37.5	42.51	33.7	299.98		
11	9/29/99 2:24	56.75	62	49	37.69	40.25	34.95	301.55		ANOVA
12	9/29/99 2:40	48.25	52	45	32.43	37.21	28.72	259.43		
13	9/29/99 2:56	54.25	63	48	35.21	38.14	32.82	281.71		Regression
14	9/29/99 3:12	44.75	57	34	29	38.76	24.06	232.02		Residual
15	9/29/99 3:28	54.5	70	39	32.44	40.85	23.54	259.51		Total
16	9/29/99 3:44	48.25	60	37	33.68	40.62	28	269.41		
17	9/29/99 4:00	43.38	64	35	27.91	33.89	24.81	223.25		
18	9/29/99 4:16	45.25	60	32	28.86	33.58	24.09	230.9		Intercept
19	9/29/99 4:32	45.88	52	42	30.38	35.03	26.98	243.04		MaxU
20	9/29/99 4:48	50.88	65	41	30.78	37.69	26.21	246.27		MinU
21	9/29/99 5:04	48.12	60	41	31.04	34.74	27.77	248.35		AvgQ
22	9/29/99 5:20	56.5	73	42	34.81	43.73	28.41	278.5		MaxQ
23	9/29/99 5:36	45.25	52	35	29.57	37.26	25.06	236.6		MinQ
24	9/29/99 5:52	46.88	59	37	28.94	33.6	23.46	231.5		SumQ
25	9/29/99 6:08	46.38	52	40	31.45	34.93	28.96	251.63		
26	9/29/99 6:24	46.12	51	40	30.51	34.2	29.16	244.11		
27	9/29/99 6:40	47.5	56	39	28.96	31.63	27.87	231.66		

Fig. 8.5. Extracted performance data from the back-end server imported into an Excel spreadsheet in preparation for multivariate regression analysis

Regression function. This function is essentially the same as the *Trendline* function used in Chap. 5 with the limitation that the assumed functional form is a *straight line* rather than a polynomial, i.e., it performs linear regression.

Indeed, the regression statistic labeled *R Square* or (R^2) in cell K6 in the output of Fig. 8.7 is called the *coefficient of determination*, and it is an important figure of merit for the regression model. It tells us how much of the variance in the data is explained by the multivariate model (8.1). In this case, better than 98% of the variance is explained by our model. A higher R^2 value can be produced by adding more regressors. Another figure of merit is the $SignificanceF$ value in cell O13. The smaller this value, the better. Higher F values are produced by fewer regressors.

8.6.2 Automation Using Spreadsheet Macros

A Perl script, like that in Sect. E.1 of Appendix E, extracts the raw SE Percolator data (Sect. 8.5.2) and averaging it over 15-minute samples of the relevant time-stamped performance metrics for each day of interest. The extracted data is then read directly into a spreadsheet using the Excel Web Query facility. This produces about 100 rows of data in the spreadsheet. Two macros are then applied to this data.

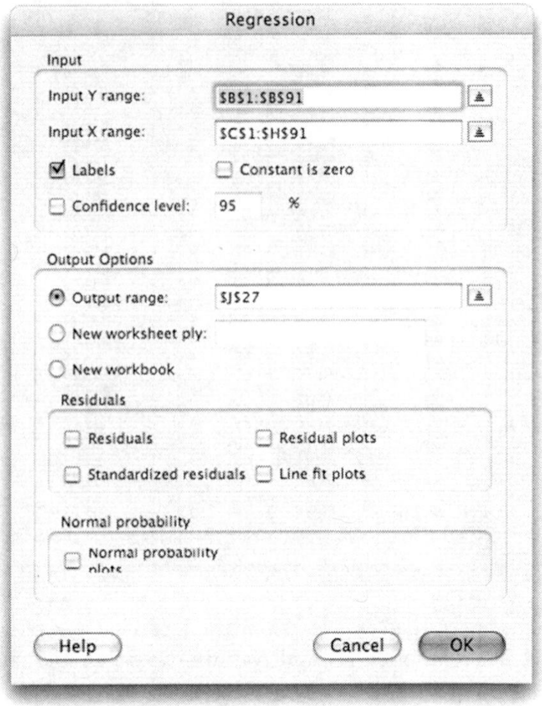

Fig. 8.6. Dialog box for the Excel regression tool. The *Input Y range* field is identified with the measured average processor utilization. These data reside in column B of Fig. 8.5 and provide values for the *dependent* or *response* random variable in the calculation of the α coefficients. The *Input X range* is identified with the set of six extracted performance metrics. These *independent* random variables $X_1, X_2, \ldots$ or *regressor* variables in (8.1) reside in columns C through H. Since labels are used for each of the columns in Fig. 8.5 the *Labels* box is checked. The *Output range* field can be a single cell which defines the top left cell of Fig. 8.7

The first of these filter out any row if it contains a measured CPU utilization of 95% or greater. Such rows are eliminated from the ANOVA calculations as being too biased for use by (8.1). The regressor variables (labeled X_1 through X_6 in (8.1) are then used by the macro in Sect. E.2 of Appendix E to calculate the coefficients of (8.1). Once these coefficients are known, the estimated value of the server utilization U_{eff} is computed for each row of the spreadsheet in Fig. 8.5 using (8.1), and then inserted as a new column into the same spreadsheet. In general, the estimated and measured utilization will be fairly close until it gets near to saturation (e.g., 95% or greater), in which case significantly larger values of are estimated, as shown in Fig. 8.8.

	J	K	L	M	N	O	P	Q
1								
2	SUMMARY OUTPUT							
3								
4	*Regression Statistics*							
5	Multiple R	0.99216266						
6	R Square	0.98438674						
7	Adjusted R Squa	0.98325807						
8	Standard Error	1.11808743						
9	Observations	90						
10								
11	ANOVA							
12		*df*	*SS*	*MS*	*F*	*Significance F*		
13	Regression	6	6541.86692	1090.31115	872.165542	9.6049E-73		
14	Residual	83	103.759919	1.2501195				
15	Total	89	6645.62684					
16								
17		*Coefficients*	*Standard Error*	*t Stat*	*P-value*	*Lower 95%*	*Upper 95%*	*Lower 95.0%*
18	Intercept	1.3240455	0.75942325	1.74348822	0.08495121	-0.18641722	2.83450822	-0.1864172
19	MaxU	0.22818773	0.02407508	9.47817141	7.2199E-15	0.18030335	0.27607211	0.1803033
20	MinU	0.25784123	0.02501249	10.3084996	1.6063E-16	0.20809238	0.30759008	0.2080923
21	AvgQ	26.0945498	39.6325319	0.65841238	0.51209543	-52.7329836	104.922083	-52.732983
22	MaxQ	-0.05100836	0.09029699	-0.56489552	0.57366849	-0.23060549	0.12858876	-0.2306054
23	MinQ	-0.15435786	0.11931225	-1.29373015	0.19934731	-0.3916652	0.08294948	-0.391665
24	SumQ	-3.14335044	4.95763341	-0.63404253	0.52779665	-13.0038866	6.7171857	-13.003886
25								
26								
27								

Fig. 8.7. Coefficients $\alpha_1, \alpha_2, \ldots, \beta$ for the effective utilization model (8.1), as calculated by Excel, appear at the bottom of column J. The labels used for these coefficients are the same as the headers for columns C–H in Fig. 8.5

8.7 Long-Term Capacity Planning

Summary statistics from the short-term multivariate model described in Sect 8.6 are then taken over into a weekly spreadsheet. About eight weeks worth of these summary statistics are needed to make reasonable long-term growth predictions.

8.7.1 Nonlinear Regression of Weekly Data

For this phase of the exercise, a nonlinear regression model was also constructed using spreadsheet macros. The maxima of the weekly effective demands U_W, calculated from the multivariate model in Sect. 8.6, were fitted to a an exponential model:

$$U_W = U_0 \, e^{\Lambda W} \tag{8.2}$$

which has only a single parameter Λ. An exponential growth model, chosen to reflect the expected server capacity, is likely to be needed to accurately forecast capacity beyond simple linear growth. Similar nonlinear models are often used for financial projections of business growth, and there was some additional evidence for exponential growth in the measured data for inbound network traffic.

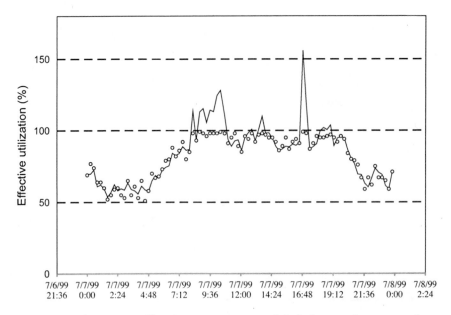

Fig. 8.8. Daily server utilization measurements (*circles*) over the course of one week. These data cannot exceed 100%, by definition. As explained in Sect. 8.2, the effective utilization U_{eff} calculated from a statistical performance model (*solid line*) is unbounded, by definition. The spike in the effective utilization near 16:48 hr indicates that more than 1.5 servers were needed theoretically to service the user demand at that time

The long-term capacity consumption U_W is expressed in terms of the numbers of weeks W since the data analysis began. The constant U_0 is the server utilization at the zeroth week when the capacity study commenced, and the parameter Λ is fitted using the *Trendline* function in Excel. Λ specifies the growth rate or curvature of the exponential curve. For the data in Fig. 8.9 the fitted parameters are $U_0 = 133.12$ and $\Lambda = 0.03090$.

8.7.2 Procurement Curves

The final task is to extrapolate the results from the analysis of weekly growth in effective demand into a set of requirements for server upgrade procurement. This kind of forecast is best expressed as a set of curves corresponding to different possible CPU configurations, cache sizes, and clock speeds. Since the multivariate regression model only pertains to measurements on the current system configuration, we need a way to extrapolate to other possible CPU configurations. This can be accomplished using the methods of Chaps. 4–6.

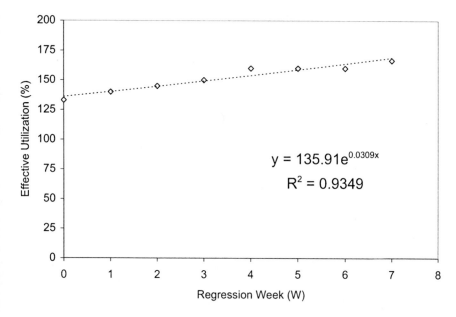

Fig. 8.9. Exponential regression (*dashed line*) on 8 weeks of peak effective utilization (*circles*) statistics carried over from the short-term multivariate model. The curvature parameter is $\Lambda = 0.0309$

8.7.3 Estimating Server Scalability

Recall from Sect. 4.4 that the normalized capacity $C(p)$ of a server with p physical processors is defined by the function

$$C(\sigma, \kappa, p) = \frac{p}{1 + \sigma(p-1) + \kappa p(p-1)}. \qquad (8.3)$$

This function can be fitted to the throughput data measured on an arbitrary set of processor configurations. The actual throughput $X(p)$ for a particular configuration can be predicted by multiplying $C(p)$ by $X(1)$. Fitting (8.3) to a set of throughput measurements produces estimates for the two parameters σ and κ.

The question becomes one of finding appropriate throughput measurements of the Web site applications of interest for capacity planning. At the time, the developers of this Web site were not in a position to characterize their own Web application in any consistent way. A useful fallback position, in this situation, is to look for similar measurements of application performance from other groups, such as quality assurance (QA). Unfortunately, this Internet company was only in the early stages of setting up a load test and a software QA group. If either of these groups had been further advanced in their data collection, it might have been possible to use those measurements to

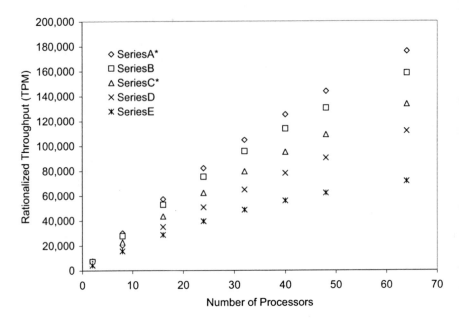

Fig. 8.10. Vendor performance data for a suite of processor products. The data used in this chapter belong to the particular products denoted *Series A* and *Series C*

improve some of the following capacity projections. In the meantime, this Web site needed to make some fiscally challenging decisions regarding server procurement and they needed to make those decisions quickly—a typical Guerrilla situation where a sense of direction is more important than a compass bearing (see Chap. 1).

In lieu of doing Web site-specific workload characterization, it was decided to approach the server vendor for some initial input regarding the scalability of their platforms. The result was that they delivered a set of company-internal measurements like those shown in Fig. 8.10, which can be regarded as being similar to renormalized throughput values for the TPC-C benchmark (www.tpc.org). These data were fitted using the scalability model (8.3) to calculate the respective scalability parameters, viz., $\sigma = 0.0061$ and $\kappa = 0.0016$. These parameters were then used to estimate the corresponding capacity gains summarized in Table 8.1.

8.7.4 Calculating Capacity Gains

The back-end servers at this Web site were running a database management system with CPU configurations up to a 64-way. The vendor scaling estimates in Table 8.1 indicate that adding 12 more Series C processors to the existing 52-way configuration would produce a 15% gain in CPU headroom. Alter-

Table 8.1. Throughput numbers are derived from vendor-supplied data in Fig. 8.10. Reading horizontally corresponds to increasing the processor clock frequency (ΔCLK) for the same CPU configuration, while reading vertically corresponds to increasing the number of physical processors (ΔCPU) with the same clock speed. These differences are also expressed as ratios. The most important ratio is the bold number in the bottom right-hand corner. It is the maximum possible upgrade ratio formed from the *bold numbers* along the diagonal. The difference between the 52-way Series C (base configuration) in column 2 and the 64-way Series A (maximal configuration) in column 3 produces the bold value in column 4. That number is then expressed as a ratio in column 5 relative to the base configuration

Vendor performance data for upgrading from Series C to Series A				
N-way	Series C	Series A	ΔCLK	Ratio
52-way	**115,755**	152,432	3,667	0.316850
64-way	133,629	**175,969**	4,234	0.316847
ΔCPU	17,874	23,537	**60,214**	–
Ratio	0.154412	0.154410	–	**0.520185**

natively, keeping the CPU configuration fixed at 52-way and increasing the CPU model from Series C to Series A shows a 32% gain. Performing both upgrades simultaneously shows a 52% gain. These capacity projections seem rather optimistic for a database application.

Table 8.2. Recalibrated vendor throughput based on adjusted parameters σ and κ in Eqn.(8.3). The table is read in the same way as described for Table 8.1. The maximum possible upgrade ratio is the *bold number* in the bottom right-hand corner, and the smaller value (cf. vendor-derived value in Table 8.1) reflects the higher expected overhead for database accesses

Recalibrated performance data for upgrading from Series C to Series A				
N-way	Series C	Series A	ΔCLK	Ratio
52-way	**57,605**	75,859	18,254	0.316882
64-way	60,875	**80,165**	19,290	0.316879
ΔCPU	3,270	4,306	**22,560**	–
Ratio	0.056766	0.056763	–	**0.391633**

In my experience, the contention factor (σ) for database management systems (e.g., ORACLE) is typically around 3% (i.e., $\sigma = 0.030$) while the coherency term is highly dependent on other factors. Here, it appears to be relatively small. It was decided, therefore, to adjust the σ value in this way and leave the κ more or less the same. The impact of this adjustment on overall scalability can be seen in the envelopes of Fig. 8.11.

This adjustment to the scalability parameters allowed for the more realistic estimate of capacity factors shown in Table 8.2 for the server configurations of

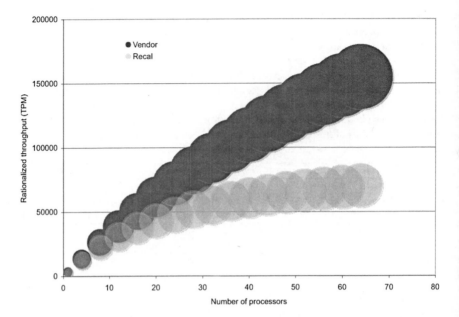

Fig. 8.11. Comparison of predicted scalability based on the vendor data (*dark disks*) in Fig. 8.10 and (8.3) using recalibrated σ and κ parameters (*light disks*). The envelope formed by the disks in each case represents a region where actual throughput might be measured. The upper side of each envelope corresponds to scalability using the highest performance *Series A* processor, while the lower side corresponds to the current *Series C* processor configuration

interest. Using these more conservative estimates, we see that adding 12 more CPUs to the 52-way Series C, at the same clock speed, predicts a 6% gain in headroom. Keeping the CPU configuration fixed at 52-way but increasing the CPU clock speed from Series C to Series A shows a 32% gain in headroom. Performing both of these upgrades together produces a 39% headroom gain.

We consider upgrading from a Series-C to a Series-A clock while maintaining a 52-way configuration on the backplane and using the vendor scaling data in Table 8.2.

Example 8.2. We first calculate the increase in processor capacity ΔCPU from the tabulated throughput values:

$$\Delta\text{CPU}_{52} = \frac{X_A - X_C}{X_C},$$
$$= \frac{75,859 - 57,605}{57,605},$$
$$= 0.32, \tag{8.4}$$

which is the ratio in column 5 of Table 8.2.   □

Next, this increase in processor capacity is used to adjust the weekly growth curve U_w in (8.2) downward so that the new curve takes longer to reach saturation.

Example 8.3. At week 20, the effective utilization is $U_C(20) = 246.97$ for the baseline server. By maximally upgrading to Series A, we know Series A ΔCPU = 0.3169, and therefore the corresponding decrease in the effective demand is given by:

$$U_A(20) = U_C(20) \, (1 - \Delta\text{CPU}) \,,$$
$$= 246.97 \, (1 - 0.3169) \,,$$
$$= 168.71\% \tag{8.5}$$

The expected server utilization at week 20 is only 168.71% (or approximately one and two-thirds servers) after the upgrade rather than 246.97% (or almost two and one-half servers) without the upgrade. □

The long-term growth envelopes are shown in Fig 8.12. The x-axis shows the number of weeks since the data analysis was begun, and week 20 corresponds to a fiscal-year boundary. The horizontal gridlines can also be interpreted as the number of servers being consumed in a given week. Each of these scenarios could have been made more accurate if actual workload measurements had been available.

8.7.5 Estimating the Doubling Period

A more intuitive grasp of the significance of the growth parameter $\Lambda = 0.0309$ evaluated in Sect. 8.7.1 comes from calculating the time it takes to double the load on the database server. The *doubling period* can be calculated very simply by dividing the natural logarithm of two by the value of Λ as it is displayed in Fig. 8.9:

$$T_2 = \frac{\ln(2)}{\Lambda} = 22.43 \,, \tag{8.6}$$

which corresponds to approximately 6 months. In other words, every six months, twice as much server capacity (Fig. 8.13) will be consumed as is being consumed now!

This the growth rate is extremely fast. It is at least an order of magnitude faster than the growth of typical mainframe data processing workloads and three times faster than Moore's law, which states that the number of transistors that can be packed into VLSI circuitry doubles roughly every 18 months. Nonetheless, this startling rate of growth agrees with growth of network traffic measured at this website.

Referring back to the Guerrilla attributes listed in Table 1.1, a plot like Fig. 8.13, which shows the number of servers that need to be procured stacked up every six months, may be a more significant *Guerrilla graph* than the more technical rendition of exponential doubling presented in Fig. 8.12. Fully

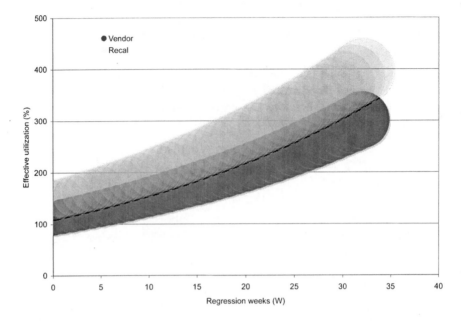

Fig. 8.12. Projected long-term capacity envelopes predicted by the vendor (*gray*) and our more conservative analysis (*black*). The *horizontal gridlines* can also be interpreted as the number of servers being consumed in a given week

loaded, high-end database servers cost many millions of dollars each. A doubling period of six months, even for the most lucrative of today's Web sites, would constitute a serious financial burden. So much for the view that capacity planning is not necessary for today's Web sites.

8.8 Summary

In this chapter we have shown how multivariate regression can used to analyze short-term effective demand in highly variable data. The effective demand is a measure of the work that is being serviced as well as the work that could be serviced if more capacity was available. Daily data was collected and the effective demand calculated using spreadsheet macros. A weekly summarization of the peak effective demand was then used to generate a nonlinear regression model for long-term capacity consumption and to further characterize that consumption by introducing the doubling period as a growth metric. This metric provides a convenient basis for describing procurement curves.

A doubling period of six months was immediately recognized by management as having potentially devastating implications for the fiscal longevity of the Web site, and additional servers were ordered. In the meantime, several software engineering actions (that were not predicted by this capacity

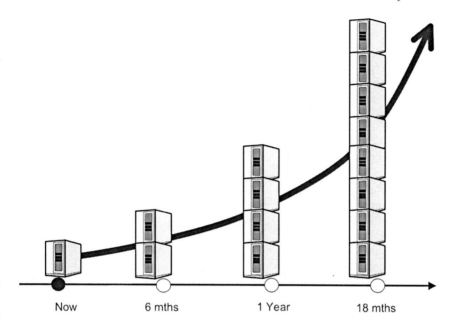

Now   6 mths   1 Year   18 mths

Fig. 8.13. Schematic representation of the financial burden presented by the exponential doubling in server capacity. When presenting your capacity planning conclusions, this may be a more significant *Guerrilla graph* than the technical form of exponential doubling presented in Fig. 8.12

planning model) were immediately undertaken to provide some additional breathing space since procurement was already behind where it should have been.

Almost all the significant traffic at this Web site was discovered to be coming from two time zones in North American with very little coming from other regions. Such regionally localized web traffic is responsible for the dominant single peak discussed in Sect. 8.2. This profile is common to many websites in North America. As Web applications continue to flourish, operations management must think beyond the immediate visual feedback of standard performance monitoring and develop a longer-term capacity plan like the one presented in this chapter.

Gargantuan Computing—GRIDs and P2P

9.1 Introduction

In this chapter we are going to consider GCaP capacity planning techniques for gargantuan-scale computer systems such as so-called peer-to-peer (P2P) networks and computational GRID networks. One of the best known working examples of a GRID-style computing system is SETI@Home (Search for Extraterrestrial Intelligence at Home), where a scientific workload, viz., processing radio-telescope signals, is farmed out to a gargantuan number of floating-point operations per second (FLOPS) in the guise of millions of otherwise idle personal computers—many being home PCs.

One of the best known working examples of a P2P-style computing system is *Skype* (www.skype.com), which allows millions of people to use their PCs like a free telephone by forming its own gargantuan network (Fig. 9.1) which supports the voice over Internet Protocol (VOIP). Other well-known P2P architectures include Gnutella, Napster, Freenet, Limewire, Kazaa, BitTorrent, instant messaging, WiFi, PDAs and even cellphones. Mnay of these architectures have progressed from simple file transfer protocols to a viable means for distribution of applications such as games, movies, and even operating systems.

This class of system offers the potential for very large-scale implementations. Consequently, it is appropriate to draw on the concepts of system scalability developed in Chap. 4 as well as the concepts of virtualization developed in Chap. 7. The general goal for these architectures is to enable scalable virtual organizations that can provide a set of well-defined services.

Key to the performance of these systems is the particular choice of network topology and its associated bandwidth. To assess the scalability of network bandwidth, this chapter draws on performance bounding techniques described in (Gunther 2005a, Chap. 5). We shall apply those same techniques to the performance analysis of a particular P2P network called *Gnutella* (commencing in Sect. 9.3) since the pros and cons of its capacity have been so well docu-

mented. First, we review some of the distinctions between GRIDs and P2P
networked computer systems.

9.2 GRIDs vs. P2P

P2P networks and GRIDs share the common focus of harnessing resources
across multiple administrative domains. Therefore, they may be distinguished
in the following way:

GRID: Supports a variety of applications with a focus on providing infrastructure with quality of service to moderate-sized, homogeneous, and partially trusted communities (Foster 2005). Grid toolkits provide secure services for submitting batch jobs or executing interactive applications. The
network architecture tends to be more centralized, hierarchical, and static.

P2P: Support intermittent participation in vertically integrated applications
for much larger communities of untrusted, anonymous individuals. P2P
systems provide protocols for sharing and exchanging data among nodes.
The network architecture tends to be more decentralized, and dynamics
require resource discovery.

It should be kept in mind that both these technologies are very much in the
process of evolving and have by no means reached a final form. Because they
are likely to become more ubiquitous, it is important for our purpose as GCaP
planners to understand something about them.

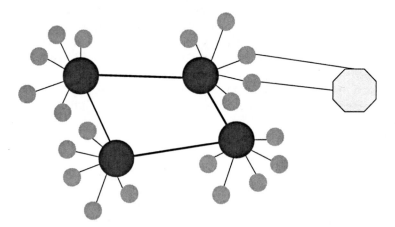

Fig. 9.1. The Skype network showing the network connectivity between its three
main entities: supernodes (*black circles*), ordinary nodes (*gray circles*), and a login
server (*gray octagon*)

GRID computing is focused on scientific and engineering applications and attempts to provide diverse resources that interoperate. The concept behind the GRID is analogous to the electrical power grid. It is available on demand and it does not matter where you are. When you throw the switch, you expect the light to come on. Consequently, GRIDs should be built from standard interfaces and protocols, and the Open Grid Services Architecture (OGSA) provides *The Globus Toolkit* as an implementation of such a standard based on Web services and technologies. OGSA is a product of the GRID community at large, and it has a major focal point in the Global Grid Forum (GGF). Members of the Globus Alliance have made significant contributions to the development of OGSA. The interested reader can find more information about goals, toolkits, and implementations at the OGSA website `www.globus.org/ogsa`.

These technologies are not mutually exclusive. The P2P model could help to ensure GRID scalability. Architects could employ P2P technologies and techniques to implement decentralized GRID systems in order to avoid or alleviate performance bottlenecks. A recent example of this approach is *GRID-nut* (Talia and Trunfio 2004) based on Clip2, the original Gnutella protocol specification `www9.limewire.com/developer/gnutella_protocol_0.4.pdf`, to which we now turn our attention.

9.3 Analysis of Gnutella

The Gnutella network is a class of open-source virtual networks known as *peer-to-peer* networks. Compared to the more ubiquitous client–server distributed architectures, every P2P node (or *servant*) can act as both a client and a server. Many client-server applications, e.g., commercial databases, have multiple clients accessing a centralized server (see Gunther 2005a, Chap. 9). Conversely, P2P network applications are usually completely decentralized.

Finding applications that can make efficient use of P2P is the current gating factor for their widespread adoption. So far, P2P networks have been employed for such applications as the Napster (`www.napster.com`) music file-sharing service and the SETI@Home project (`setiathome.berkeley.edu`), although both those implementations rely on a significant centralized server component.

The initial release of Gnutella in 2000 led to the perception that the intrinsic architecture may not be capable of scaling to meet the sharing demands of millions of anticipated[1] users. Similar concerns about scalability have arisen in the context of hypergrowth traffic impinging on popular e-commerce Web sites (see Chap. 8). Based on measurements of popular queries, it was proposed that Gnutella scaling problems could be ameliorated through the implementation of appropriate caching strategies. Other measurements indicated that

---

[1] In 2001, the size of the Napster network was 160,000 simultaneous users, down from a peak of 1.6 million reported by Webnoize in February, 2001.

there were more readers than writers involved in file sharing. They suggested that a propensity for reading could lead to higher than expected load on the P2P network, thereby degrading its performance as well as increasing its vulnerability to fragmentation.

A mathematical analysis by Ritter (2002) (one of the original developers of Napster) presented a detailed numerical argument demonstrating that the Gnutella network could not scale to the capacity of its competitor, [2] the Napster network. Essentially, that model showed that the Gnutella network is severely bandwidth-limited long before the P2P population reaches a million peers. In each of these previous studies, the conclusions have overlooked the intrinsic bandwidth limits of the underlying topology in the Gnutella network: a Cayley tree (Rains and Sloane 1999) (see Sect. 9.4 for the definition).

Trees are known to have lower aggregate bandwidth than higher dimensional topologies, e.g., hypercubes and hypertori. Studies of interconnection topologies in the literature have tended to focus on hardware implementations (see, e.g., Culler et al. 1996; Buyya 1999), which are generally limited by the cost of the chips and wires to a few thousand nodes. P2P networks, on the other hand, are intended to support from hundreds of thousands to millions of simultaneous peers, and since they are implemented in software, hyper-topologies are relatively unfettered [3] by the economics of hardware.

In this chapter, we analyze the scalability of several alternative topologies and compare their throughput up to 2–3 million peers. The virtual hypercube and the virtual hypertorus offer near-linear scalable bandwidth subject to the number of peer TCP/IP connections that can be simultaneously kept open. We adopt the abbreviation *hypernet* for these alternative topologies. The assumptions about the distribution of peer activity are similar to those employed by Ritter (2002). This is appropriate since our purpose is to rank the relative performance of these hypernets rather than to predict their absolute performance.

9.4 Tree Topologies

In the subsequent discussion, the P2P network is treated as a graph, i.e., a set nodes or vertices connected by a set of edges or links. The nodes correspond to network peers, and the links to the links to network connections.

Because the tree structure of the Gnutella network has been such a hidden determinant underlying the conclusions drawn in previous scalability studies, we commence our performance comparisons by distinguishing clearly among

---

[2] At the height of the media attention, Napster's legal problems drove some 50,000 users per day over to Gnutella such that peers connected by 56 Kbps phone lines caused the P2P network to fragment into disconnected "islands" of about 200 peers.

[3] As the `SETI@Home` project has demonstrated, 2.8 million desktops (and 10 PetaFLOPS) can be harnessed for free.

the relevant tree topologies. Topologically, all trees are planar and thus have $d = 2$ spatial dimensions.

9.4.1 Binary Tree

The binary tree is familiar in the computing context by virtue of its ubiquity as a parsing and storage data structure. There is a unique root node that is connected only to two sibling nodes, and each of those siblings is connected to another pair of sibling nodes, and so on. At each level h in the tree, there are 2^h nodes. Therefore, the number of nodes grows as a binary exponential number. Because of its relatively sparse nodal density, the binary tree is rarely employed as a bona fide interconnection network.

9.4.2 Rooted Tree

A rooted tree is simply the generalization of a binary tree in which each node (other than the root) has a vertex of degree v. The total number of nodes is the sum of a geometric series:

$$N_{bin}(h) = \frac{v^h - 1}{v - 1}.$$

(9.1)

9.4.3 Cayley Tree

A Cayley tree (Rains and Sloane 1999) has no root. Recalling the binary tree, what was the root of the parent binary tree now has a link to an another binary subtree of height one less than the parent. All nodes thus become trivalent with $v = 3$ at every level. More generally, for a v-valent tree, the total number of nodes is given by:

$$N_{cay}(h) = 1 + \sum v \, (v - 1)^{h-1},$$

(9.2)

and therefore is denser than the number of nodes in (9.1).

This is the central formula used in the scalability analysis of Ritter (2002). The network he analyzed is thus a Cayley tree with vertex degree v corresponding to the number of open network connections per servant. Ritter analyzed valences in the range $v = 4 \ldots 8$; the former value being the default setting in the original Gnutella release, and the latter more closely resembling the number of peers claimed for the contemporaneous Napster network.

9.5 Hypernet Topologies

An alternative to bandwidth-limited trees is a topology with higher dimensionality. We examine the performance attributes of two hypernets in particular: the binary hypercube and the hypertorus, each in d dimensions.

9.5.1 Hypercube

In a Boolean or binary hypercube each node forms the vertex of a d-dimensional cube. The number of nodes is simply 2^d, and the degree of each vertex v is equal to the dimensionality d of the network. Hence, each node can be enumerated or addressed using a base-2 (binary) d-digit number. Moreover, since neighboring nodes differ in address by only 1 digit, sending a message on the hypercube becomes a simple matter of shifting successive bits as the binary address passes each node between source and destination.

In $d = 3$ dimensions the hypercube is simply a cube. Each vertex has degree $v = 3$, so there are $2^3 = 8$ nodes. A 4-dimensional hypercube, can be visualized as spatially translating a 3-cube such that the locus of its four vertices trace out the additional connections.

9.5.2 Hypertorus

A d-dimensional hypertorus is a d-dimensional grid with each node connected to a ring of nodes in each of the d orthogonal dimensions. The hypertorus reduces to the binary hypercube when there are only two nodes in each ring. The simplest visualization is, once again, in three dimensions. A two-dimensional grid is first wrapped about one axis such the edges join to form a tube. The tube is wrapped about the orthogonal axis to form a ring such that the open ends of the tube become joined. The result is a 3-torus, otherwise known as a donut.

All of these topologies fall into a class known as single stage networks, and they are relatively easy to implement in software. The more exotic topologies, such as cube-connected cycles, butterflies, and other multistage networks, are not considered here because they are likely to be more difficult to implement.

9.6 Capacity Metrics

9.6.1 Network Diameter

The notion of a network diameter is analogous to the diameter for a circle. There, it is the maximum chordal length between two points on the circumference. For a network, it is the maximum number of communication links that must be traversed to send a message to any node along the shortest path. It represents a lower bound on the latency to propagate messages throughout the entire network. In 1997 the Web was estimated to comprise more than half a million sites (Gray 1996). By 2001, it was estimated (OCLC 2004) to have grown to 3.1 million publicly accessible sites.

The diameter of the Web has been estimated to be about 20 hops. If the Web is modeled as a Cayley tree, its height would be half the diameter, i.e., $h = \delta/2 = 10$ hops (Table 9.1). A vertex degree of 5 (connections per node) would contain just under half a million nodes, while a vertex degree of 6 would contain nearly 3 million (2,929,687) nodes.

Table 9.1. Network diameter

Topology	δ
Tree	$2h$
Hypercube	d
Torus	$dN^{1/d}/4$

9.6.2 Total Nodes

Next, we determine the total number of peer nodes in the P2P network. For a binary tree:

$$N(h) = \sum_{k=1}^{h} 2^{k-1}. \tag{9.3}$$

For a d-dimensional binary hypercube the number of nodes is 2^d.

9.6.3 Path Length

The path length is the maximal distance between a leaf node and the root. For a tree, it is half the diameter. The path length corresponds the peer horizon used by (Ritter 2002) in his analysis. A better measure of network latency is the average number of hops H, which we shall define shortly.

9.6.4 Internal Path Length

The internal path length is the total number of paths between all nodes. For a binary tree of depth h, the total number of paths is:

$$P(h) = \sum_{k=1}^{h} k \, N(k). \tag{9.4}$$

9.6.5 Average Hop Distance

Since the network diameter is a maximal distance, it tends to overestimate message latency. A better measure is the average number of hops between source and destination. This quantity is found by dividing the internal path length in (9.4) by the total number of nodes in (9.3)

$$H = \frac{P}{N}. \tag{9.5}$$

It corresponds to the average number of network hops traversed by a P2P query.

9.6.6 Network Links

This is a measure of the number of physical network links. As revealed in Table 9.2, L scales with the number of physical nodes N for the topologies we are considering.

Table 9.2. Number of network links

Topology	L
Tree	N_{tree}
Hypercube	$dN_{cube}/2$
Torus	dN_{torus}

9.6.7 Network Demand

The transit frequency across a link f_{link} is a measure of the average query size per link. Under the assumption of uniform message routing, it can be defined as:

$$f_{link} = \frac{H}{L} . \tag{9.6}$$

If the latency across a link is denoted by S_{link}, then the total service demand (Gunther 2005a, Chap. 2) is:

$$D_{link} = f_{link}\, S_{link} . \tag{9.7}$$

For simplicity and without loss of generality, we normalize the network demand to unit periods, i.e., $S_{link} = 1$.

9.6.8 Peer Demand

In a manner similar to the definition for the time spent on a link S_{link}, we define S_{peer} for node latency. Under the assumption of uniform message routing:

$$f_{peers} = \frac{1}{N} , \tag{9.8}$$

and the total peer service demand is:

$$D_{peers} = \frac{S_{peer}}{N} . \tag{9.9}$$

Again, we normalize the peer demand to unit periods ($S_{peer} = 1$) in the subsequent discussion.

9.6.9 Bandwidth

It follows from Little's law, $U = XD$ (Gunther 2005a, p. 44) that when any node in the network reaches saturation i.e., $U = 1$, the maximum in the system throughput is determined by:

$$X_{\text{max}} = \frac{1}{Max(D_{\text{peers}}, D_{\text{link1}}, D_{\text{link2}}, ...)} \, . \qquad (9.10)$$

The node with the longest service demand D_{max} is the system bottleneck. The service demand at the bottleneck therefore determines the maximum system throughput. With these metrics defined, we are in a position to compare the asymptotic performance of each of the topologies described in Sects. 9.4 and 9.5.

9.7 Relative Bandwidth

Since we are interested in network scalability up to a few million peers, it is sufficient to base the comparison on the asymptotic network throughput defined in (9.10). In particular, we will rank the above hypernets according to their relative maximal bandwidth,

$$X_{\text{relative}} = X_{\text{max}}(N)/N \, , \qquad (9.11)$$

where N is the number of peers in the horizon (Table 9.3 at the end of this section). $X_{\text{relative}} = 1.0$ corresponds to linear scalability since $X_{\text{max}} = N$ in (9.11).

In several respects our approach is similar to that taken by (Culler et al. 1996) for their LogP model of assessing parallel hardware performance. In both approaches, the respective network topology enters into the performance model via the network demand defined in Sects. 9.7 and 9.9.

9.7.1 Cayley Trees

First, we consider the relative performance of tree topologies. Figure 9.2 shows the normalized bandwidths of a fourth-degree rooted tree, a 4-valent Cayley tree and an 8-valent Cayley tree.

The 4-valent Cayley tree represents the default peer connectivity in the original release of Gnutella. Similarly, the 8-valent Cayley tree corresponds to Ritter's comparison with Napster scalability. The curves in Fig. 9.2 terminate at different peer populations because the population is an integral multiple which is dramatically affected by the vertex degree and the height of the tree.

We see immediately that the 8-valent Cayley tree has the greatest bandwidth up through 2 million peers. The 4-valent Cayley tree has the lowest bandwidth, even lower than the rooted tree. This follows from the fact that at its root the 4-tree has the same connectivity as the 4-Cayley tree, but all its descendants have vertices of 5 degrees. Even for the 8-Cayley, at 2 million peers the bandwidth is less than one quarter of linear scalability.

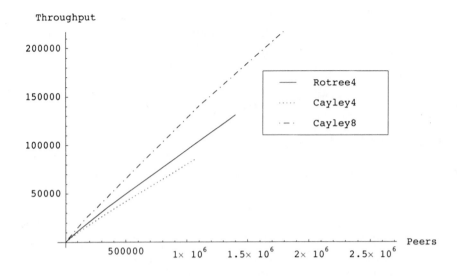

Fig. 9.2. Relative throughput of binary and Cayley trees

9.7.2 Trees and Cubes

We next consider the relative performance of high-degree trees and hypercubes. In particular, Fig. 9.3 shows the normalized bandwidths for an 8-Cayley

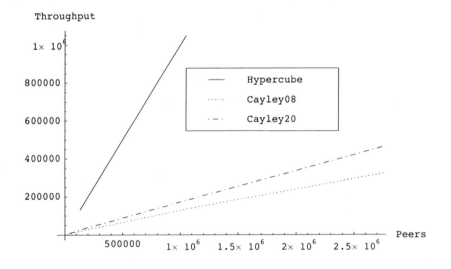

Fig. 9.3. Relative throughput of Cayley trees and hypercubes

(the best throughput of the trees considered in Fig. 9.2), a 20-Cayley, and a binary hypercube. The d-dimensional hypercube clearly exhibits superior scalability.

9.7.3 Cubes and Tori

Of these high-order topologies, the binary hypercube offers linearly scalable bandwidth beyond one million active peers (Fig. 9.4). The ten-dimensional hypertorus has comparable scalability up to one million peers but degrades beyond that point. The three-dimensional hypertorus is also shown for com-

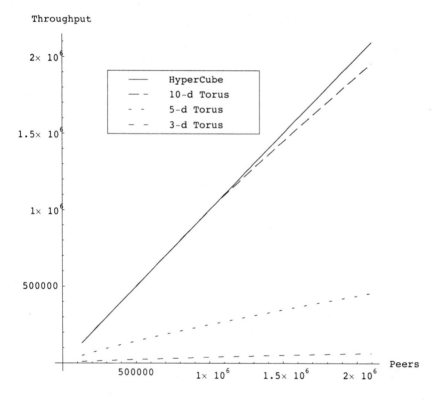

Fig. 9.4. Relative throughput of hypercubes and hypertori

parison since that topology has been used in large-scale hardware implementations up to several hundred nodes per cluster, e.g., HP NonStop s88000 server (formerly the Tandem Himalaya).

9.7.4 Ranked Performance

The main results of our analysis are summarized in Table 9.3, which shows each of the topologies ranked by their relative bandwidth as defined in (9.11). The 20-dimensional hypercube outranks all other contenders on the basis of query throughput. For an horizon containing 2 million peers, each servant must maintain 20 open connections, on average. This is well within the capacity limits of most TCP/IP implementations. The 10-dimensional hypertorus is comparable to the 20-hypercube in bandwidth up to an horizon of 1 million peers but falls off by almost 10% at 2 million peers. The 10-torus is also arguably a more difficult topology to implement.

Table 9.3. Topologies ranked by maximal relative bandwidth

Network topology	Connections per peer	Hops to horizon	Peers $\times 10^6$ in horizon	Relative (%) bandwidth
20-Cube	20	10	2.1	100
10-Torus	20	11	2.1	93
5-Torus	10	23	2.1	22
20-Cayley	20	6	2.8	16
8-Cayley	**8**	**8**	**1.1**	**13**
4-Tree	4	11	1.4	12
3-Torus	6	96	2.1	10
4-Cayley	**4**	**13**	**1.1**	**8**

The 20-valent Cayley tree is included since the number of connections per peer is the same as that for the 20-cube and the 10-torus. An horizon of 6 hops was used for comparison because the peer population is only 144,801 nodes at 5 hops. Similarly for 8-Cayley, a 9-hop horizon would contain 7.7 million peers. These large increments are a direct consequence of the high vertex degree per node.

The 4-Cayley (modeling early Gnutella) and 8-Cayley (modeling the Napster population) show relatively poor scalability at 1 million peers. Even doubling the number of connections per peer produces slightly better than 50% improvement in throughput. This confirms the conclusions reached by Ritter (2002) and, moreover, supports our proposal to consider hypernet topologies.

9.8 Summary

Previous studies of Gnutella scalability have tended to overlook the intrinsic bandwidth limits of the underlying tree topology. The most thorough and accurate of these studies is that presented by Ritter (2002). Unfortunately, his analysis could be accused of straining at a gnat. As a viable candidate for massively scalable bandwidth, our analysis demonstrates that trees are essentially dead wood.

Conversely, by going to higher dimensional virtual networks (and the hypercube in particular) near linear scalability can be achieved for populations on the order of several million peers each with only 20 open connections. According to Sect. 9.6, this level of scalability would already match the number of nodes present in the entire Web.

The dominant constraint for hardware implementations of high-dimensional networks is the cost of the physical wires on the interconnect backplane. Since the hypernets discussed here would be implemented in software, no such constraints would prevent reaching the desired level of scalability. In this sense, hypernets appear to offer good (g)news for Gnutella-like P2P networks.

10

Internet Planning

> *Mountains are not cones, clouds are not spheres, trees are not cylinders, neither does lightening travel in a straight line. Almost everything around us is non-Euclidean.*
>
> —Benoit Mandelbrot

10.1 Introduction

In Chap. 4 we considered the fundamental concepts of scaling. In particular, we observed that a material volume not only occupies space, but it has a mass, and that mass has weight. As the volume is scaled up (by multiplying each of its three linear dimensions), its weight increases until, at some point, the volume will weigh so much that it literally crushes itself. Therefore, there must be a *critical* size that an object can attain before it finally collapses. This is the concept of allometric scaling, and the relationship between a physical quantity like material strength (y) and the weight (x) is given by a power law of the form:

$$y = x^\alpha \tag{10.1}$$

where $0 < \alpha < 1$. For the discussion in Chap. 4, we found $\alpha = 0.3333$.

In this chapter, we shall see that power laws of the form:

$$y = x^{-\alpha} \tag{10.2}$$

(note the negative exponent) can be used to explain a peculiar form of recursive scaling observed in many types of Internet traffic and often associated with Pareto distributions (see, e.g., Downey 2001; Park and Willinger 2000).

Fractals are a mathematical object that scale according to (10.2), so they have become a kind of common currency for explaining so-called *self-similar* traffic (see, e.g., Crovella and Bestavros 1997). This is important because (10.2) also belongs to a class of functions that have persistent correlations. Correlations of this type produce long packet-trains that can potentially overflow buffers in routers and servers on the Internet. From the Guerrilla capacity planning standpoint the question is, How big should these buffers be sized so as to accommodate the possibility of such large packet trains?

Moreover, the fractal nature of these correlations also means that many of the conventional assumptions used to develop queue-theoretic models (see, e.g., Gunther 2005a) are in serious jeopardy. Strong correlations violate the usual Poisson independence assumptions invoked to make queueing network models soluble. If not queueing models, how should we do capacity planning for these effects?

Surprisingly, as crucial as this knowledge would appear, it has remained inscrutable to many of those who could use it most—performance engineers and capacity planners. This is strikingly reminiscent of the impenetrability of queueing theory for performance engineers, which led me to write books (Gunther 2000, 2005a) that made that topic a little more transparent and directly applicable. That is another purpose of this chapter: to make the concepts behind self-similar Internet traffic approachable enough for you to draw your own conclusions regarding how you should take it into account to size buffers for your local routers and Web servers. In the last couple of years some new insights have emerged that indicate the fear, uncertainty, and doubt about how to model networks that has been generated in the literature over the past decade may have been overplayed.

10.2 Bellcore Traces

The genesis of this subject goes back to certain network measurements taken at Bellcore (now morphed into Lucent Technologies) in the late 1980s and early 1990s (Leland et al. 1993). The motivation for these measurements came from AT&T wanting to understand the nature of *broadband* network usage for both voice and data. Broadband at that time meant Broadband Integrated Services Digital Network (B-ISDN) or just ISDN. ISDN is a set of CCITT/ITU standards for digital transmission over ordinary telephone copper wire as well as over other media.

An example of the network probe architecture used by Bellcore engineers is shown in Fig. 10.1. The Ethernet local area network (LAN) comprised some 140 hosts and routers which served Bellcore researchers engaged in everything from software development to prototyping new services for the telephone system. The traffic was mostly from services that used the internet protocol (IP) to perform such things as remote login or email, and Network File System (NFS) file services from NFS servers to workstations. Some audio from a local radio station was also carried on the Ethernet LAN.

Notice that the probe is an Ethernet monitor on their local network and the Ethernet connection to the Internet is via a separate IP router. The network probe recorded packet traces over an initial period of 3–4 years, with trace files ranging in size from about 50 MB to 15 GB (Fig. 10.2).

The monitor was programmed to gather the packets off the network being studied as they arrive, place them in buffers, and record a timestamp and status information for each packet. For each packet seen on the Ethernet under

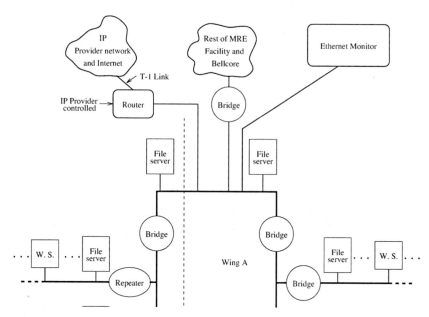

Fig. 10.1. Network schematic showing the location of the ethernet probe for the January 1990 measurements (Leland et al. 1993)

study, the monitor recorded a time stamp consisting of a 48-bit integer number of 4-μs intervals since the start of the trace. This time stamp represents the arrival time of the end of the packet rather than the time the packet was placed on the Ethernet; the latter can easily be calculated. The monitor also recorded the packet length, the status of the Ethernet interface (which contains information about whether the packet is well-formed or whether packets were lost since data on the last one was taken), and finally the first 60 bytes of data in each packet. The system delivered time stamps accurate to within 20 μs for the arrival time of each packe; the system was used to gather the most recent data set used in the analysis.

Some tools capable of capturing and analyzing IP packets, include:

Columbia: www.cs.columbia.edu/~hgs/internet/tools.html
Ethereal: www.ethereal.com
LASS: www.samsi.info/TR/tr2004-07.pdf
LBL tools: ita.ee.lbl.gov/html/software.html
LBL traces: ita.ee.lbl.gov/html/traces.html
SELFIS: www.cs.ucr.edu/~tkarag/Selfis/Selfis.html
Web traces: www.web-caching.com/traces-logs.html

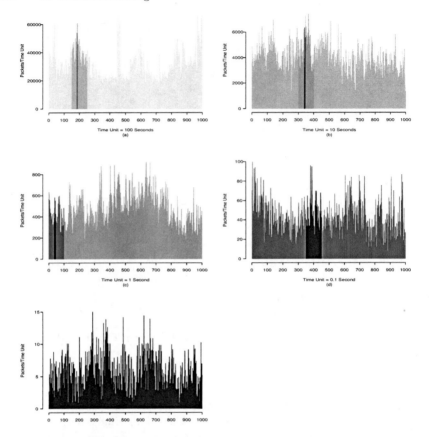

Fig. 10.2. Evidence of self-similarity: Ethernet traffic (packets per time unit) on five different time scales. (Different gray levels are used to identify the same segments of traffic on the different time scales (Leland et al. 1993)

10.3 Fractals and Self-Similarity

It has been known for a long time that the coastlines of different countries (presumably as measured in an atlas) fall along different straight lines with very similar negative slopes (Mandelbrot 1983). As S gets smaller, L gets bigger. From the axes in Fig. 10.3, we see that the relationship is linear and therefore can be written as:

$$\log(L) = -D \log(S) , \tag{10.3}$$

where D is a constant of proportionality. But this is the same as:

$$\log(L) = \log(1/S)^D . \tag{10.4}$$

Taking the antilogarithm of both sides of (10.4) produces:

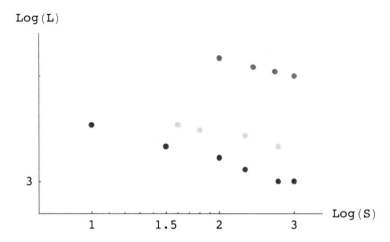

Fig. 10.3. Log-log plot of Lewis Richardson's coastline data (Mandelbrot 1983) for the Australian coast (top band), the German land frontier (middle band), and the west coast of Britain (bottom band). The x-axis is the step size S (e.g, separation of compass legs) and the y-axis is the estimated length L of the respective coastline in an atlas. Note that each band appears to fall along a set of approximately parallel lines sloping downward from left to right

$$L = \frac{1}{S^D} = S^{-D} . \qquad (10.5)$$

Formally speaking, this function is a hyperbola.

Remark 10.1. If we had plotted $\log(L)$ against $\log(1/S)$ in Fig. 10.3, we would have produced straight lines with positive slopes. Both representations are equivalent. The positive slope matches that seen in the Bellcore data (Fig. 10.4).

The quantity D in (10.3) represents the slope of any one of the lines in Figs. 10.3 and 10.4, and since (10.5) has the same form as (10.2), it represents power law scaling. For the Bellcore data in Fig. 10.4 the y-axis, labeled $log10(r/s)$, corresponds to a quantity called the *rescaled range*. It is the ratio of the range r of the data, i.e., minimum to maximum, and the sample standard deviation s. This is the logical equivalent of the coastline length. The x-axis, labeled $log10(d)$, is the logarithm of the sample size d. It is the logical equivalent of the step size.

Example 10.1. If the sample consisted of 10 measurements, you could take pairs ($d = 2$), or triples ($d = 3$), and so on. For Bellcore traces, the samples are: 100s, 1000s, etc. On a logarithmic scale they become: $\log(d) = 2$, $\log(d) = 3$, etc. □

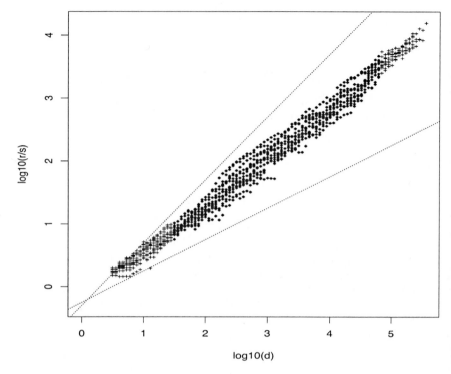

Fig. 10.4. Log–log plot of rescaled range data from a Bellcore trace file. Data clusters around a straight having an estimated slope of $D = 0.79$ (Leland et al. 1993)

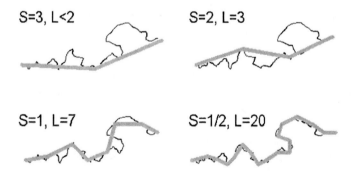

Fig. 10.5. Schematic representation showing how the inverse relationship between the step size S and the estimated length L arises. As S gets smaller it can get into more nooks and crannies, so the length L of the irregular line becomes longer. It also explains the downward slope of the bands corresponding to irregular coastlines in Fig. 10.3

In the unbounded hyperbola (10.5), L becomes infinite as S approaches the origin, and conversely L approaches zero as S goes to infinity. This is a signal of infinite variance and long-range correlations seen in both the Bellcore data and the ragged coastlines. We discuss this further in Sect. 10.4. Figure 10.5 shows how the inverse relationship given in (10.5) arises. As the step size S gets smaller it can fit into more nooks and crannies, so the estimated length L of the irregular line increases. This is the connection between traditional Euclidean geometry and the non-Euclidean behavior of fractals alluded to in the rubric to this chapter. It also explains the downward slope of the bands corresponding to irregular coastlines in Fig. 10.3.

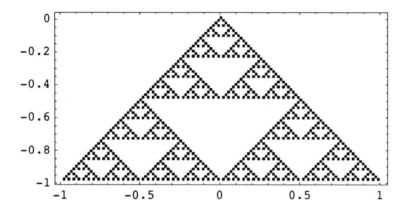

Fig. 10.6. Example of a geometrical fractal with $D = -1.5849$

What are the defining features of a fractal like the one shown in Fig. 10.6? They all start with *an initiator* and *a generator* and an iterating procedure that is applied to the initiator repetitively. In addition, fractals possess:

Iteration: Some aspect of the iterated limiting object is *infinite* e.g., total length, perimeter, or surface area. Some aspect of the limiting object remains *finite* e.g., area of the covering triangle in Fig. 10.6.

Self Similarity: At any step in the iteration, a piece of the object resembles a scaled down but otherwise identical copy of the previous iteration. It appears *self-similar* (SS).

The fractal dimension D is a nonspatial dimension that measures the degree to which a fractal curve fills space. It also called the *Hausdorff measure* (Mandelbrot 1983).

10.4 Fractals in Time

Many readers will have seen the phrase "second-hand smoke" in the popular press. This phrase refers to the risk of suffering deleterious health effects from cigarettes that someone else is smoking. For example, you are in a restaurant, a train, or some other confined space when suddenly, you become aware of pungent cigarette smoke entering your nose. Although the smell can be quite strong and may seem like the cigarette is very close by, you often have to scan around carefully to see that the source of the smoke is actually coming from a smoker on the other side of the room. Since there is no breeze in a confined space, how did *their* cigarette smoke get into *your* nose? The answer is, *diffusion*. Diffusion, in this case, refers to the process of smoke moving from a region of high concentration (the cigarette) to a region of low concentration (the extremities of the room in general and your nose in particular). The modern explanation of diffusion in terms of the smoke particles being spread by incessant collisions with air molecules would have been met with skepticism just 100 years ago.

10.4.1 Short-Range Dependence

1905 was a very good year for Albert Einstein because he wrote several seminal scientific papers, one of which explained how smoke particles (among other things) diffuse. In that paper (see English translation in Einstein 1956), he proposed that the smoke particles do not simply drift across the room with some average speed. Rather they are jostled back and forth in an entirely erratic way by means of a gargantuan number of independent microscopic shocks from unseen air molecules (Fig. 10.7). These stochastic shocks are associated with a probability distribution whose variance σ^2 was shown by Einstein to vary linearly with the elapsed time t:

$$\sigma^2(t) = 2Dt. \tag{10.6}$$

Here, D is the so-called diffusion coefficient; a quantity that can be measured directly. Equation (10.6) leads to what has become known as the Einstein relation:

$$\sigma(t) = \sqrt{2Dt}. \tag{10.7}$$

Previous attempts to measure the average speed or velocity of smoke particles had failed because their instantaneous zig-zag motion meant the velocity is essentially infinite.

Using the same notation as (Gunther 2005a), where $E(X)$ denotes the expected or mean value of a random variable X, the mean displacement in the one dimension is:

$$\mu(t) = E(X(t)), \tag{10.8}$$

and the variance $Var(X)$ about that mean is given by:

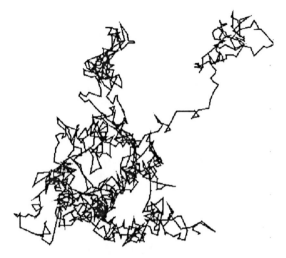

Fig. 10.7. A sample path for a random walk process—a discrete space version of the diffusion process. Although the overall displacement is not great, there are a multitude of small steps taken to get there. These small steps have a common mean free path between events that correspond to collisions of a smoke particle with surrounding air molecules

$$\sigma^2(t) \equiv Var(X(t)) = E(X^2(t)) - \mu^2(t) \,. \qquad (10.9)$$

If we place the cigarette at the origin, then a smoke particle has equal probability of being knocked to the left or the right, so that $\mu(t) = 0$ and the variance reduces to the mean squared displacement $E(X^2(t))$. In other words, (10.7) states that the average spreading of the smoke particles is proportional to the square root of the elapsed time since they left the cigarette ($H = 0.5$ in Fig. 10.8). Technically speaking, we are considering just one short puff on the cigarette.

More important, Einstein showed that his physical model given by (10.7) held independently of the size of the smoke particles and the size of the surrounding particles in which they were immersed. The only thing that changed was the time scale over which they spread; bigger particles take longer to spread over the same average displacement. In fact, the smoke particles could be as big as dust particles, which can be seen more easily under a microscope, and those dust particles could be suspended in a liquid like water, rather than a gas like air. In that case, when viewed under a microscope, the dust particles can be seen literally jiggling around erratically as if they were alive (which was once thought to be the explanation). This stochastic motion (Fig. 10.7) is called Brownian motion (Einstein 1956) after its original observation by Robert Brown in 1828. Using (10.7), Einstein calculated that a typical size dust particle immersed in water would undergo an average displacement of about 6 μm at room temperature. Within a year, this prediction was con-

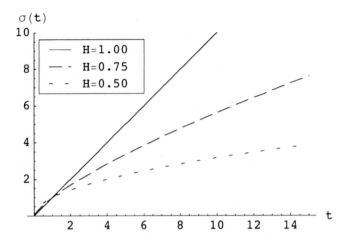

Fig. 10.8. Stochastic spread of $\sigma(t)$ as a function of elapsed time corresponding to various Hurst parameter values $H = 0.5$ (diffusion), $H = 0.75$, and $H = 1.0$

firmed experimentally and together with the fact that Einstein's model was as simple as possible but no simpler (see Sect. F.2 in Appendix F), it convinced most skeptics that atoms and molecules must really exist despite the fact that they could not be observed directly.

For the purposes of this chapter, the invariance of Einstein's model to particle size means that Brownian motion is fractal-like or SS. Going to smaller and smaller time subdivisions produces the same kind of erratic path. It is essentially a fractal in time.

Writing (10.7) in a slightly more skeletal form as:

$$\sigma(t) \sim t^{\frac{1}{2}}, \tag{10.10}$$

we can consider generalizing the exponent in (10.10) to something that can take on values greater then $\frac{1}{2}$. Physically speaking, the random walk in Fig. 10.7 develops large excursions or "jumps" that are greater than the typical mean free path between collisions (see Fig. 10.9). These jumps are known as *Levy flights* and can be simply described by introducing a new parameter, the Hurst parameter $H \in (\frac{1}{2}, 1)$, into the exponent of (10.10). This extension can be written symbolically as:

$$\sigma(t) = \underbrace{t^{0.5}}_{Einstein} \longrightarrow \underbrace{t^{H}}_{Levy} \tag{10.11}$$

10.4.2 Long-Range Dependence

One mechanism that has been proposed to explain the generalized power law in (10.11) is a multisource on/off Pareto model (Crovella and Bestavros

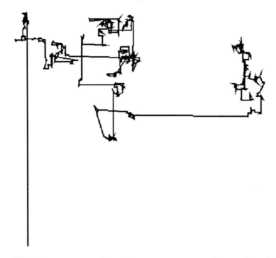

Fig. 10.9. Levy flights correspond to the occurrence of occasional large excursions or jumps. Compare this with the mean displacement in Brownian motion (Fig. 10.7) which results from a multitude of relatively small steps taken in succession

1997). The idea is that to produce traffic with long-range dependent (LRD) correlations on the Internet requires multiplexing many different sources (user-initiated requests) into a network segment or network router, and that each source causes the emission of files that are sometimes very large (*mammoths*) and other times relatively small (*mice*) according to a Pareto-like distribution in time.

The relationship between LRD and SS is subtle, and one has approach these attributes with caution because there are SS processes that are not LRD (e.g., Brownian motion), and it is possible to have time series with long-term correlations that are not SS. This ambiguity can be removed by judicious choice of definitions from time series analysis (see, e.g., Box et al. 1994), which leads to Theorem 10.1. Using (10.8) we define the *autocovariance* as:

$$\gamma(s,t) \equiv Cov(X(s), X(t)) = E([X(s) - \mu(s)][X(t) - \mu(t)]). \qquad (10.12)$$

Definition 10.1 (Weak Stationarity). *A time series is called* second-order *or* weakly *stationary if it satisfies the following conditions:*

1. $\mu(t) = \mu$ and $\sigma^2(t) = \sigma^2$ for all t.
2. $\gamma(s,t) = \gamma(s+k, t+k)$; (10.12) is time-translation invariant.

Definition 10.2 (Weak Self-Similarity). *Weak SS requires that the auto-covariance satisfy*

$$\gamma(k) = \frac{1}{2}\sigma^2\left[(k+1)^{2H} - 2k^{2H} + (k-1)^{2H}\right], \qquad (10.13)$$

where H is the Hurst parameter.

Theorem 10.1 (Equivalence of SS and LRD). *For a weak SS process, if $H \in (\frac{1}{2}, 1)$ in (10.13) then SS $\Leftrightarrow$ LRD.*

Proof. The interested reader can find a detailed proof of this equivalence in (Leland et al. 1993) and (Park and Willinger 2000, Chap. 1).

The autocorrelation function is defined as:

$$\rho(k) = \frac{\gamma(k)}{\sigma^2}. \tag{10.14}$$

For $H \in (\frac{1}{2}, 1)$ (10.14) behaves asymptotically $(k \to \infty)$ as:

$$\rho(k) \sim k^{-\beta}, \tag{10.15}$$

where $\beta \in (0, 1)$.

In summary:

- Aggregated time series are analyzed using the autocorrelation function.
- LRD time series are analyzed using the autocovariance function.
- LRD in the frequency domain (inverse time) are analyzed using the power spectra (see Sect. 10.6).

10.5 Impact on Buffer Sizing

Usually, one expects to apply basic queueing theory (see, e.g., Gunther 2005a, Chap. 2) to estimate the size of a buffer required to hold a waiting line of packets that are to be processed by a single-server router.

10.5.1 Conventional Buffer Sizing

The usual assumption is that the arrival of packets is statistically independent. In other words, the occurrence of arrival events follows a Poisson distribution, and therefore the mean time between arrivals (denoted by λ^{-1}) is *exponentially* distributed. This kind of statistical independence property of the exponential distribution means that what happened in the past has no influence in the current period. For this reason such statistical independence in time is called a *memoryless* process or *Markovian* processes (denoted M) (see Gunther 2005a, Appendix C). If the mean interarrival period λ^{-1} and the the mean service period S both belong to an exponential distribution, then a queue of this type is denoted in Kendall symbols as $M/M/1$; the first M refers to the Markovian arrival process and the second M referrs to the Markovian service process with a single server (Fig. 10.10).

As packets arrive at the router, the expected time to be routed, i.e., the residence time, consists of two components:

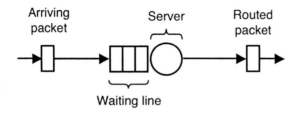

Fig. 10.10. Simple $M/M/1$ queueing model of an Internet router showing the waiting line or buffer and the service facility that does the routing. The queue length Q refers to the total number of packets in the buffer plus the one that is currently being routed with server utilization $\rho \in (0, 1)$

1. The expected time to process packets already waiting for service, i.e., the queueing component.
2. The expected service time for the arriving packet, i.e., the service component.

If we assume that the mean service time S is the same for every packet and the average queue length is Q, the expected time for the arriving packet to reach the server is QS. The two components of the residence time can then be written as:

$$R = QS + S. \tag{10.16}$$

If there are no packets ahead of the arriving packet, then $Q = 0$ (no queueing) and the residence time is precisely $R = S$. Otherwise, the arriving packet has to join the end of the line and wait.

Substituting Little's law ($Q = \lambda R$) into (10.16) produces:

$$R = (\lambda R) S + S, \tag{10.17}$$

and solving for R we find:

$$R = \frac{S}{1 - \lambda S}. \tag{10.18}$$

A further substitution of the utilization law ($\rho = \lambda S$) into the denominator of (10.18) leads to:

$$R = \frac{S}{1 - \rho}. \tag{10.19}$$

Equation (10.19) allows us to determine the average residence time, even if the arrival rate is not known. The measured utilization of the server can be used instead.

We can also interpret (10.19) as an inflated service time. The inflation factor is $(1 - \rho)$ for a single server. Since ρ can be interpreted as the fraction of time the server is busy during any measurement interval, the quantity $(1-\rho)$

can be interpreted as the fraction of time the server is available. If the server is available ($\rho = 0$), then $R = S$ because there is no queueing.

Multiplying both sides of (10.19) by λ produces:

$$Q = \frac{\rho}{1 - \rho}, \tag{10.20}$$

which is the average queue length expressed entirely as a function of the server utilization ρ. It is also equivalent to the mean number of requests in the system—a single buffer and a single router in this case. Since the utilization is bounded $\rho \in [0, 1)$, it follows that $Q = 0$ when $\rho = 0$, whereas the buffer rapidly approaches an infinite length as $\rho \to 1$. This happens because the queue length becomes unbounded when the stability condition $\lambda < S^{-1}$ is no longer satisfied at $\rho = 1$.

Convential rules of thumb for $M/M/1$ buffer sizes are:

$$Q = 0, \text{ when } \rho = 0;$$
$$Q = 1, \text{ when } \rho = 1/2;$$
$$Q = 3, \text{ when } \rho = 3/4;$$

based on (10.20). These rules are also visually evident for the curve labeled $H = 0.5$ in Fig. 10.11.

These conventional rules of thumb become invalid, however, if a router is subjected to packet arrivals that are not Markovian due to LRD effects.

10.5.2 LRD Buffer Sizing

To get some idea of how radically different buffer sizing considerations become under the influence of LRD effects, Norros (1994) generalized (10.20) to include the Hurst parameter H in the following model:

$$Q = \frac{\rho^{\frac{1}{2(1-H)}}}{(1 - \rho)^{\frac{H}{1-H}}}. \tag{10.21}$$

The dramatic significance of (10.21) for sizing packet buffers is shown in Fig. 10.12. Moreover, a comparison with actual network measurements in Fig. 10.12 shows strikingly good agreement.

In this model, the "burstiness" of Internet packet arrivals is characterized the by Hurst parameter $H \in (\frac{1}{2}, 1)$. For $H = \frac{1}{2}$, (10.21) is identical to the $M/M/1$ sizing model (10.20). For $H > \frac{1}{2}$, however, the highly correlated arrivals of LRD traffic produce both very large and very small packet trains, sometimes referred to as the *mammoth and mouse* effect. The shocking conclusion of this model is that such fractal-like correlations between packets can cause buffers to grow unbounded at intermediate traffic intensities! In other

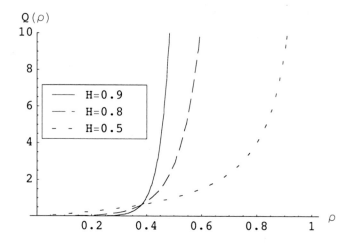

Fig. 10.11. Queue length of the generalized buffer model (10.21) as a function of network traffic load. Compared to the statistically independent traffic $(M/M/1)$ corresponding to $H = 0.5$, highly clustered packets represented by $H > 0.5$ cause the mean queue length to grow very rapidly at much lower loads

words, buffer overflow becomes a significant possibility at relatively low traffic intensities. This not only defies conventional queueing theory, it is completely counter intuitive. This is yet another reason good capacity planning models are important.

10.6 New Developments

The conclusions of Sect. 10.5.2 appear devastating for sizing buffers in local routers and servers and Internet capacity planning in general (Paxson and Floyd 1995), including the inability to use simulation tools (Paxson and Floyd 1997).

The dim prospect of this conclusion is so alarming, in fact, that I undertook to interviewing various network engineers, especially those responsible for monitoring and planning large-scale websites, to determine what methodologies they employed to address these important LRD phenomenon. To my great surprise, the results of my unscientific poll indicated that buffer overflows of the type discussed in Sect. 10.5 are either never observed, or, if they are present, they are too subtle to be measured. Contrast this with the well-known, frequent occurrence of so-called *denial-of-service* attacks that can also cause buffer overflows in the TCP/IP listen queues of Internet servers.

Moreover, it was suggested to me by several network engineers that even if LRD clustering of IP packets occurred on the Internet backbone, those packet trains would simply lead to a higher than average drop rate, which would, in

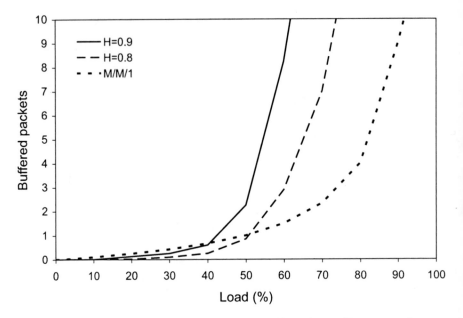

Fig. 10.12. Measured buffer occupancy due to self-similar traffic generated on an isolated test network. Note the resemblance to the buffer model in Fig. 10.11

turn, cause the dropped packets to be retransmitted. This is precisely how it is supposed to be in order to maintain routing stability. The further implication is that any serious LRD effects are therefore likely to be much more localized on the Internet, e.g., within a given website.

10.6.1 Ethernet Packetization

Add to this list of counterexamples a recent publication (Field et al. 2004) in which the authors not only measured *localized* network traffic, but monitored traffic on their 1000Base-T switched ethernet LAN, which was coupled to the Internet via a router. This is very similar to the monitoring architecture for the original Bellcore traces. Comparing the Bellcore monitoring architecture in Fig. 10.1 with the 1000Base-T network monitored near the Web server Network Interface Card (NIC) in Fig. 10.13, these authors discovered a number of interesting results that may be summarized briefly as:

- External packet arrivals from the router into the Web server are typically Markovian rather than fractal. In other words, since the arriving packets were Poisson, they alone could not be responsible for any measured power law behavior.

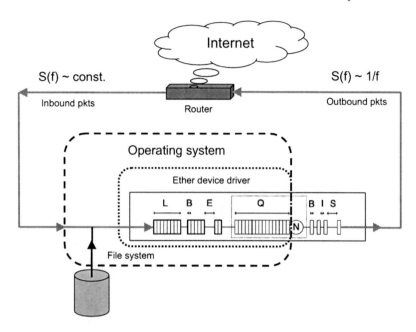

Fig. 10.13. Ethernet switch measurement architecture reported in Field et al. (2004). The power spectrum $S(f)$ being constant on the input side corresponds to Poisson arrivals, but it is power law $S(f) \sim f^{-1}$ on the output side of the Web server. This implies the power law behavior typically associated with self-similar traffic is due to the Ethernet packetization process

- Packetization interarrival periods (E in Fig. 10.13) within the operating system (Linux in these experiments) *are* power-law, like (10.2), and, in particular, they are Cauchy distributed.
- Requested file sizes (L in Fig. 10.13) are also Cauchy distributed (i.e., power law or fractal-like).
- Ethernet frame sizes (or packet sizes B in Fig. 10.13) occur as 1518 Byte multiples (or less for padding).
- Outbound packet *are* LRD correlated with $1/f$ power spectrum.

The conclusion that follows from these observations is that the Ethernet packetization process alone appears to be responsible for the LRD behavior seen in the outbound packet traces, and it is relatively insensitive to the interarrival periods between packetization requests. This result sits in stark contrast to the multisource on/off Pareto model mentioned in Sect. 10.4.

K. Christensen (private communication, 2005) has been able to corroborate the findings of Field et al. (2004) for nonaggregated arrivals using his own Ethernet simulations (private communication, 2005). This ethernet simulation model has been extensively validated and data generated by it was presented to the IEEE 802.3 working group. A switched Ethernet simulation is equivalent to a single-station shared-bus model with no CSMA/CD or binary exponential backoff, and going from 10 Mbps to 1 Gbps is just a parameter scaling.

10.6.2 LRD and Flicker Noise

Based on Sect. 10.6.1 we now understand that LRD packet trains do not require that the arrivals be power law, rather the power-law correlations are more closely associated with a so-called "flicker noise" or "pink noise" or "$1/f$" noise, which has a spectral density $S(f)$ given by:

$$S(f) \sim \frac{1}{f}, \tag{10.22}$$

where f is the frequency of the measurement periods in Fig. 10.14. This formulation is the frequency-domain counterpart of the time-domain fractals discussed in Sect. 10.4. Flicker noise has been known for a long time and was studied by Schottky in 1918 because of its presence in thermionic tubes and other early electrical circuits.

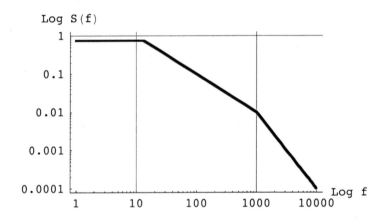

Fig. 10.14. Log–log plot of the frequency spectrum $S(f)$ as a function of frequency f showing white noise (*left*), "flicker noise" (*center*), and Brownian noise (*right*). Compare these curves with the coastline fractal data in Fig. 10.3

More generally, the spectral density or power spectrum $S(f)$ is Fourier transform of autocorrelation function $\rho(t)$. If $\rho(t) \sim t^{\alpha-1}$ then (10.22) becomes:

$$S(f) \sim \frac{1}{f^\alpha}, \tag{10.23}$$

which has the same form as (10.2) with x replaced by the frequency f. The form of (10.23) on a log–log plot is shown in Fig. 10.14, and like Figs. 10.3 and 10.4 the slope is determined by the value of the exponent α.

The following noise models can also be associated with the value of exponent in (10.23):

White noise: $\alpha \to 0$
Flicker noise: $\alpha \to 1$
Brownian process: $\alpha \to 2$

as depicted in Fig. 10.14. In this way, several apparently different random processes can be unified by virtue of the power law exponent α. At the time of writing, there is still no universal physical model of $1/f$ noise.

10.7 Summary

In this chapter we have tried to provide an overview of an important topic regarding the peculiar impact of self-similar Internet traffic on buffer sizing for routers and servers. The reason this is potentially very important for capacity planning is due to LRD clustering of Internet packets of the type first observed in the Bellcore measurements circa 1990. Such fractal-like clustering potentially leads to buffer overflow at much lower than conventionally expected traffic intensities.

Unfortunately, most of the details concerning LRD effects are contained in academic papers that are mathematically very sophisticated and impenetrable to the typical network capacity planner. This chapter has attempted to provide a simpler mathematical treatment than is generally available, but without any loss in accuracy. We concluded with some recent measurements and analysis that indicate the severity of these LRD effects may have been overestimated. Nonetheless, even if LRD effects are less important now than is currently portrayed, the wise GCaP planner will use the tools listed in Sect. 10.2 to monitor Internet traffic for their appearance in the future as multi-media payloads become more commonplace.

11

Going Guerrilla—A Case Study

Contributed by James A. Yaple

11.1 Introduction

This chapter presents an account of the real-world experience of applying Guerrilla capacity Planning (GCaP) techniques to the management of Sun Solaris UNIX platforms deployed at the United States Department of Veteran's Affairs.[1] We review some basic concepts, pertinent issues, and risks together with an assessment of the open source toolsets we employed to deliver results at low cost and in a timely fashion. Solaris-specific tools, such as the *SE toolkit* (SEtk) and the open source *Orca* data collection package, are discussed in detail. We also describe how these collected performance data were aggregated and uploaded to a z/900 mainframe for later processing with SAS statistical software.

The overall objective of this project was not to establish a *best practice*, but rather to convey the experience of using a guerrilla-style approach to capacity planning. The Austin Automation Center (AAC) began with essentially no budget and a desire for results on an accelerated schedule. As described in Chap. 1, the focus was on quickly determining a *sense of direction* as opposed to spending a lot of time getting a fix on a *compass bearing* using an expensive global positioning (GPS) device. From the perspective of management, they just wanted to know which city they should fly to, not how to read GPS coordinates and fly the aircraft themselves.

11.2 Guerrilla Monitoring Phase

In the summer of 2003, I read several online articles that Dr. Neil Gunther had written for the professional organization known as the Computer Measurement Group (www.cmg.org). In some of these articles, Gunther (2003) introduced

---

[1] James Yaple is with the Austin Automation Center, US Department of Veteran's Affairs in Austin, Texas. This chapter is an updated version of (Yaple 2004).

the notion of *Guerrilla Capacity Planning*. A central notion leverages the fact that many of the factors in performance management are unknown or uncertain (including monitored performance data), so aiming for a high degree of accuracy gains little and therefore tends to waste a lot of time. The Guerrilla approach (Chap. 1), on the other hand, aims to provide managers and other decision makers with a less accurate but more immediate sense of direction, rather than a precise, but late, compass bearing. According to Gunther (2003), performance management can be partitioned into three evolutionary phases:

1. performance monitoring
2. performance analysis
3. performance prediction

Performance monitoring, therefore, is the foundation component in the development of any Guerrilla capacity plan. Moreover, performance monitoring typically gets the most attention within the overall performance management effort because it is easiest to address with scripts developed by administrators or commercial tools.

But what about those situations where performance monitoring is a requirement, but commercial tools have not been selected and deployed, and consistent home-grown scripts do not exist? How can performance measurements be made consistently across dozens of production systems? Can a Guerrilla approach be applied in this case?

This was the case at the ACC. The AAC is a recognized, award-winning federal data center within the Department of Veterans Affairs (VA). As one of six VA Enterprise Centers, the AAC provides e-government solutions and enterprise *best practices* to support the information technology needs of customers within the federal sector. The AAC transitioned into a fee-for-service enterprise operation in 1994. This allows the Center to record a "profit" for identifying efficiencies, managing service levels, and implementing recovery and chargeback policies.

The AAC had realized for some time that *if you do not measure it, you cannot manage it*. Consequently, the ACC had already been involved in a large-scale competitive analysis to procure and implement a commercial performance monitoring facility. Unfortunately, the procurement cycle turned out to be long and would have taken months before a final vendor was selected and a suitable monitoring solution implemented. A different strategy was needed to get capacity planning data in the short term. The essence of this chapter is to demonstrate how an enterprise application-hosting center was able to implement a guerrilla-style approach to developing the monitoring phase of performance management for its UNIX systems.

In accordance with Gunther's prescription, our Guerrilla approach exploited opportunism, and developed tiny tools with little or no available budget (cf. Sect. 1.3). The final result, including data collection, aggregation, and alerting will ultimately be replaced with a commercial package. However, by sharing the AACs experiences with other organizations, it was felt that they might also be able to improve their own attempts at GCaP.

11.3 The Basic Solution

In 2001, the AAC began to explore how to keep track of an increasing number of UNIX servers, mostly Sun Solaris. The process at that time was a mixture of system administrator scripts and a rapid response if new data were required. There was no budget for sophisticated tools, and the number of servers that needed to be managed was growing rapidly.

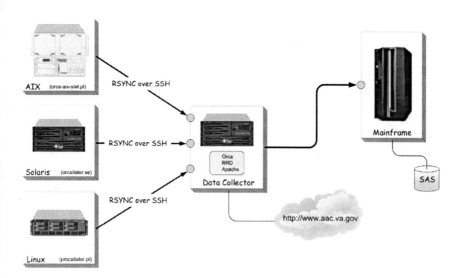

Fig. 11.1. ACC monitoring architecture

The core of the solution (Fig. 11.1) was based on an open source package known as *Orca* (www.orcaware.com/articles/1999_07_01_sunworld.html), originally developed by Blaire Zajac. Orca was intended to meet the following requirements:

- The ability to monitor many systems.
- Measure and display short (daily) and long term (yearly) trends.
- Allow easy comparison of the same type of measurement between different systems.
- Allow easy viewing of all system measurements on different time scales.
- Plots are always up to date and always available.
- The act of measuring a system should not adversely affect it (e.g., by placing a large additional load on the CPUs and degrading throughput).

Generically, an Orca implementation consists of several functions. First and foremost is the data collector, which typically accesses the /proc table and other UNIX kernel data structures. Second, a method is needed to aggregate these data into a single location. Yet another component takes these raw data and generates graphical output on a Web page. Viewing the results is then performed with a Web browser.

11.3.1 Implementation Details

The AAC started with a relatively generic Orca configuration. Since the target environment was mostly Solaris, data collection was accomplished using orcallator.se developed by Zajac from the Solaris SEtk (Cockcroft and Pettit 1998) component known as percollator.se (cf. Sect. 8.5.2). Data from multiple clients was moved to a central server using the open source tool rsync (samba.anu.edu.au/rsync). Orca, with embedded round robin database (RRD) (rrfw.sourceforge.net). library functions processed the aggregated data and produced the files for display. Apache HTTP server 1.3 provided a suitable Web display.

The orcallator.se program, written in the SymbEL scripting language, traces its lineage back to the SEtk written by Cockcroft and Pettit (1998). Orcallator is an enhanced version of SEtk percollator.se, which, in turn, collects most of the measurements shown in the SEtk zoom.se script (Cockcroft and Pettit 1998). Data collected by orcallator.se are appended as a single line to a text file every five minutes for later processing and viewing. The data are columnar with a varying number of columns based on the system configuration. A configuration with more disks or network interfaces would have more columns of data, but each observation is still contained on a single line. Data are transferred from those hosts running the data collector to a central host using rsync, an open-source utility for fast incremental file transfer which is freely available under the GNU General Public License, version 2. The use of rsync for this purpose is described in "Capacity Planning for the Masses—Using the SE Toolkit and Orca" (www.samag.com/documents/s=8965/sam0314a/0314a.htm). At AAC, files are transferred using a secure shell (ssh) configuration for encryption of the data stream.

The final component is the Orca script itself. Orca is a Perl script that reads a configuration file (orcallator.cfg), describing where its input text data files are located, the general format of the input data files, where its RRD data files should be located, and the root of the HTML tree to be generated. The orcallator.cfg file contains an informational link to the Orcaware Web site. The link appears as a hyperlink in the resulting Web presentation, describes the data being plotted, and offers some guidelines on what might constitute a good or bad performance value. The AAC has found these guidelines to be somewhat generic, but they often provide a good starting point

for further analysis as well as historical information on the evolution of the
orcallator.se counters.

11.3.2 Orca Output Examples

The previous sections explained the circumstances and motivation for the
Guerrilla approach. Figures 11.2–11.6 show a collection of graphical Orca
outputs which demonstrate its versatility in helping us achieve our Guerrilla
monitoring plan.

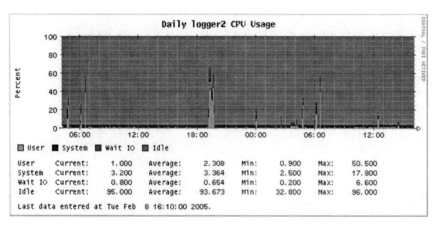

Fig. 11.2. CPU utilizations broken down by user, system, wait IO, and idle per-
centages for the host logger2. Each metric can be displayed in its own color (not
shown here). Each value is provided at the current time, as well as a minimum,
maximum, and average for the specific time period. This is a daily graph, showing
the pattern of metric behavior over some 20 h. In this case, each major grid line
represents one hour

11.3.3 Round-Robin Database

The ability to read the collected data files and generate GIF plots is facilitated
by Orca through the use of the RRD library written by Tobias Oetiker. Some
users of tools such as the Multi Router Traffic Grapher (MRTG) may be
familiar with RRD. It provides a flexible binary format for the storage of
numerical data measured over time.

A convenient function provided by RRD is *data consolidation*. Consolidation of input data reduces the amount of disk space required for long-term
data storage. The consolidated data is used by Orca when it creates charts
that span long periods, e.g., yearly plots of performance data. Consolidation

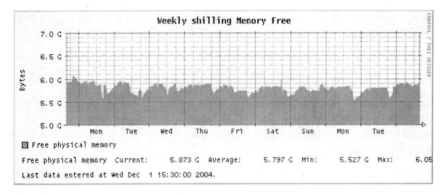

Fig. 11.3. Free memory on the Solaris host shilling is displayed across one week. This metric is physical bytes of free memory. On a Linux system using the procallator data collector, this metric is shown as a percentage of memory free. Each metric is provided as a current value, as well as a minimum, maximum, and average for the specific time period. In this case, each major grid line represents six hours

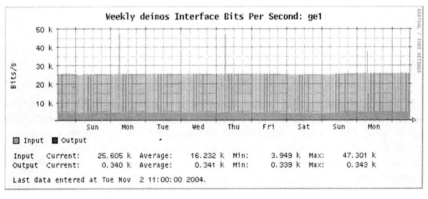

Fig. 11.4. Weekly graph of Ethernet input and output bits per second on the ge1 interface of host deimos. Each metric is provided as a current value, as well as a minimum, maximum, and average for the specific time period, and can be displayed in its own color (not shown here). Major grid lines represent six hours

is one of the key features of RRD: The data files do not grow significantly over time. In Orca's case, 5-minute data are kept for 200 h, 30 min averaged data are kept for 31 d, 2 h averaged data are kept for 100 days, and daily averaged data for 3 years. Such a data file is typically about 50 KB. Another feature of RRD is that it can read an arbitrary number of RRD files and generate GIF plots. Plots will either show a daily, weekly, monthly, or yearly view of the data in question.

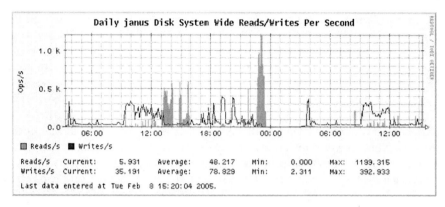

Fig. 11.5. System-wide disk activity for host janus. Read and Write activity can be presented in a specific color (not shown here) as an area graph. Each metric is provided as a current value, as well as a minimum, maximum, and average for the specific time period. In this case, each major grid line represents one hour

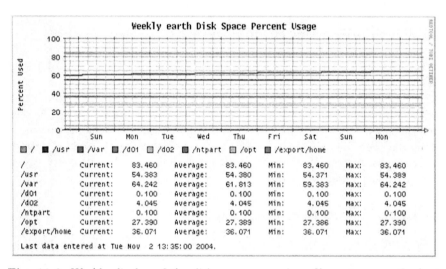

Fig. 11.6. Weekly display of the disk usage on various file systems on the host earth. Each file system can be shown in its own color (not shown here). Each metric is provided as a current value, as well as a minimum, maximum, and average for the specific time period. In this case, each major grid line represents six hours

In its normal mode, Orca runs continuously, sleeping until new data are placed by `orcallator.se` into the output data files. Once new data are written to a file by `orcallator.se`, Orca updates the RRD data files and recreates any dependent GIF charts. By starting with a basic Orca installation, the AAC realized several advantages very quickly. Orca is freely available in terms of cost and access to the source code. Open source allows sites to adjust parameters in response to local needs, and provides access to the experiences of other users via e-mail support lists and user contributions to the project. The `orcallator.se` script runs as a single process on each system and does not fork any new processes. In this way it collects performance data from each system without becoming one of the performance problems that needs to be investigated. Orca is able to work with almost any text data file. The AAC accepted some of the basic limitations in the data collection portion, `orcallator.se` and the SEtk. For now, these tools are only available on SPARC and x86 Solaris platforms. To support Orca monitoring on new platforms, a new data collection tool would have to be deployed.

11.4 Extending the Basic Solution

While the AAC uses Orca to provide some level of monitoring, additional needs demanded further extensions be made to the basic implementation. Most of the AAC performance and capacity planning staff were mainframe-oriented and had been schooled in classic methods and techniques. The data consolidation functions within Orca and RRD helped control the volume of data, but there was a desire to maintain the entire history of collected data. In addition, the burden of manually reviewing performance data on every system was extremely time-consuming.

11.4.1 Mainframe Data Processing

The AAC addressed the first issue by creating a method to feed data into mainframe datasets, where it could be stored, analyzed, and managed according to the existing volume management practice.

On a daily basis, the individual data files, each representing a host, are consolidated into a single data file on the central Orca collection platform by a locally developed Perl script. The script uploads the combined data file to the mainframe by secure FTP. The AAC typically maintains several months of data online before archiving it to tape. Each day, a mainframe job runs to consolidate the data from the 5-minute Orca intervals to 15-minute slices in SAS format (see Sect. 11.1). This collection of generational datasets constitutes the open systems performance database (PDB) that allows reports and graphs to be generated by the existing staff without requiring the mastery of a completely new toolset.

Additional jobs, such as a consolidation of seven-day data into a single file, along with reports and graphs, were developed on an ad hoc basis. The acknowledged limitation of loading data to the mainframe is the time delay incured. Data can be up to 24 hours old before it is analyzed and reported.

11.4.2 Guerrilla Planning Phase

The third phase of performance management described in Sect. 11.2 is performance prediction. Collection of historical performance data over long periods (in the monitoring phase) provided the foundation for performance projections by AAC capacity planning staff for future system upgrades and budgeting. Here we see the fruition of the Guerrilla approach to capacity planning. For example, data collated on the mainframe were processed in Excel to produce a chart of CPU utilization (Fig. 11.7) for one customer.

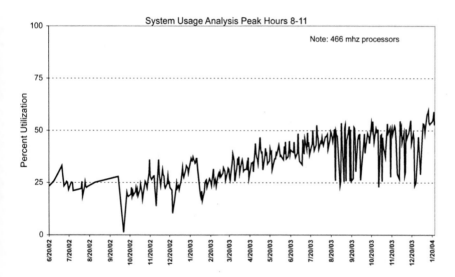

Fig. 11.7. Tracking production CPU utilization

The customer's application runs on a Sun E10000 production domain with 24-way processors. Their application is BEA Tuxedo transaction processing, which presents a load of about 4 million services per day. The application servers access an Oracle database located on the same domain. This customer was very interested in maintaining overall performance and invested considerable development effort in capturing the elapsed service times for each transaction. Over time, the AAC identified a specific server/transaction type that maps to overall performance of the system. Used as a benchmark, it shows significant degradation in performance when aggregate CPU utilization exceeds 80%. The 80% threshold was used as an upgrade indicator.

In true Guerrilla fashion, this is not an exact number, but it is sufficient to provide managers with a general sense of direction (cf. Sect. 11.2). There are limitations to this justification. Since this is based on a daily average, there may be times where the system exceeds 80% utilization. The staff must continually monitor the system to identify changes in activity, and work with the customer to identify application deployment plans. In addition, other factors, such as disk I/O rates and memory usage, enter into the upgrade discussion.

Based on the data in Fig. 11.7 and excellent cooperation from the customer about their plans for future deployment, the AAC was able to predict that this system would come close to the upgrade point somewhere around March 2005. Since the customer operated on an annual budget, this estimate was sufficient. The lead time for identifying capital requirements is long, but by utilizing historical data in the way described here, a general time frame can be determined and a greater sense of direction provided.

11.4.3 Monitoring With ORCAlerts

The volume of data Orca collected across a large number of platforms continued to grow, and the ability to regularly review key metrics on all of the systems being monitored became problematic. To assist in prioritizing the review of Orca data, an idea arose to analyze and respond to data as it was collected via a script that had the ability to notify staff via e-mail or text pager. The AAC calls these notifications ORCAlerts. For example, as usage on a specific file system on a particular host exceeds 90%, the Orca process in place reports the data to the collection point. Using a script to evaluate the collected data, crossing the 90% threshold is detected, and an email or page is generated for human analysis and possible action.

The key elements required for ORCAlerts included the identification of metrics to monitor and trigger an alert as well as the ability to set values on an individual host basis. Several additional elements, such as logging, message filters, and suppression of repeat alerts for the same conditions, were also implemented. As noted in Sect. 11.3.1, system data for each host is appended as a single line to a text file every five minutes for later processing and viewing. Based on AAC hardware configurations, current text lines range from less than 200 columns to about 1000 columns.

The code required to manipulate such a large number of columns tends to be beyond what the Guerrilla approach considers *tiny* tools as described in Chap. 1. However, included with the Orca distribution is the orcallator_ column.pl Perl script, which provides the ability to isolate a list of columns for individual analysis, thereby allowing individual data elements to be selected. The specific line modified is reproduced below:

```
my @default_column_regexs =
    qw(usr% sys% wio% idle% 5runq scanrate smtx/cpu ncpus
       swap_avail freememK tcp_estb disk_runp_*);
```

Since the existing Orca data on the collection platform resided in a directory hierarchy (e.g. /orca/data/orcallator_clients/⟨project_name⟩/⟨host\ _name⟩), it was an easy scripting task to recursively descend the directory and evaluate the last line of the collected output file. Using the <project_name> and <host_name>, thresholds specific to each host can be determined. The most recent five-minute data were examined subject to the following constraints:

- CPU %usr + %sys > 80%
- CPU %sys > 20% and > %usr
- CPU %iowait > %usr
- CPU smtx > 500/CPU
- Disk space > 90% in use
- Disk space > 50% increase usage over last 4 h
- Free memory < lotsfree
- Page scans > 200 pages over 5 min
- TCP connections > 50% over weekly high-water mark
- Processes in run queue > number of CPU over last 15 min

When the AAC first activated the ORCAlert script, there was a large volume of notifications. For several weeks, the staff met regularly to determine the causes. In response, many of the threshold values triggering the alerts for specific systems have been readjusted. It is expected that the experience of evaluating thresholds will be valuable during the future implementation of commercial monitoring tools.

There is a level of alerting built in to the basic orcallator.se data collector for Solaris. This is visible as the character string wwwwwwwggwg in each line of observed data. It is an indicator of the *color*, or severity, of various counters, as identified in the SEtk documentation. By examining this string, various threshold violations can be detected. While this approach can be used in a Solaris implementation, it is not supported by data collection scripts for other platforms.

11.5 Future Developments

It is not clear what role our Guerrilla monitoring and planning solution, based on Orca, will take in the future plans of the AAC. The organization is in the process of rolling out a commercial solution. However, there are also plans for performance monitoring to be charged back to the customer, and it is not clear what percentage of them will be able to justify a business case for those charges. The initial implementation of the commercial performance management solution will focus on shared AAC components, e.g., enterprise wide backup systems, file and print services as well as email services. Many of these facilities reside on Microsoft Windows platforms for which there is no

Orca port. Orca will likely remain a part of the UNIX performance monitoring picture for the foreseeable future.

Recently, several customers initiated plans to develop and launch projects on platforms other than Sun Solaris. Future deployments will includes variations of Linux and AIX. These plans already escalated an identified issue with the existing solution because the original Orca data collector only runs on the Solaris operating system.

Fortunately for Linux platforms, the Orcaware site www.orcaware.com/orca/ also provides a Perl data collector called procallator.pl as part of its distribution. Community input and contributions are a common benefit of many open-source projects. When a need arises, one or more people contribute a solution. For Linux data collection, Guilherme Carvalho Chehab stepped forward with the solution. The AAC is very close to implementing the Linux collector into the existing Orca data collection, storage, presentation, and alerting infrastructure. On the AIX platform, a similar solution was provided by Jason D. Kelleher and Rajesh Verma. The current version of orca-aix-stat.pl supports AIX 4.3 and 5.

11.6 Summary

The AAC has now implemented Orca-based monitoring on IBM AIX 5.2 and RedHat Linux AS 3.0 servers. While this has uncovered several issues related to how the various UNIX operating systems collect and populate their kernel performance counters, the support from the Orca community has been effective.

The Orca-based solution is not for everyone. It requires some level of analysis for a successful implementation. In its basic form, it can provide a significant amount of information about certain aspects of system health. In our environment (Sect. 11.4.1), Orca-based data collection also provided a foundation for some level of alerting and capacity planning. However, Orca will not put any of the commercial monitoring companies out of business. Those tools provide richer data collection agents, analysis tools, and performance-modeling capabilities. That said, if your organization is interested in using an open-source approach to gather capacity planning data, Orca can be a worthy component of that effort.

Moreover, based on the experience reported here, the AAC can now make the case that using Orca for Guerrilla monitoring helped to refine the process of selecting and implementing a commercial monitoring product. By knowing what data elements are commonly collected, it made it easier to distinguish when a tool vendor was really adding value with their product. The effort and discussions involved in identifying key metrics and thresholds for alerting can be transferred into any implementation of a commercial product. In addition, the ease of manipulating historical data using familiar tools required the vendors to better justify the value of the proprietary components in their products.

Implementing a GCaP solution was valuable for quickly instantiating a data collection and planning framework under rather severe time and budget constraints. So it enabled us to meet the intended goal, but it is only the first step on an otherwise long road. Now that we have established a performance database, the focus will be on managing it and using it to provide more value to the organization in the future.

A

Amdahl and the Repairman

This Appendix reveals the connection between Amdahl's law and the repairman queue-theoretic model. In particular, Sect. A.3 contains the proof of Theorem 6.2.

A.1 Repairman Queueing Model

The *machine repairman* model (Allen 1990; Gunther 2005a) is a closed queueing network comprised of a finite number of machines N (shown in the upper part of Fig. A.1) that break down after a mean lifetime Z and queue for repairs at a single repairman (lower part of Fig. A.1) who takes a mean time S to service them. Our interest is in expressions for the system throughput

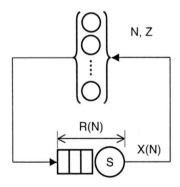

Fig. A.1. Repairman queueing model with N workstations

$X(N)$ and residence time $R(N)$. Subsequently, we shall relate these quantities to Amdahl's law.

Because the closed queue in Fig. A.1 is a self-regulating, negative-feedback loop, the arrival rate into the repair station is not constant. Of the N total machines, there are $X \times Z$ machines (on average) still "up", and $Q(N)$ "down," such that the mean throughput is the difference:

$$X(N) = \frac{1}{Z} \left(N - Q(N) \right) . \tag{A.1}$$

Since there is no independent analytic expression for $Q(N)$, we cannot evaluate $X(N)$ directly. An alternative approach is to apply mean value analysis (MVA) techniques (Lazowska et al. 1984; Gunther 2005a).

Remark A.1 (Repairman Asymptote). For a large number of stations $N \to \infty$, the repairman becomes saturated, i.e., the utilization becomes $\rho = XS = 1$, and the throughput X approaches the asymptote $1/S$ (cf. Theorem 4.1).

Definition A.1 (Round-Trip Time). *The mean time to tour the entire circuit in Fig. A.1 is called the round-trip time (RTT). It is the sum of the workstation lifetime Z and the residence time R at the repairman:*

$$\mathrm{RTT} = R(N) + Z = \frac{N}{X(N)} . \tag{A.2}$$

Equation (A.2) can be derived from Little's law $Q = XR$ (Lazowska et al. 1984; Gunther 2005a) by writing $N = \mathrm{RTT} \times X$.

Definition A.2 (Mean Throughput). *The mean throughput can be expressed by a simple rearrangement of (A.2):*

$$X(N) = \frac{N}{R(N) + Z} . \tag{A.3}$$

We now derive Amdahl's law from the repairman queueing model. In fact, there are two possible derivations of Amdahl's law related to the duality Theorem 4.2. One follows from the conventional representation for parallel subtasks (Sect. A.2), while the other follows from the representation for concurrent multitasking (Sect. A.3). The former could be considered as the *hardware* perspective, whereas the latter might be regarded as the *software* perspective.

A.2 Amdahl's Law for Parallel Subtasks

In this section, the repairman queueing variables are interpreted as follows:

- N represents the number of physical processors or parallel subtasks.
- Workstation lifetime Z represents the mean execution time of a task.
- Repair time S represents an unspecified serial delay.
- RTT (A.2) represents the elapsed time T_N.

Consider a succession of parallel workloads starting with a single task.

A.2.1 Single Task

Amdahl's law, as derived in Sect. 4.3.2, assumes that the amount of work has a *fixed* total size. The round-trip time for $N = 1$ is simply:

$$\text{RTT} = S + Z \,. \tag{A.4}$$

From Definition 4.4, the speedup (4.13) is:

$$S(N) = \frac{T_1}{T_N} = \frac{S + Z}{S + Z} \,. \tag{A.5}$$

Since there is only one task $S(1) = 1$ in (A.5), so there is no speedup.

A.2.2 Two Subtasks

Divide the single unit of work in two halves, so that the mean execution time is also halved, i.e., $Z \rightarrow Z/2$. This corresponds to $N = 2$ workstations in the repairman model or two separate processors in a multiprocessor model. The serial delay, however, remains fixed because, although there are two equal subtasks, their service times are also assumed to be halved, viz., $S \rightarrow S/2$. The round-trip time (A.2) becomes:

$$\text{RTT} = 2\left(\frac{S}{2}\right) + \frac{Z}{2} \,, \tag{A.6}$$

and the speedup corresponding to (A.5) is:

$$S(N) = \frac{S + Z}{S + \frac{Z}{2}} > 1 \,. \tag{A.7}$$

A.2.3 Multiple Subtasks

Generalizing to N subtasks executing on N processors results in the following expression for the speedup:

$$S(N) = \frac{S + Z}{S + \frac{Z}{N}} \,. \tag{A.8}$$

Comparing (A.8) with Eqn.(4.14), leads to the identifications:

$$S = \sigma \, T_1 \quad \text{and} \quad Z = (1 - \sigma) \, T_1 \tag{A.9}$$

Remark A.2. As the number of subtasks N becomes large, the repairman speedup (A.8) approaches the asymptote:

$$\lim_{N \to \infty} S(N) = \frac{S + Z}{S} \,. \tag{A.10}$$

Definition A.3. *From Theorem 4.1, $S(p) \sim \sigma^{-1}$ as $p \to \infty$. Comparison with (A.10) suggests:*

$$\sigma = \frac{S}{S+Z}, \tag{A.11}$$

which expresses the serial fraction (Definition 4.3) in terms of purely queue-theoretic variables.

Rewriting (A.5) as

$$\frac{Z}{S+Z} = 1 - \frac{S}{S+Z}, \tag{A.12}$$

and substituting (A.11) for the second term, produces:

$$\frac{Z}{S+Z} = 1 - \sigma. \tag{A.13}$$

Combining (A.11) with (A.13), the ratio

$$\frac{1-\sigma}{\sigma} = \frac{Z}{S}, \tag{A.14}$$

is the repairman *service ratio* (see, e.g., Highleyman 1989, p. 129) expressed in terms of the Amdahl serial-fraction parameter.

Dividing the speedup (A.8) by S produces:

$$S(N) = \left(\frac{S+Z}{S}\right)\frac{1}{1+\left(\frac{Z}{S}\right)\frac{1}{N}}. \tag{A.15}$$

Substituting the identities (A.11) and (A.14) into (A.15) leads to the simplification:

$$S(N) = \left(\frac{1}{\sigma}\right)\frac{1}{1+\left(\frac{1-\sigma}{\sigma}\right)\frac{1}{N}}, \tag{A.16}$$

$$= \frac{1}{\sigma + \frac{1-\sigma}{N}}, \tag{A.17}$$

which, on rearrangement, gives Amdahl's law:

$$S(N) = \frac{N}{1+\sigma(N-1)}, \tag{A.18}$$

corresponding to Eqn.(4.15) with $p = N$.

Amdahl's law for parallel speedup results from partitioning the fixed-size workload $N = 1$ into shorter duration subtasks $Z \to Z/N$ while the serialization delay S remains fixed. Under these conditions the only queueing is within the server and no waiting line forms.

A.3 Amdahl's Law for Concurrent Multitasks

In this section, rather than partitioning the original fixed-size workload into N smaller subtasks, N identical units of work are added to the system. Consider the synchronous throughput where $R(N) = NS$. Then, from Definition A.2 we can write the synchronous throughput as:

$$X_{\text{syn}} = \frac{N}{NS + Z}. \tag{A.19}$$

Remark A.3. Although the bound (A.19) is noted in (Lazowska et al. 1984), its connection with Amdahl's law has apparently gone unnoticed.

The concurrent speedup can be defined in terms of the normalized throughput ratio:

$$S(N) = \frac{X_{\text{syn}}(N)}{X_{\text{syn}}(1)}, \tag{A.20}$$

which, using (A.19), becomes

$$S(N) = \frac{N}{NS + Z} \times (S + Z), \tag{A.21}$$

$$= \frac{NS + NZ}{NS + Z}. \tag{A.22}$$

Equation (A.22) can be expanded as:

$$S(N) = \frac{N(D + Z)}{D + Z + ND - D}, \tag{A.23}$$

$$= \frac{N}{1 + (\frac{D}{D+Z})N - (\frac{D}{D+Z})}. \tag{A.24}$$

Substituting the identity (A.11) into the denominator leads to the simplification:

$$S(N) = \frac{N}{1 + \sigma N - \sigma} = \frac{N}{1 + \sigma(N - 1)}, \tag{A.25}$$

which proves Theorem 6.2.

Amdahl speedup for concurrent tasks results from increasing serialization time $S \to NS$ due to synchronous queueing, while the mean execution time per task Z remains fixed. The fact that (A.18) and (A.25) are formally identical is another manifestation of the duality Theorem 4.2.

A.4 Note On Nelson's Approach

L. Williams (private communication, 2006) asked me to compare Theorem 6.2 with the work of Nelson (1996). The distinctions are marked but subtle, so I summarize them briefly here.

The motivation of Nelson's paper is quite different from my own. His purpose (along with many other authors) is to find clever ways to *defeat* Amdahl's law; mine is to *understand* it. Ironically, we both end up resorting to queue-theoretic models to gain more insight into the various issues; an *open* queue in Nelson's analysis, a *closed* queue in mine. There are two parts to Nelson's paper:

1. An attempt to *unify* (4.15) and (4.30) into a single speedup function.
2. *Extend* that new speedup function with a measure of waiting time.

The overarching goal is to find waiting-time optima for this unified speedup function. Unification is achieved by purely algebraic manipulations and does not rest on any queue-theoretic arguments. The connection with an open queueing model is introduced later, also in a rather ad hoc fashion, to incorporate waiting time based on queue length. His analysis thereafter is based mostly on simulations and departs radically from my goals.

Conversely, I have shown elsewhere (Gunther 2005b) that both Amdahl's law (4.15) and Gustafson's law (4.30) are unified by the *same* queueing model; the repairman model. Theorem 6.2 tells us that Amdahl's law corresponds *identically* to synchronous throughput of the repairman. Synchronous throughput is worst case because it causes maximal queueing at the repairman (Fig. A.1) or bus. In that sense, Theorem 6.2 represents a *lower* bound on throughput and therefore is worse than the *mean* throughput. Once this interpretation understood, it follows immediately that Amdahl's law can be defeated, much more easily than proposed in (Nelson 1996), by simply requiring that all requests be issued *asynchronously*!

B

Mathematica Evaluation of NUMA Parameters

This Appendix shows how to calculate the parameters σ and κ using *Mathematica* applied to the scalability data in Chap. 5. *Mathematica* employs infinite precision numbers and this highlights a limitation of using Excel, which seriously underestimates κ and overestimates p^*.

B.1 Mathematica Packages

We note the version of *Mathematica* being used in all of the following calculations.

```
$Version
```

```
5.1 for Mac OS X (October 25, 2004)
```

```
<< Statistics`NonlinearFit`
```

B.2 Import the Data

```
cpuRawData = ReadList["/Users/njg/Books/Springer GCAP/
GCaP Mathematica/NLFit/Hardware-X1/NUMAdata.txt",
  Number, RecordLists → True]
```

```
{{1, 20}, {4, 78}, {8, 130}, {12, 170}, {16, 190},
  {20, 200}, {24, 210}, {28, 230}, {32, 260}, {48, 280}, {64, 310}}
```

We check that the first column is the processor p-configuration, and that the second column contains the measured throughput values by reformatting the output in *TableForm*.

B.3 Tabulate the Data

cpuRawData // TableForm

1	20
4	78
8	130
12	170
16	190
20	200
24	210
28	230
32	260
48	280
64	310

This data agrees with Table 5.1. For regression analysis, it is necessary to extract the single processor throughput value $X(1)$ to provide the correct normalization.

X1 = Flatten[cpuRawData][[2]]

20

B.4 Plot Normalized Data

ListPlot[cpuNormData, PlotStyle → PointSize[0.025],
PlotRange → {0, 16}, AxesLabel → {"p", "C(p)"}];

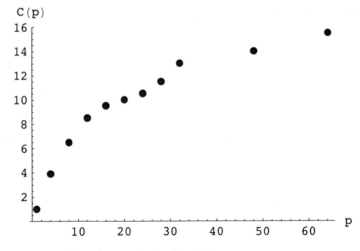

This plot agrees with the scatter plot in Fig. 5.2.

B.5 Nonlinear Regression

Mathematica has the powerful ability to directly fit the regression parameters to a rational-function (see Definition 4.8). Applying *NonlinearRegress* to the universal scalabilty model (5.1):

```
NonlinearRegress[cpuNormData,

         p
    ─────────────────────, {p}, {{σ, 0, 0.1}, {κ, 0, 0.01}},
    1 + σ (p - 1) + κ p (p - 1)

RegressionReport → {BestFitParameters}]
```

```
{BestFitParameters → {σ → 0.0497973, κ → 0.0000114344}}
```

B.6 ANOVA Report

If the *RegressionReport* argument is not suppressed, *NonlinearRegress* also displays the complete set of analysis of variance (ANOVA) statistics.

```
NonlinearRegress[cpuNormData,

         p
    ─────────────────────, {p}, {{σ, 0, 0.1}, {κ, 0, 0.01}}]
    1 + σ (p - 1) + κ p (p - 1)
```

{BestFitParameters → {σ → 0.0497973, κ → 0.0000114344}, ParameterCITable →

	Estimate	Asymptotic SE	CI
σ	0.0497973	0.00320716	{0.0425422, 0.0570524}
κ	0.0000114344	0.0000693348	{-0.000145412, 0.000168281}

EstimatedVariance → 0.242613,

		DF	SumOfSq	MeanSq
	Model	2	1166.53	583.263
ANOVATable → Error		9	2.18352	0.242613,
	Uncorrected Total	11	1168.71	
	Corrected Total	10	187.327	

$$\text{AsymptoticCorrelationMatrix} \to \begin{pmatrix} 1. & -0.927523 \\ -0.927523 & 1. \end{pmatrix},$$

		Curvature
FitCurvatureTable →	Max Intrinsic	0.0292726
	Max Parameter-Effects	0.0705461
	95. % Confidence Region	0.484701

For comparison, the parameters calculated using Excel are shown in Table B.1. Using the algorithms in Chap. 3, $\sigma = 0.0500$ is sufficiently close to the *Mathematica* value $\sigma = 0.04979$ after rounding the latter with Algorithm 3.2. The Excel value $\kappa = 0.5 \times 10^{-5}$, however, is an underestimate of the *Mathematica* value $\kappa = 1.14344 \times 10^{-5}$ by more than a factor of two.

Table B.1. Model parameters calculated using Excel from Sect. 5.6.2

Parameter	Value
σ	0.0500
κ	5×10^{-6}
p^*	435

B.7 Maximal CPU Configuration

$$\sqrt{\frac{1-\sigma}{\kappa}}$$

```
288.271
```

As a consequence of the underestimation of κ by Excel in Sect. B.6, the corresponding value of p^* in Table B.1 is overestimated by about 50% because $\sqrt{\kappa}$ appears in the denominator of Eqn.(4.33).

B.8 Plot of Regression Model

```
Show[
  Block[{$DisplayFunction = Identity},
    {ListPlot[cpuNormData,
      PlotStyle → PointSize[0.025], AxesLabel → {"p", "C(p)"}],
     Plot[univModel, {p, 1, 64}]}]
];
```

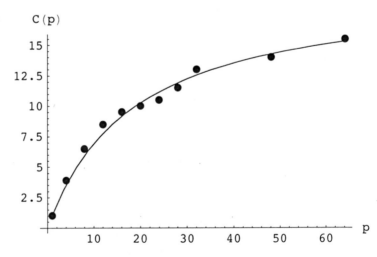

This plot can be compared with Fig. 5.8.

C

Abbreviations and Units

C.1 SI Prefixes

Throughout this book we use the conventions of the basic International System
of Units (SI) for physical quantities summarized in Table C.1.

Table C.1. Prefixes for general SI units

Large			Small		
Symbol	Name	Factor	Symbol	Name	Factor
da	deka	10^1	d	deci	10^{-1}
h	hecto	10^2	c	centi	10^{-2}
k	kilo	10^3	m	milli	10^{-3}
M	mega	10^6	μ	micro	10^{-6}
G	giga	10^9	n	nano	10^{-9}
T	tera	10^{12}	p	pico	10^{-12}
P	peta	10^{15}	f	femto	10^{-15}
E	exa	10^{18}	a	atto	10^{-18}
Y	yotta	10^{24}	y	yocto	10^{-24}

C.2 Time Suffixes

Table C.2 summarizes the conventional units for time. The units in the lower
half of Table C.2 are not officially a part of the SI unit system but occur
frequently enough to be accepted implicitly.

Table C.2. Units of time

Symbol	Name	SI unit
s	second	10^0 s
ms	millisecond	10^{-3} s
μs	microsecond	10^{-6} s
ns	nanosecond	10^{-9} s
min	minute	60 s
h	hour	60 m = 3,600 s
d	day	24 h = 86,400 s

C.3 Capacity Suffixes

Units of digital computer capacity present some ambiguities. Although physical quantities like cycles per second (Hz) are measured in base-10 (decimal) units, digital quantities involving binary digits are measured in base-2 (binary) units. The International Electrotechnical Commission (IEC) published unambiguous computing technology units in 1998. Further details are available at the NIST web site (http://physics.nist.gov/cuu/Units/index.html). This proposed convention has not yet been widely adopted in the industry, so we do not use it either. For completeness, we summarize the usual computer industry units that we do use, together with the IEC units in Table C.3. A

Table C.3. Units of computer capacity

Symbol	Name	IEC symbol	IEC name	Decimal unit	Power of 2
b	bit	b	bit	1 b	2^0 b
B	byte	B	byte	8 b	2^3 b
KB	kilobyte	KiB	kibibyte	1,024 B	2^{10} B
MB	megabyte	MiB	mebibyte	1,048,576 B	2^{20} B
GB	gigabyte	GiB	gibibyte	1,073,741,824 B	2^{30} B
TB	terabyte	TiB	tebibyte	$1.099,511,6 \times 10^{12}$ B	2^{40} B

kilobyte refers not to 1,000 bytes but the *power of two* closest to that number viz. 1,024 bytes = 2^{10} B; similarly for the other prefixes shown in Table C.3. Therefore, one has to know the context to know which interpretation of *kilo* applies. The strict SI convention introduces a new set of prefixes to remove this ambiguity. For example, 1,024 B would be referred to as a *kibibyte* (meaning, a kilobinary byte) and denoted 1 KiB.

D

Programs for Chapter 3

D.1 Determine SigDigs in VBA

```
Function SigFigs(number)
    ' Assumes EXCEL 2000 or later.
    ' Created by Neil J. Gunther, Wed Jun  5 18:02:29 2002
    ' Updated by Neil J. Gunther, Tue Jun 18 10:00:06 2002
    Dim numString As String
    Dim numParts As Variant

    'Treat the number as a string literal
    numString = CStr(number)

    If (numString Like "*.*") Then 'check for decimal point
        'Separate integer and fractional parts
        numParts = Split(numString, ".")
        'Concatenate sans decimal point
        digString = numParts(0) & numParts(1)
        nlength = Len(digString)
        i = 1
        'Match FORWARDS from LEFTmost digit...
        'non-zero digit preceding zero or more digits
        patString = "[1-9]*"
        Do While i < nlength
            If (digString Like patString) Then
                Exit Do
            End If
            'prepend any digit metacharacter
            patString = "?" & patString
            i = i + 1
        Loop
        SigDigs = nlength - i
    Else 'no decimal point so, scan number as is ...
        nlength = Len(numString)
```

```
            i = 0
            'Match BACKWARDS from RIGHTmost digit...
            'zero or more digits preceding a non-zero digit
            patString = "*[1-9]"
            Do While i < nlength
                If (numString Like patString) Then
                    Exit Do
                End If
                'append any digit metacharacter
                patString = patString & "?"
                i = i + 1
            Loop
            SigDigs = nlength - i
        End If

    SigFigs = SigDigs 'Return result to spreadsheet cell
End Function
```

D.2 Determine SigDigs in Mathematica

```
SigFigs[] :=
  (* Created by Neil J. Gunther, Tue Jun 18 09:18:54 2002 *)
  (* Updated by Neil J. Gunther, Tue Jun 18 16:29:01 2002 *)
  Module[
    {numString, digString, intList, realList},
    numString = InputString[": "]; (* force string literal *)
    If[StringMatchQ[numString, "*.*"],
      (*** must be REAL - valued ***)
      (* elide decimal point *)
      digString = StringReplace[numString, "." -> ""];
      realList = ToExpression[Characters[digString]];
      (* Walk list from LEFTmost digit *)
      While[Length[realList] != 0,
        If[First[realList] == 0,
            realList = Rest[realList], (* delete from head *)
            (* first non-zero digit! *)
            Return[{FullForm[numString], Length[realList]}]
            ];
        ],
      (*** Else: must be an INTEGER ***)
      intList = ToExpression[Characters[numString]];
      (* Walk list from RIGHTmost digit *)
      While[(len = Length[intList]) != 0,
        If[Last[intList] == 0,
            intList = Take[intList, len - 1], (* delete from tail *)
            (* first non-zero digit! *)
            Return[{FullForm[numString], Length[intList]}]
            ];
```

```
        ];
      ] (* end of If *)
    ] (* end of Module *)
```

D.3 Determine SigDigs in Perl

```perl
#! /usr/bin/perl/ -w
#
# Created by Neil J. Gunther, Tue Jun  4 22:55:41  2002
# Updated by Neil J. Gunther, Tue Jun 18 12:27:16  2002
# Available from www.perfdynamics.com/Tools/sigfigs.txt

# Read the number in from the keyboard.
print "Enter a number: ";
$numstring = <STDIN>;
chomp($numstring); # Toss the carriage return
$skipzero = ''; $i = 0;

# Check for presence of decimal point
if ($numstring =~ /\./) {
        # Separate integer and fractional parts
        ($int, $frac) = split(/\./, $numstring);
        # Concatenate sans decimal point
        $digstring = $int . $frac;
        $numfigs = length($digstring);
        # Find position of first non-zero digit
        while ($i < $numfigs ) {
                # Compare FORWARDS from LEFTmost digit ...
                if ($digstring =~ /^$skipzero(\d)/) {
                        $sigfigs = $numfigs - $i;
                        last if ($1 ne '0');
                }
                $skipzero = $skipzero . '.';
                $i++;
        }
}
else {  # No decimal point, so just scan the integer...
        $numfigs = length($numstring);
        # Find position of first non-zero digit
        while ($i < $numfigs) {
                # Compare BACKWARDS from RIGHTmost digit ...
                if ($numstring =~ /(\d)$skipzero$/) {
                        $sigfigs = $numfigs - $i;
                        last if ($1 ne '0');
                }
                $skipzero = $skipzero . '.';
                $i++;
        }
```

```
}

# Print out the result.
print "The number '$numstring' contains $sigfigs significant
digits.\n";
```

E

Programs for Chapter 8

E.1 Example Data Extractor in Perl

```perl
#! /usr/local/bin/perl
#
# Parse data collector logs over fifteen min intervals
# to make output format compatible with EXCEL macro input.
#
# Created by Neil J. Gunther
# Performance Dynamics Company

use Time::Local;

while (<>) {
    next if ($_=~/Time$/);

    ($dummy, $load, $dummy, $dummy, $dummy, $sys, $usr, $dummy,
    $dummy, $dummy, $dummy, $dummy, $dummy, $dummy, $dummy, $dummy,
    $dummy, $dummy, $dummy, $dummy, $dummy, $dummy, $dummy, $dummy,
    $localt) = split(/\t/);
    ($date, $hms) = split(" ", $localt);
    ($month, $mday, $year) = split("/", $date);
    ($hr, $minute, $second) = split(/:/, $hms);
    $timestamp = timelocal($second, $minute, $hr, $mday, $month-1,
        $year-1900);
    $starttime=$timestamp;
    $endtime=($timestamp + 1800);
    $hour=($hr . ":" . $minute);
    $busy=($usr + $sys);
    $count{$hour}++;
    $cpu{$hour}+=$busy;
    $load{$hour}+=$load;
    $cpumax{$hour}=$busy;
    $cpumin{$hour}=$busy;
```

```perl
    $loadmax{$hour}=$load;
    $loadmin{$hour}=$load;

    while (($timestamp < $endtime)) {
        if (!eof) {
            $d=<> ;
            ($dummy, $load, $dummy, $dummy, $dummy, $sys, $usr, $dummy,
            $dummy, $dummy, $dummy, $dummy, $dummy, $dummy, $dummy,
            $dummy, $dummy, $dummy, $dummy, $dummy, $dummy, $dummy,
            $dummy, $dummy, $localt) = split(/\t/,$d);
            ($date, $hms) = split(" ", $localt);
            ($month, $mday, $year) = split("/", $date);
            ($hr,$minute,$second)=split(/:/,$hms);
            $timestamp = timelocal($second, $minute, $hr, $mday,
            $month-1, $year-1900);

            if (($timestamp < $endtime)) {
                $busy=($usr + $sys);
                $count{$hour}++;
                $cpu{$hour}+=$busy;
                $load{$hour}+=$load;
                # find min, max
                ($cpumax{$hour}=$busy) if ( $busy > $cpumax{$hour} );
                ($cpumin{$hour}=$busy) if ( $busy < $cpumin{$hour} );
                ($loadmax{$hour}=$load) if ( $load > $loadmax{$hour} )
                ($loadmin{$hour}=$load) if ( $load < $loadmin{$hour} )
            } else {
                $starttime=$timestamp;
                $endtime=($timestamp + 1800);
                $hour=($hr . ":" . $minute);
                $busy=($usr + $sys);
                $count{$hour}++;
                $cpu{$hour}+=$busy;
                $load{$hour}+=$load;
                $cpumax{$hour}=$busy;
                $cpumin{$hour}=$busy;
                $loadmax{$hour}=$load;
                $loadmin{$hour}=$load;
            }
        } else {
                last;
        }
    }
}

print "Date      Time     AvgU     MaxU     MinU     AvgQ     MaxQ     MinQ
    SumQ\n";

foreach $time (sort(keys %count)) {
```

```
      printf ("%s\t%s\t%.2f\t%.2f\t%.2f\t%.2f\t%.2f\t%.2f\n",
      $date,
      $time,
      ($cpu{$time}/$count{$time}),
      $cpumax{$time},
      $cpumin{$time},
      ($load{$time}/$count{$time}),
      $loadmax{$time},
      $loadmin{$time},
      $load{$time},
      );
}
```

E.2 VBA Macro for Calculating U$_{\text{eff}}$

```
Sub DoDaily()
'
' Daily Macro created by Neil J. Gunther
'
' This macro performs regression analysis on 24 hours worth of
' extracted web DB server metrics.
'
'
' Make sure stats Add-Ins are installed in EXCEL
    AddIns("Analysis ToolPak").Installed = True
    AddIns("Analysis ToolPak - VBA").Installed = True

' Declare globals
    Dim ddepth As Integer
    Dim fdepth As Integer
    Dim lastDayRow As Integer
    Dim DailyMax As Integer
    DayMax = 7 * 90 ' some nominal value < 100 intervals
    Dim regYcol As Integer
    Dim regXcol1 As Integer
    Dim regXcol2 As Integer
    Dim tval As String
    Dim bookName As String
    bookName = "MulitVarRegression.xls"  ' Current name of model
    Dim sheetName As String
    sheetName = "Hourlys"
    Dim chartName As String
    chartName = "Hourlys Chart"

' Check if Dailys chart already created
    Application.DisplayAlerts = False
    For Each chartObj In Workbooks(bookName).Charts
        If chartObj.Name = chartName Then
```

```
                    answer = MsgBox("Remove current Hourly chart? ",
                        vbOKCancel)
                    If answer = vbOK Then
                        chartObj.Delete
                        Exit For
                    End If
                End If
            Next chartObj
            Application.DisplayAlerts = True


    ' Insert selection criteria
        Worksheets(sheetName).Activate
        Range("J1").Value = "MinU"
        Range("K1").Value = "MaxU"
        Range("J2").Value = ">1"
        Range("K2").Value = "<90"


    ' Cut and paste filtered data
        Range("A1:H300").Select
        Range("A1:H300").AdvancedFilter _
            Action:=xlFilterCopy, _
            CriteriaRange:=Range("J1:K2"), _
            CopyToRange:=Range("L1:S300"), _
            Unique:=False


    ' How many rows of data are there?
    ' Input data column depth ...
        Range("A1").Select
        Cells(1, ActiveCell.Column).End(xlDown).Select
        ddepth = ActiveCell.Row
    ' Filtered data column depth ...
        Range("L1").Select
        Cells(1, ActiveCell.Column).End(xlDown).Select
        fdepth = ActiveCell.Row
    ' Which row to append to in Dailys?
        Worksheets("Dailys").Select
        Range("A1").Select
        tval = ActiveCell.Value
        If tval = "DateTime" Then
            Cells(1, ActiveCell.Column).End(xlDown).Select
            lastDayRow = ActiveCell.Row
        Else ' nothing copied there yet
            lastDayRow = 1
        End If
        lastDayRow = lastDayRow + 1


    ' Calculate regression coeffs ...
        Worksheets(sheetName).Select
        Range("N1").Select
```

```
        regYcol = ActiveCell.Column
        Range("P1").Select
        regXcol1 = ActiveCell.Column
        Range("S1").Select
        regXcol2 = ActiveCell.Column

        Application.Run "ATPVBAEN.XLA!Regress", _
            ActiveSheet.Range(Cells(1, regYcol),
                Cells(fdepth, regYcol)), _
            ActiveSheet.Range(Cells(1, regXcol1),
                Cells(fdepth, regXcol2)), False, True, , _
            ActiveSheet.Range("$W$1") _
            , False, False, False, False, , False

' Insert model results
        Range("c1:c300").Insert (1)
        Range("c1").Value = "Ueff"
        Range("c2").Select
        Range("c2").NumberFormat = "#,##0.00"
        ActiveCell.Formula = _
            "=$Y$17+$Y$18*F2+$Y$19*G2+$Y$20*H2+$Y$21*I2"
        Range("c2").Copy Destination:= _
            Range(Cells(3, 3), Cells(ddepth, 3))

' Plot the results
        Range(Cells(1, 1), Cells(ddepth, 5)).Select
        Charts.Add
        With ActiveChart
            .ChartType = xlXYScatterSmoothNoMarkers
            .SetSourceData Source:=Sheets(sheetName).Range("A1:E91"), _
                PlotBy:=xlColumns
            .Location Where:=xlLocationAsNewSheet, Name:=chartName
            .HasTitle = False
            .Axes(xlCategory, xlPrimary).HasTitle = False
            .Axes(xlValue, xlPrimary).HasTitle = True
            .Axes(xlValue, xlPrimary).AxisTitle.Characters.Text = _
                "%Ucpu"
            .HasLegend = True
            .Legend.Select
            Selection.Position = xlBottom
        End With

' Append to Dailys ?
        answer = MsgBox("Update Dailys? ", vbYesNo)
        If answer = vbYes Then
            'Check if there's already 7 contiguous days inserted
            If lastDayRow >= DayMax Then
                MsgBox "Dailys is full with 1 week of data. Move it to
                    Weeklys!"
```

```
            Exit Sub
        End If

        ' Paste the fieldnames anyway ...
        Worksheets(sheetName).Select
        Application.CutCopyMode = True
        Worksheets(sheetName).Range(Cells(1, 1), Cells(1, 5)).Copy
        Worksheets("Dailys").Select
        Range(Cells(1, 1), Cells(1, 5)).Select
        ActiveSheet.Paste
        Application.CutCopyMode = False

        ' Copy data from Hourlys ...
        Worksheets(sheetName).Select
        Application.CutCopyMode = True
        Worksheets(sheetName).Range(Cells(2, 1), Cells(ddepth, 5)).Copy

        ' and append it to the Dailys ...
        Worksheets("Dailys").Select
        Range(Cells(lastDayRow, 1), _
            Cells((lastDayRow - 2) + ddepth, 5)).Select
        Selection.PasteSpecial Paste:=xlValues, Operation:=xlNone,
            SkipBlanks:= _
        False, Transpose:=False
        Application.CutCopyMode = False
        Range("A2:A700").NumberFormat = "m/d/yy h:mm"
        Range("B2:C700").NumberFormat = "#,##0.00"
        Worksheets("Dailys").Activate
    End If

    'Cleanup Hourly data ...
    Worksheets(sheetName).Select
    Application.CutCopyMode = True
    Worksheets(sheetName).Range(Cells(2, 3), Cells(ddepth, 3)).Copy
    Range(Cells(2, 3), Cells(ddepth, 3)).Select
    Selection.PasteSpecial Paste:=xlValues, Operation:=xlNone,
        SkipBlanks:= _
        False, Transpose:=False
    Application.CutCopyMode = False
    Range(Cells(2, 3), Cells(ddepth, 3)).NumberFormat = "#,##0.00"
    ' Range("K1:AE50").Delete
    Range(Cells(1, 11), Cells(fdepth, 30)).Delete
    Worksheets(sheetName).Activate

End Sub
```

F

The Guerrilla Manual

Management resists, the guerrilla planner retreats;
Management dithers, the guerrilla planner proposes;
Management relents, the guerrilla planner promotes;
Management retreats, the guerrilla planner pursues.

Hit-and-Run Tactics You Can Use on Your Boss or Throw Around in a Tiger Team Meeting

This chapter is both a preview and a summary. It is a preview of what is contained in this book, if you have not read it before; it is a summary of all the important points, if you have. The intent is to provide you with an authoritative list of key ideas and aphorisms from which you can draw at any time to underscore your Guerrilla capacity planning point for those who need to be convinced by something more than a verbal discussion. This material is also available online at www.perfdynamics.com.

F.1 Weapons of Mass Instruction

The following distillations have been extracted from the chapters in this book, my training classes of the same name, as well as my other book, *Analyzing Computer System Performance with Perl::PDQ* (Gunther 2005a).

Why Go Guerrilla? The planning horizon is now 3 months, thanks to the gnomes on Wall Street. Only Guerrilla-style *tactical planning* is crazy enough to be compatible with that kind of insanity.

Selling Prevention: Capacity planning is about prevention and someone told me "You can't sell prevention!" Then explain the multibillion dollar dietary-supplements industry!

Why Capacity Planning is Nontrivial: Capacity planning is complicated by your brain thinking *linearly* about a computer system that operates *nonlinearly*.

Capacity planning techniques, such as the *universal scalability model* (in Sect. F.3), help us to describe and predict these nonlinearities.

The Performance Homunculus: Capacity management is to systems management as the homunculus (sensory proportion) is to the human body (geometric proportion). See Fig. 1.1 in Chap. 1.

Capacity management can rightly be regarded as just a subset of systems management, but the infrastructure requirements for successful capacity planning (both the tools and knowledgeable humans to use them) are necessarily out of proportion with the requirements for simpler systems management tasks like software distribution, security, backup, etc. It is self-defeating to try doing capacity planning on the cheap.

Self Tuning Applications: Self-tuning applications are not ready for prime time. How can they be when human performance experts get it wrong all the time!?

Performance analysis is a lot like a medical examination, and medical *Expert Systems* were heavily touted in the mid 1980s. You do not hear about them anymore. And you know that if it worked, HMOs would be all over it. It is a laudable goal but if you lose your job, it will not be because of some expert performance robot.

Squeezing Capacity: Capacity planning is not just about the future anymore.

Today, there is a serious need to squeeze more out of your current capital equipment.

When Wrong Is Right: Capacity planning is about setting expectations. Even *wrong* expectations are better than no expectations!

Planning means making predictions. Even a wrong prediction is useful. It means either (i) the understanding behind your prediction is wrong and needs to corrected, or (ii) the measurement process is broken somewhere and needs to be fixed. Start with a SWAG. Next time, try a G. If you aren't making iterative predictions throughout a project life cycle, you will only know things are amiss when it is too late!

The Overengineering Gotcha: Hardware *is* cheaper today, but a truckload of PCs will not help one iota if all or part of the application executes single-threaded.

My response to the oft-heard platitude: "We don't need no stinkin' capacity planning. We'll just throw more cheap iron at it!" The *capacity* part is easy. It is the *planning* part that is subtle.

Network Performance: It is never the network!

If the network is out of bandwidth or has interminable latencies, fix it! Then we will talk performance of your application.

Can't Beat This! If the measured round-trip times (RTTs) for an application produce a relatively flat or concave curve (like that in Fig. 1.5) as a function of increasing load, SHIP IT! Only if you do not understand basic queueing theory would you press on in spite of such data.

Modeling Errors: When I am asked, "But, how accurate are your performance models?" my canonical response is, "Well, how accurate are your performance *data*!?"

Most people remain blissfully unaware of the fact that *all* measurements come with errors, both systematic and random. An important capacity planning task is to determine and track the magnitude of the errors in your performance data. Every datum should come with a "±" attached (which will then force you to put a number after it).

Data are Not Divine: Treating performance data as something divine is a sin.

Data comes from the devil, only models come from God.

Just Digging the Hole Deeper: Busy work does not accrue enlightenment.

Western culture too often glorifies hours clocked as productive work. If you do not take time off to come up for air to reflect on what you are doing, how are you going to know when you are wrong?

Little Things: Little's law means a lot! Learn $Q = XR$ by heart.

I use it almost daily to *cross-check* that throughput and delay data are consistent, no matter whether those data come from measurements or models. More details about Little's law can be found in (Gunther 2005a, Chap. 2), *Analyzing Computer System Performance with Perl::PDQ*. Another use of Little's law is calculating service times, which are notoriously difficult to measure directly. See the Rules of Thumb in Sect. F.2.

Bigger is Not Always Better: Beware the SMP wall!

The *bigger* the symmetric multiprocessor (SMP) configuration you purchase, the *busier* you need to run it. But only to the point where the average run-queue begins to grow. Any busier and the user's response time will rapidly start to climb through the roof.

If They Snooze, You lose: Spend as much time on developing the presentation of your capacity planning conclusions as you did reaching them.

If your audience does not get the point, or things go into the weeds because you did not expend enough thought on a visual, you just wasted a lot more than your presentation time-slot.

Bottlenecks: You never *remove* a bottleneck, you just shuffle the deck.

Benchmarks: All benchmarks represent institutionalized cheating.

Consolidation: Gunther's law of consolidation: Remove it and they will come!

Control Freaks Unite! Your own applications are the last refuge of performance engineering.

Control over the performance of hardware resources, e.g., processors and disks, is progressively being eroded as these things simply become commodity black boxes, viz., multicore processors and disk arrays. This situation will only be exacerbated with the advent of Internet-based application services. Software developers will therefore have to understand more about the performance and capacity planning implications of their designs running on these black boxes. (see Sect. F.3)

Best Practices: Best practices are an admission of failure.

> Copying someone else's apparent success is like cheating on a test.
> You may make the grade but how far is the bluff going to take you?

F.2 Capacity Modeling Rules of Thumb

Here are some ideas that might be of help when you are trying to construct your capacity planning or performance analysis models.

Keep It Simple: A performance model should be as simple as possible, but no simpler!
> I now tell people in my GCaP classes, despite the fact that I repeat this rule of thumb several times, you *will* throw the kitchen sink into your performance models; at least, early on as you first learn how to create them. It is almost axiomatic: the more you know about the system architecture, the more detail you will try to throw into the model. The goal, in fact, is the opposite.

More Like The Map Than The Metro: A performance model is to a computer system as the BART map (Fig. 1.2) is to the BART rail system.
> The BART map is an abstraction that has very little to do with the physical train. It encodes only sufficient detail to enable transit from point A to point B. It does not include a lot of irrelevant details such as altitude of the stations, or even their actual geographical proximity. A performance model is a similar kind of abstraction.

The Big Picture: Unlike most aspects of computer technology, performance modeling is about deciding how much detail can be *ignored!*

Look for the Principle: When trying to construct the performance representation of a computer system (which may or may not be a queueing model), look for the principle of operation. If you cannot describe the principle of operation in 25 words or less, you probably do not understand it yet.
> As an example, the principle of operation for a time-share computer system can be stated as: *Time-share gives every user the illusion that they are the ONLY user active on the system.* All the thousands of lines of code in the operating system, which support time-slicing, priority queues, etc., are there merely to support that illusion.

Guilt is Golden: Performance modeling is also about spreading the guilt around.
> You, as the performance analyst or planner, only have to shine the light in the right place, then stand back while others flock to fix it.

Where to Start? Have some fun with blocks; *functional blocks!*
> One place to start constructing a PDQ model is by drawing a *functional block diagram*. The objective is to identify where time is spent at each stage in processing the workload of interest. Ultimately, each

functional block is converted to a queueing subsystem like those shown above. This includes the ability to distinguish sequential and parallel processing. Other diagrammatic techniques e.g., UML diagrams, may also be useful. See (Gunther 2005a, Chap. 6).

Inputs and Outputs: When defining performance models (especially queueing models), it helps to write down a list of INPUTS (measurements or estimates that are used to parameterize the model) and OUTPUTS (numbers that are generated by calculating the model).

Take Little's law $Q = XR$, for example. It is a performance model, albeit a simple equation or operational law, but a model nonetheless. All the variables on the *right* side of the equation (X and R) are INPUTS, and the single variable on the *left* is the OUTPUT. A more detailed discussion of this point is presented in (Gunther 2005a, Chap. 6).

No Service, No Queues: You know the restaurant rule: "No shoes, no service!" Well, this is the PDQ modeling rule: no service, no queues. In your PDQ models, there is no point creating more queueing nodes than you have measured service times for.

If the measurements of the real system do not include the service time for a queueing node that you think ought to be in your PDQ model, then that PDQ node cannot be defined.

Estimating Service Times: Service times are notoriously difficult to measure directly. Often, however, the service time can be calculated from other performance metrics that are easier to measure.

Suppose, for example, you had requests coming into an HTTP server and you could measure its CPU utilization with some UNIX tool like *vmstat*, and you would like to know the service time of the HTTP Gets. UNIX will not tell you, but you can use Little's law ($U = XS$) to figure it out. If you can measure the arrival rate of requests in Gets/sec (X) and the CPU %utilization (U), then the average service time (S) for a Get is easily calculated from the quotient U/X.

Change the Data: If the measurements do not support your PDQ performance model, change the measurements.

Closed or Open Queue? When trying to figure out which queueing model to apply, ask yourself if you have a finite number of requests to service or not. If the answer is yes (as it would be for a load-test platform), then it is a *closed* queueing model. Otherwise use an *open* queueing model.

Opening a Closed Queue: How do I determine when a closed queueing model can be replaced by an open model?

This important question arises, for example, when you want to extrapolate performance predictions for an Internet application (open) that are based on measurements from a load-test platform (closed).

An open queueing model assumes an infinite population of requesters initiating requests at an arrival rate λ (lambda). In a closed model, λ (lambda) is approximated by the ratio N/Z. Treat the thinktime Z

as a free parameter, and choose a value (by trial and error) that keeps N/Z constant as you make N larger in your PDQ model. Eventually, at some value of N, the OUTPUTS of both the closed and open models will agree to some reasonable approximation.

Steady-State Measurements: The steady-state measurement period should on the order of 100 times larger than the largest service time.

Transcribing Data: Use the timebase of your measurement tools. If it reports in seconds, use seconds, if it reports in microseconds, use microseconds. The point being, it is easier to check the digits directly for any transcription errors. Of course, the units of ALL numbers should be normalized before doing any arithmetic.

Workloads Come in Threes: In a mixed workload model (multiclass streams in PDQ), avoid using more than three concurrent workstreams whenever possible.

Apart from making an unwieldy PDQ report to read, generally you are only interested in the interaction of two workloads (pairwise comparison). Everything else goes in the third (AKA "the background"). If you cannot see how to do this, you are probably not ready to create the PDQ model.

F.3 Scalability on a Stick

The following points explain how to quantify notions of scalability:

1. A lot of people use the term "scalability" without clearly defining it, let alone defining it quanitatively. Computer system scalability must be quantified. If you cannot quantify it, you cannot guarantee it. The *universal law of computational scaling* provides that quantification.

2. One the greatest impediments to applying queueing theory models (whether analytic or simulation) is the inscrutibility of service times within an application. Every queueing facility in a performance model requires a service time as an input parameter. As noted in Sect. F.2, *No service time, no queue*. Without the appropriate queues in the model, system performance metrics like throughtput and response time, cannot be predicted. The *universal law of computational scaling* leapfrogs this entire problem by NOT requiring ANY low-level service time measurements as inputs.

F.3.1 Universal Law of Computational Scaling

The relative capacity $C(N)$ (the dashed line in Figs. 6.3 or 6.5) is given by:

$$C(N) = \frac{N}{1 + \alpha N + \beta N(N-1)} \tag{F.1}$$

where N is either:

1. The number of users or load generators on a fixed hardware configuration. In this case, the number of users acts as the independent variable while the CPU configuration remains constant for the range of user load measurements.
2. The number of physical processors or nodes in the hardware configuration. In this case, the number of user processes executing per CPU (say, 10) is assumed to be the same for every added CPU. Therefore, on a 4 CPU platform you would run 40 virtual users.

with α the *contention* parameter, and β the *coherency-delay* parameter. The latter accounts for the retrograde throughput seen in Fig. 6.3, for example.

- The objective of using Eq.(F.1) is *not* to produce a curve that passes through every data point. That is called curve fitting and that is what graphics artists do with splines. As von Neumann said, "Give me four parameters and I will fit an elephant. Give me five and I will make its trunk wiggle!" (At least I only have two).
- When the coherency-delay parameter vanishes i.e., $\beta = 0$, Eq.(F.1) reduces to Amdahl's law, as expcted. See Eq.(4.15) in Chap. 4.

F.3.2 Areas of Applicability

This universal model has wide spread applicability. Some areas are:

- Modeling such effects as VM thrashing, and cache-miss latencies.
- Modeling disk arrays, SANs, and multicore processors.
- Modeling certain types of network I/O.
- User-load performance testing is one of the most common applications.
- Using it in combination with measurement tools like LoadRunner, Benchmark Factory, etc.

That is why Eq.(F.1) is called *universal*.

F.3.3 How to Use It

Virtual Load Testing: The universal model in Eq.(F.1) allows you take a sparse set of load measurements (4–6 data points) and determine how your application will scale under larger user loads than you may be able to generate in your test lab. This can all be done in a spreadsheet like Excel. See, e.g., Fig. 1.3 in Chap. 1 and Fig. 5.3 in Chap. 5.

Detecting measurement problems: Equation (F.1) is not a crystal ball. It cannot foretell the onset of broken measurements or intrinsic pathologies. When the data diverge from the model, that does not automatically make the model wrong. You need to stop measuring and find where the inconsistency lies.

Performance Heuristics: The relative sizes of the α and β parameters tell you respectively whether contention effects or coherency effects are responsible for poor scalability.

Performance Diagnostics: What makes Eq.(F.1) easy to apply also limits its diagnostic capability. If the parameter values are poor, you cannot use it to tell you what to fix. All that information is in there alright, but it is compressed into the values of those two little parameters. However, other people, e.g., application developers (the people who wrote the code), the systems architect, may easily identify the problem once the universal law has told them they need to look for one.

Bibliography

Acree, N., Howard, J., and Wohlgemuth, D. (2001). "How to communicate and define the value of performance in dollars and cents". In *Proc. CMG Conf.*, pages 781–787, Anaheim, CA.

Allen, A. O. (1990). *Probability, Statistics, and Queueing Theory with Computer Science Applications*. Academic Press, San Diego, 2nd. edition.

Amdahl, G. (1967). Validity of the single processor approach to achieving large scale computing capabilities. *Proc. AFIPS Conf.*, 30:483–485.

Atkison, T., Butler, L. A., and Miller, E. (2000). "Comparing CPU performance between and within processor families". In *Proc. CMG Conf.*, pages 421–430, Orlando, FL.

Barham, P. T., Dragovic, B., Fraser, K., Hand, S., Harris, T. L., Ho, A., Neugebauer, R., Pratt, I., and Warfield, A. (2003). "Xen and the art of virtualization". In *SOSP (ACM Symposium on Operating Systems Principles)*, pages 164–177.

Bass, J. (2000). "A look at eight-way server scalability: The Dell PowerEdge 8450 gives a good bang for the buck". *Network World*.

Bertsekas, D. and Gallager, R. (1987). *Data Networks*. Prentice-Hall, Englewood Cliffs, NJ.

Box, G. E. P., Hunter, W. G., and Hunter, J. S. (1978). *Statistics for Experimenters: An Introduction to Design, Data Analysis, and Model Building*. Wiley, New York.

Box, G. E. P., Jenkins, G. M., and Reinsel, G. C. (1994). *Time Series Analysis*. Prentice-Hall, Engelwood Cliffs, NJ, third edition.

Brady, J. F. (2005). Virtualization and CPU wait times in a Linux guest environment. *J. Computer Resource Management*, 116:3–8.

Buch, D. K. and Pentkovski, V. M. (2001). Experience in characterization of typical multi-tier e-Business systems using operational analysis. In *Proc. CMG Conf.*, pages 671–681, Anaheim, CA.

Buyya, R., editor (1999). *High Performance Cluster Computing: Architectures and Systems*, volume 1. Prentice-Hall.

Cockcroft, A. and Pettit, R. (1998). *Sun Performance and Tuning*. SunSoft Press, Mountain View, California, 2nd. edition.

Crovella, M. E. and Bestavros, A. (1997). "Self-similarity in world wide web traffic: Evidence and possible causes". *IEEE/ACM Transactions on Networking*, 5(6):835–846.

Culler, D. E., Karp, R. M., Patterson, D., Sahay, A., and Santos, E. E. (1996). "LogP: A practical model of parallel computation". *Comm. ACM*, 39(11):79–85.

Ding, Y., Bolker, E. D., and Kumar, A. (2003). "Performance implications of hyper-threading". In *Proc. CMG Conf.*, pages 21–29, Dallas, TX.

Downey, A. B. (2001). "Evidence for long-tailed distributions in the internet". In *Proc. ACM SIGCOM Conf.*, pages 1037–1044, Atlanta, GA.

Einstein, A. (1956). "On the movement of small particles suspended in a stationary liquid demanded by the molecular-kinetic theory of heat". In Fürth, R. and Cowper, A. D., editors, *Investigations on the Theory of the Brownian Movement*, pages 1–18. Dover, New York, USA.

Faraway, J. J. (2004). *Linear Models with R*. CRC Press, Boca Raton, FL.

Fernando, G. (2005). "To V or not to V: A practical guide to virtualization". In *Proc. CMG Conf.*, pages 103–116, Orlando, FL.

Field, T., Harder, U., and Harrison, P. (2004). "measurement and modeling of self-similar traffic in computer networks". Technical report, Imperial College, London, UK.

Forst, F. (1997). "Latent demand: The hidden consumer". In *Proc. CMG Conf.*, pages 1011–1017, Orlando, FL.

Foster, I. (2005). "Service-oriented science". *Science*, 308:814–817.

Galilei, G. (1638). "Discourses and mathematical demonstrations concerning two new sciences pertaining to mechanics and local motions". In Drake, S., editor, *Two New Sciences*. Wall & Emerson, Toronto, Canada (2000), 2nd edition.

Gelenbe, E. (1989). *Multiprocessor Performance*. Wiley, NY.

Gilbert, L., Tseng, J., Newman, R., Iqbal, S., Pepper, R., Celebioglu, O., Hsieh, J., and Cobban, M. (2005). "Performance implications of virtualization and hyper-threading on high energy physics applications in a grid environment". In *Proc. 9th IEEE International Parallel and Distributed Processing Symposium*, page 32a, Denver, CO.

Gray, M. K. (1996). "Web growth summary". `www.mit.edu/people/mkgray/net/web-growth-summary.html`.

Gunther, N., Christensen, K., and Yoshigoe, K. (2003). "Characterization of the burst stabilization protocol for the RR/CICQ switch. In *IEEE Conf.*

on Local Computer Networks, Bonn, Germany.

Gunther, N. J. (1993). "A simple capacity model for massively parallel transaction systems". In *Proc. CMG Conf.*, pages 1035–1044, San Diego, CA.

Gunther, N. J. (1995). "Thinking inside the box: The next step in TPC benchmarking". *TPC Quarterly Report*, 12:8–17.

Gunther, N. J. (1996). "Understanding the MP effect: Multiprocessing in pictures". In *Proc. CMG Conf.*, pages 957–968, San Diego, CA.

Gunther, N. J. (1997). "Shooting the RAPPIDs: Swift performance techniques for turbulent times". In *Proc. CMG Conf.*, pages 602–613, Orlando, Florida.

Gunther, N. J. (1998). *The Practical Performance Analyst*. McGraw-Hill, New York, NY.

Gunther, N. J. (1999). "Capacity planning for Solaris SRM: All I ever wanted was my unfair advantage (And why you cant get it!)". In *Proc. CMG Conf.*, pages 194–205, Reno, NV.

Gunther, N. J. (2000). *The Practical Performance Analyst*. iUniverse, Lincoln, NE, Reprint edition.

Gunther, N. J. (2001). "Performance and scalability models for a hypergrowth e-Commerce Web site". In Dumke, R., Rautenstrauch, C., Schmietendorf, A., and Scholz, A., editors, *Performance Engineering: State of the Art and Current Trends*, volume # 2047, pages 267–282. Springer–Verlag, Heidelberg.

Gunther, N. J. (2002a). "A new interpretation of Amdahl's law and Geometric scalability". xxx.lanl.gov/abs/cs.DC/0210017.

Gunther, N. J. (2002b). "Hit-and-run tactics enable guerrilla capacity planning". *IEEE IT Professional*, July–August:40–46.

Gunther, N. J. (2003). "Guerrilla capacity planning: Hit-and-run tactics for website scalability". www.cmg.org/measureit/issues/mit02/m_2_2.html, www.cmg.org/measureit/issues/mit04/m_4_7.html.

Gunther, N. J. (2004a). "Celebrity boxing and sizing: Alan Greenspan vs. Gene Amdahl". Invited presentation. CMG 2002, Reno, NV.

Gunther, N. J. (2004b). "On the connection between scaling laws in parallel computers and manufacturing systems". Canadian Operations Research Society Conference, Banff, CANADA.

Gunther, N. J. (2005a). *Analyzing Computer System Performance with Perl::PDQ*. Springer-Verlag, Heidelberg, Germany.

Gunther, N. J. (2005b). "Unification of Amdahl's law, LogP and other performance models for message-passing architectures". In *IASTED 17th Intl. Conf. on Parallel and Distributed Computer Systems*, pages 569–576, Phoenix, AZ.

Gunther, N. J. and Shaw, J. G. (1990). "Path integral evaluation of ALOHA network transients". *Information Processing Letters*, 33(6):289–295.

Gunther, N. J. and Traister, L. M. (1995). "Implementing performance flight-recorders in a distributed computing environment with A+UMA". *IEEE TCOS (Technical Committee on Operating Systems) Bulletin*, (7)3.

Haldane, J. B. S. (1928). "On being the right size". `www.physlink.com/Education/essay_haldane.cfm`.

Hennessy, J. L. and Patterson, D. A. (1996). *Computer Architecture: A Quantitative Approach*. Morgan Kaufmann, San Francisco, CA, 2nd. edition.

Highleyman, W. H. (1989). *Performance Analysis of Transaction Processing Systems*. Wiley, New York.

Holtman, J. (2004). "Using R for system performance analysis". In *Proc. CMG Conf.*, pages 791–802, Las Vegas, NV.

Jain, R. (1990). *The Art of Computer Systems Performance Analysis*. Wiley, New York, NY.

Johnson, S. (2003). "Measuring CPU time from hyper-threading enabled Intel processors". In *Proc. CMG Conf.*, pages 369–378, Dallas, TX.

Karp, A. H. and Flatt, P. H. (1990). "Measuring parallel processor performance". *Comm. ACM*, 33(5):539–543.

Kay, J. and Lauder, P. (1988). "A fair share scheduler". *Comm. ACM*, 31:44–55.

Kleban, S. D. and Clearwater, S. H. (2003). "Hierarchical dynamics, interarrival times and performance". In *Proc. SuperComputer2003*, pages 28–34, Phoenix, AZ.

Kumar, R., Tullsen, D., Jouppi, N., and Ranganathan, P. (2005). "Heterogeneous chip multiprocessors". *IEEE Computer*, 38(11):32–38.

Lazowska, E. D., Zahorjan, J., Graham, G. S., and Sevcik, K. C. (1984). *Quantitative System Performance: Computer System Analysis Using Queueing Network Models*. Prentice-Hall, Engelwood Cliffs, NJ. Out of print but available online at `http://www.cs.washington.edu/homes/lazowska/qsp/`. Cited Jun 12, 2004.

Leland, W. E., Taqqu, M. S., Willinger, W., and Wilson, D. V. (1993). "On the self-similar nature of ethernet traffic" (extended version). Technical report, Bellcore, NJ, Morristown. DRAFT.

Levine, D., Berenson, M., and Stephan, D. (1999). *Statistics for Managers Using Microsoft EXCEL*. Prentice–Hall, New Jersey, 2nd. edition.

Lilja, D. J. (2000). *Measuring Computer Performance: A Practitioner's Guide*. Cambridge University Press, Cambridge, UK.

Mandelbrot, B. B. (1983). *The Fractal Geometry of Nature*. W. H. Freeman, New York.

Nelson, R. D. (1996). Including queueing effects in Amdahl's law. *Comm. ACM*, 39(12es):231–238.

Norros, I. (1994). "A storage model with self-similar input". *Queueing Systems*, 16:387–396.

OCLC (2004). "Web characterization: Size and growth statistics ". www.oclc.org/research/projects/archive/wcp/stats/size.htm.

OpenGroup (1997). Systems management: Universal measurement architecture. www.opengroup.org/bookstore/catalog/c427.htm.

OpenGroup (2002). The application response measurement. www.opengroup.org/tech/management/arm/.

Park, K. and Willinger, W., editors (2000). *Self-Similar Network Traffic and Performance Evaluation*. John Wiley & Sons, Inc., New York, NY.

Paxson, V. and Floyd, S. (1995). "Wide area traffic: The failure of Poisson modeling". *IEEE/ACM Transactions on Networking*, 3(3):226–244.

Paxson, V. and Floyd, S. (1997). "Why we don't know how to simulate the internet". In *Proc. Winter Simulation Conf.*, pages 1037–1044, Atlanta, GA.

Press, W. H., Flannery, B. P., Teukolsky, S. A., and Vetterling, W. T. (1988). *Numerical Recipes in C.* Cambridge Univ. Press, Cambridge, U. K.

Rains, E. M. and Sloane, N. J. A. (1999). "On Cayley's enumeration of alkanes (or 4-valent trees)". *Journal of Integer Sequences.*

Ritter, J. (2002). "Why Gnutella can't scale. No, really.". www.darkridge.com/~jpr5/doc/gnutella.html.

Rudd, C. (2004). *An Introductory Overview of ITIL.* itSMF Ltd., Reading, UK.

Strong, P. (2005). "Enterprise grid computing". *ACM Queue*, 3:50–59.

Sutter, H. (2005). "The free lunch is over: A fundamental turn toward concurrency in software". *Dr. Dobb's Journal*, 30(3).

Taber, R. (1969). *The War of the Flea: A Study of Guerrilla Warfare Theory and Practice.* Paladin, London, UK.

Talia, D. and Trunfio, P. (2004). "A P2P grid services-based protocol: Design and evaluation". In *10th International Euro-Par Conf. on Parallel Processing*, pages 1022–1031, Pisa, Italy.

Vahalia, U. (1996). *UNIX Internals: The New Frontier.* Prentice-Hall, Upper Saddle River, NJ.

Venables, W. N. and Ripley, B. D. (2002). *Modern Applied Statistics with S.* Springer, New York, NY, 4 edition.

VMware (2005). "ESX server performance and resource management for CPU-intensive workloads". www.vmware.com/pdf/ESX2_CPU_Performance.pdf.

Ware, W. (1972). The ultimate computer. *IEEE Spectrum*, 9:89–91.

Williams, L. G. and Smith, C. U. (2004). "Web application scalability: A model-based approach". In *Proc. CMG Conf.*, pages 215–226.

Yaple, J. (2004). "A practical implementation of Guerrilla monitoring". In *Proc. CMG Conf.*, pages 715–721, Las Vegas, NV.

Index

Active Server Pages (ASP), 111
Allometric scaling, 43, 179
ALOHA network, 64
Amdahl's law, 49–51, 55–57, 62, 63, 65,
    69, 72, 81, 85, 98–101, 104, 106,
    116
Application Resource Measurement
    (ARM), 3

Bellcore
    packet traces, 180
    self-similar packets, 182
BitTorrent, 138, 165
Bottleneck law, 144

Capacity (binary) unit suffixes, 224
Cayley tree, 138, 140, 168–170, 173, 174
Clusters, *see* Scalability clusters
Coefficient of determination, 153
Concave function, 58
Concurrency, VIII, 53, 58, 102, 115,
    127, 137, 217
Concurrent programming, 102, 116
Concurrent users, 103, 106, 112, 113,
    217, 240
Convex function, 58
Coxian server, 63
Critical size, 45

Dell PowerEdge 8450, 108
Doubling period, 13, 161

Enterprise JavaBeans (EJB), 111
Ethernet monitor, 180

Excel, 9–11, 14–16, 104, 150, 152, 153,
    156, 225, 229, 241
Exponential model, 64

F value, 153
Fair-share scheduler, 127, 129–131, 134,
    142
Fiscal year, 162
Forecasting, 13, 144, 149, 155, 156
Fractal
    Brownian motion, 188, 193
    coastline, 185
    dimension, 185
    geometric, 179, 182, 185
    Hausdorff measure, 185
    long-range dependence, 196, 197
    power law, 179
    time-based, 186
Functional test, 22

Geometric model, 63
Geometric scaling, 41, 42
Giants, 45
Gnutella, *see* P2P
GRID
    Global Grid Forum, 167
    Globus toolkit, 167
    OGSA (Open Grid Services
        Architecture), 167
    versus P2P, 166
GRID computing, 117, 138, 139, 142,
    165, 166
Guerrilla
    attributes, 7

capacity planning, 1, 127, 138, 142
case study, 199
graph, 162
guidelines, 14
management, IX
mantra, 16
Manual, VII, 16, 235
scalability, VIII
schedules, 4
successes, IX
tactical planning, 1
tactics, VIII, 6
tools, 9–11, 13, 15
Guerrilla Capacity Planning (GCaP),
    VII–IX, 1, 9

Hardware scalability, 47
Homunculus
    medical, 6
    performance, 5
Hyper-Threading Technology (HTT),
    119
Hyperthreading, 119
Hz (SI unit), 224

Information Technology Infrastructure
    Library (ITIL)
    defined, 17
Information Technology Infrastructure
    Library(ITIL), 17, 18, 20, 25
    business perspective, 19
    capacity management, 21
    wheel of performance, 21
Integrated Services Digital Network
    (ISDN), 180, 197
Interconnect
    technology, 66
    topology, 66, 114, 165, 168–170, 172,
        173, 175, 176
Internet planning, 179
Interval arithmetic, 39

Jack and the Beanstalk, 46
Java
    bytecodes, 4
    servlet, 111
Java 2 Platform, Enterprise Edition
    (J2EE), 135

Java Database Connectivity (JDBC),
    111
Java Server Pages (JSP), 111

Linux, see Unix
Little's law, 11, 35, 191, 214
Long-Range Dependence (LRD), 188,
    192, 193, 195–197

Mathematica, XI, 14, 15, 39, 85,
    219–222, 226, 253
Minitab, XI, 15, 85
Moore's law, 161
Multi-tier architectures, 110, 116
Multicores, see Scalability chip
    multiprocessor (CMP)
Multiuser model, 52

Object-oriented programming, 102
Open Database Connectivity (ODBC),
    111

P2P
    Gnutella, 138, 165, 167
    Skype, 138, 165
Packet
    traces, 180
    trains, 182
Parameters
    coherency, 58
    contention, 55, 58
    heuristic, 62, 68
Pareto distribution, 179
Peer-to-peer, see P2P
Performance
    analysis, 6
    homunculus, 5
    monitoring, 6
    planning, 6
Perl, 202, 206, 208, 210, 227
Planning
    strategic, 6, 16
    tactical, 6, 9, 16
Power law, 41, 58, 179, 188, 194, 196,
    197

Quadratic model, 63

R, XI, 15, 85
Rational function, 42, 65, 77

Risk
  management, 2
  perception, 2

Scalability
  chip multiprocessor (CMP), 47, 66
  clusters, 66
  Guerrilla style, VIII
  hardware, 49, 52, 56, 63, 66
  multicores, 47, 66
  software, 97, 98, 100, 103, 107
  spreadsheet, 10
  symmetric multiprocessor (SMP), 47,
    52, 56
Scalability model
  Amdahl, 49
  Exponential, 64
  Geometric, 63
  Multiuser, 52
  Quadratic, 63
  software, 97
  Universal, 56
Scaling
  allometric, 43
  geometric, 41, 42
  power law, see Power law
  self-similarity, see Self-similar traffic
Schedule
  inflation, 7, 9, 15
  product, 4, 6
  success measure, 1
Self-similar traffic, 179, 180, 182, 185,
    190, 193, 197
Service Level Agreement (SLA), 20, 132
SGI
  IRIX, 74
  Origin 2000, 74
SI prefix conventions, 223
Skype, see P2P
Space elevator, 46
SPEC
  CINT2000 benchmark, 108
  SDM benchmark, 103
SQL Server
  scalability, 107
  version 6.5 vs. 7.0, 107
Sun
  E10000 server, 207
  SEtoolkit, 199, 202
  Solaris, 199, 201, 210

SPARCcenter 2000, 104
Superserial model, see Universal
    scalability

Testing
  functional, 22
  unit, 22
  virtual, 98, 110
threads, 11
Time unit suffixes, 223
Topology, see Interconnect

UltraSPARC T1, 119
Unit test, 22
Units
  capacity suffixes, 224
  SI prefixes, 223
  time suffixes, 223
Universal Measurement Architecture
    (UMA), 3
Universal scalability, 56, 71, 77, 82, 87,
    100, 103, 107
Unix
  AIX, 3, 210
  BSD, 3
  HPUX, 3
  instrumentation, 4, 142
  IRIX, 74
  Linux, 3, 8, 127, 143, 209, 210
  MacOS X, 3
  Solaris, 3, 199, 201, 202

Virtual
  load-testing, 10, 98, 110
  processing, 117
  servers, 117
Virtual machine monitors, 127
Virtual machines, 118, 119, 127, 138
VTune, 122

WebLogic, 111, 134–136
WebSphere, 111
Wheel of performance, 21
Windows
  2000 Advanced Server, 108, 123
  2000 Production Server, 126
  2003 Enterprise Edition, 135
  instrumentation, 4, 142
  NT Enterprise Edition, 108
  scalability, 107
  XP, 127

Colophon

This colophon is here to remind me and tells others what tools I used to create this book. I also want to proclaim the shear brilliance of MacOS X, Preview 3.0.7, and its intrinsic PDF image capture capability (especially from other tools such as PowerPoint, Excel, and Mathematica) for producing a camera-ready book manuscript. Combined with pdfLaTeX, MacOS X enabled me to complete the majority of this book in an aggregate time of about six months.

Why do I use LaTeX? It takes flat ASCII text[*] as its typographic source. Flat ASCII is both *the* universal program interface[†] and *the* immutable data repository. LaTeX 2_ε is also monetarily free and therefore not subject to the whimsy of commercial interests. As a consequence it also remains asymptotically bug free, and some of the best ports of LaTeX 2_ε are available on the Power Macintosh platform.

The source text for this book was composed in BBEdit 8.2.4 and typeset with pdfLaTeX 3.14159-1.10b-2.1 (via Gerben Wierda's www.rna.nl/ *i-Installer* program ii2.sourceforge.net) using Springer's *SVMono* macro package driven by OzTeX 5.3b2 as the front end. The platform was a Power-Mac model MDD equipped with a 1-GHz PowerPC G4 CPU running MacOS 10.4.7, 1.25-GB RAM, and two ATA disk drives (60-GB IBM and 80-GB Seagate). The bibliography was generated by BibTeX 0.99c using natbib and apalike styles. The index was formatted by MakeIndex 2.14. *Mathematica* programs were written using version 5.1 for both Power Macintosh and Windows XP.

---

[*] By *flat ASCII* I mean text that is devoid of any formatting or special encoding that might prevent it from being read in the future by tools that did not write it.

[†] This is aligned with an important tenet of UNIX philosophy due to Doug McIlroy, the inventor of UNIX pipes (en.wikipedia.org/wiki/Unix_philosophy), viz., write programs to handle text streams, because text is a universal programmatic interface.

Neil J. Gunther, Performance Dynamics Company,
Castro Valley, CA, USA

Analyzing Computer System Performance with Perl::PDQ

XXIII, 436 p. Hardcover
ISBN 3-540-20865-8

Analyzing computer system performance is often regarded by most system administrators, IT professionals and software engineers as a black art that is too time consuming to learn and apply. Finally, this book by acclaimed performance analyst Dr. Neil Gunther makes this subject understandable and applicable through programmatic examples. The means to this end is the open-source performance analyzer Pretty Damn Quick (PDQ) written in Perl and available for download from the author's Website: www.perfdynamics.com. As the epigraph in this book points out, Common sense is the pitfall of performance analysis. The performance analysis framework that replaces common sense is revealed in the first few chapters of Part I. The important queueing concepts embedded in PDQ are explained in a very simple style that does not require any knowledge of formal probability theory. Part II begins with a full specification of how to set up and use PDQ replete with examples written in Perl. Subsequent chapters present applications of PDQ to the performance analysis of multicomputer architectures, benchmark results, client/server scalability, and Web-based applications. The examples are not mere academic toys but are based on the author's experience analyzing the performance of large-scale systems over the past 20 years. By following his lead, you will quickly be able to set up your own Perl scripts for collecting data and exploring performance-by-design alternatives without inflating your manager's schedule.

Contents: Part I System Theory: Time – The Zeroth Performance Metric; Getting the Jump on Queueing; Queueing Systems for Computer Systems; Linux Load Average – Take a Load Off!; Performance Bounds and Log Jams.- Part II System Practice: Pretty Damn Quick: A Slow Introduction; Analyzing Multicomputer Architectures; How to Measure an Elephant with PDQ; Analyzing Client/Server Applications; Analyzing Web Applications with PDQ.– Part III Appendices: Glossary of Terms; A Short History of Buffers; Thanks for the (Lack of) Memories; Performance Metrics and Tools; List of Programs; Compendium of Queueing Equations; Solutions to Selected Exercises. – References. – Index.

CPSIA information can be obtained at www.ICGtesting.com
Printed in the USA
LVOW101023130313

323977LV00015B/333/P